THE TRIUMPH OF THE SAINTS

THE SEPARATE CHURCHES OF LONDON 1616–1649

THE TRIUMPH OF THE SAINTS

THE SEPARATE CHURCHES OF LONDON 1616—1649

MURRAY TOLMIE
ASSOCIATE PROFESSOR OF HISTORY
UNIVERSITY OF BRITISH COLUMBIA

CAMBRIDGE UNIVERSITY PRESS
CAMBRIDGE
LONDON · NEW YORK · MELBOURNE

Published by the Syndics of the Cambridge University Press
The Pitt Building, Trumpington Street, Cambridge CB2 1RP
Bentley House, 200 Euston Road, London NW1 2DB
32 East 57th Street, New York, NY 10022, USA
296 Beaconsfield Parade, Middle Park, Melbourne 3206, Australia

First published 1977

Printed in Great Britain by
Western Printing Services Ltd, Bristol

Library of Congress Cataloguing in Publication Data

Tolmie, Murray, 1931–
The triumph of the saints

Bibliography: p.
Includes index.
1. Dissenters, Religious – England – London.
2. Sects – England – London. 3. London – Church history. I. Title.
BX5205. L7T64 274.21 76–46861
ISBN 0 521 21507 2

FOR ANNE

CONTENTS

TABLES

PREFACE

The triumph of the saints of the title is the successful establishment of protestant nonconformity, in the form of permanent and enduring congregations of protestant dissenters, at the time of the puritan revolution in England. A secondary aspect of that triumph is the execution of the supreme head of the Church of England, King Charles I, in 1649.

It is customary in prefaces to claim a prior neglect for one's topic. The subject of this book has been denied existence altogether by the most learned and prolific of present day historians writing of the connection between religion and revolution in England, Christopher Hill. His perspective is established in several of his books in prefatory remarks which, like axioms, need neither discussion nor proof:

There seems to me sometimes to be as much fiction and unwarranted assumption – and sheer waste of time – in tracing the genealogy of sects as of individuals.

(*Economic Problems of the Church*, 1956, p. xii)

Secondly, most of us think that we do know all about Puritanism. But too often we are thinking – whether with conscious hostility or unconscious sympathy – not of Puritanism at all but of later nonconformity. They differ as much as vinegar does from wine.

(*Puritanism and Revolution*, 1958, p. vii)

We know, as a result of hindsight, that some groups – Baptists, Quakers – will survive as religious sects, and that most of the others will disappear. In consequence we unconsciously tend to impose too clear outlines on the early history of English sects, to read back later beliefs into the 1640s and 50s. One of the aims. . .will be to suggest that in this period things were much more blurred.

(*The World Turned Upside Down*, 1972, p. 12)

Dr Hill observes his own axioms. The people who appear in this book, the coherence of their ideas, the stability of their institutions, and the nature of their relations with the other actors in the revolution are absent from Dr Hill's perspective as it ranges across puritanism in England as far as the outer reaches of 'the lunatic fringe.' The omission of what might be termed respectable nonconformity is reinforced by other recent books, A. L. Morton's *The World of the Ranters* (1970) and B. S. Capp's *The Fifth Monarchy Men* (1972). Readers of such books are left with the impression – scarcely an argument – that organized nonconformity is a later development that, following the exuberant religious experimentation of the revolutionary period, embodied a quietism and respectability signifying the 'failure' of the religious revolution.

This impression (false, as I hope to show) perpetuates the perspective established by those older progressives, the whig historians. Often Low Churchmen, admirers of Bunyan, tolerant of but slightly condescending towards nonconformists, the whig historians saw protestant nonconformity in England as the result of the failure of the puritan revolution and of the consequent ejection of the puritan clergy from the established church in 1662. For various reasons influential nonconformist historians have shared this view, Presbyterians because they had not in fact been nonconformists before 1662, others perhaps because the clerical ejections of 1662 lent nonconformity a respectability useful in distinguishing it from the lunatic fringe. The result of this older tradition was that the 'sectaries' of the period before 1662, like the Levellers of the 1640s, were neglected. The Levellers are now restored firmly to the centre of the revolutionary picture; the sectaries continue in the shadows.

Other historiographical traditions impinge on the sectaries as well. American scholars in this century have been deeply interested in English puritanism, but for the purpose of elucidating the history of their own country. Thus Champlin Burrage ended his *Early English Dissenters* (published in 1912, and the last work to attempt a general view of our subject) in 1640, when the puritan migration to America ended. The inadvertent result is that his book presents English dissent as a movement breaking apart and losing momentum by 1640. This book argues precisely the opposite. In the influential works of Perry Miller the distinctive experience of the English nonconformist disappears as completely as in the works of Dr Hill; indeed, Miller's conception of 'non-separating congregationalism', however useful in understanding Massachusetts, has been seriously misleading in the English context.

Scholars of English literature have extensively explored the sphere of religious radicalism in which John Milton lived and, to a degree, shared; but since Milton never became a member of a sectarian congregation they have not pressed their investigations into the field of sectarian genealogy. Thus William Haller failed to free himself from the perspective of the pamphlet literature he studied so carefully, and his work expresses, uncritically, the perception of the sectaries held by hostile contemporaries as 'shifting and amorphous groups of people... congregating loosely about individual preachers and flocking from one to another.'[1] The present book attempts to prove otherwise.

There are also intrinsic difficulties. The nonconformists throughout the whole period treated in this book were engaged in illegal activities, and they covered their tracks. Even careful contemporary observers could not distinguish what they were up to, and it is this blur in the perception of contemporaries that has been vividly reconstructed for us by Professor Haller. If we are to use the most voluminous source available for our subject, the comments of hostile contemporaries, we must learn to distinguish the blur in the mind of the percipient from the sectarian activities we are attempting to reconstruct. The denominational and ecclesiastical terminology of our subject is also full of confusion; a general warning that all such terms require consideration in their context will suffice here, since particular problems are discussed in what follows. One example, however, may help readers familiar with the historical controversies of the present generation. The terms 'Independent' and 'Presbyterian' have been commonly used as designations for political groupings in the Long Parliament and defined by such things as voting patterns and committee memberships. This book is not about the members of the Long Parliament, and these terms will be used here primarily as religious designations. When religious problems encroach into the parliamentary sphere, as they must in this period, the discrepancy between the religious and the political significations of these terms must be borne in mind.

It has taken a long time to work through the historiographical and contemporary confusions surrounding the 'sectaries', and I have accumulated many debts. The Marjorie Young Bell Fund of Sackville, New Brunswick, and the Canada Council have given financial assistance, and The University of British Columbia has afforded study leave. I am grateful to Professor W. K. Jordan and to Mr W. G. Barr, the Rector of Exeter College, Oxford, for their encouragement in the early stages of this undertaking. Joan Kent interrupted her own studies in London to secure material for me. Robert C. Walton and John R. MacCormack read and commented upon sections of the manuscript. George Thomson, Dorothy Thomson, and Fritz Levy read an earlier version in its entirety and offered moral support as well as practical aid. The final version has benefited from the searching criticism of my colleague John Norris.

I also wish to place on record a more remote debt, to three distinguished professors of Dalhousie University: R. A. MacKay, who first put Tawney in my hands, William Maxwell, who introduced me to

Professor Woodhouse's book, and G. E. Wilson, who taught me to be sceptical of received accounts. I can hint at the wisdom available to my generation at that University by adding that this list does not include two men, both philosophers, to whom I owe most.

The completion of this book would not have been possible without the sacrifices and the assistance of my wife.

Vancouver, BC M.T.
July 1976

NOTE

Spelling and punctuation have been modernized in quotations. Dates are Old Style, except that the year begins on 1 January. The place of publication for works cited in the Notes, in the list of Abbreviations, and in the Bibliography is London unless otherwise stated.

INTRODUCTION

In the first half of the seventeenth century protestant dissidents successfully challenged the aspiration of the Church of England, in its projected presbyterian as well as its episcopal form, for religious uniformity in an all-embracing territorial church. This challenge was complex, ranging from the defiance of the early separatists to the indirection and concealment practised by the Independents as they gathered their churches under the noses of the Presbyterian divines of the Westminster Assembly in the 1640s. The success of the challenge was embodied in 'separate churches' which, established in considerable numbers by 1649, constitute the foundations of nonconformity in England. Built into these foundations was the premise of a protestant pluralism, that is, a diversity of protestant worship within a political order still in some sense Christian even although no longer enforcing ecclesiastical uniformity. The responsible leaders of English nonconformity recognized that only by agreeing to disagree could they afford to Christian consciences what they considered to be the fundamental right of conscience: to worship in the way it saw best. This was their contribution to the English liberal tradition of the future. Having created sectarian diversity, they sought by their political actions to preserve it – impose it, their enemies said – on the nation as a whole. This was their contribution to the English revolution.

The essence of English nonconformity was the creation of nonparochial protestant congregations, or 'separate churches' as contemporaries described them. This term, denominationally neutral, permits us to see the underlying unity of nonconformity. It also suggests the fundamental truth that the later nonconformist denominations were organized from pre-existing congregations, that the separate churches preceded the denominations in time. For purposes of analysis it is convenient to use slightly anachronistic denominational categories – Congregationalist, Particular Baptist, General Baptist – in addition to the categories used by contemporaries – Independent, Anabaptist, separatist, or Brownist. If it is remembered that it is the church that makes the denomination, not the denomination the church, the use of these denominational categories need not cause confusion.

The creation of successful and enduring separate churches was not as straightforward as it might seem to us who have been familiar with such congregations for three centuries. There were false starts and new beginnings, in both ideas and institutions. The English separatists of the late Elizabethan and early Jacobean period represent a false start, to be followed by the new beginning which is the subject of this book.

The early separatists, Henry Barrow, Francis Johnson, Henry Ainsworth, John Smyth, and John Robinson, made valiant efforts to organize and sustain separatist congregations, but by the middle of the reign of James I most of the survivors of this tradition lived in exile. Their latest historian, Dr B. R. White, has described them as 'hasty Puritans' and as 'the most impatient embodiment of Elizabethan and Jacobean Puritanism.'[1] Their impulse to reformation sprang from the same root as that of the puritans: disgust with the ceremonies and non-preaching ministry of the Church of England, and with the authoritarian ecclesiastical hierarchy that sustained these 'abuses.' Their solution was to repudiate the Church of England as a totally false church, and by diligent study of the Bible to create a true Christian worship in their separatist congregations. The premise of this programme was that there was in the Bible a single true and universally binding model of a Christian church. This premise was of the very essence of their separatism, for it was by this standard that the Church of England was condemned as a false church from which true Christians must totally separate.

This rigidity proved fatal to separatist institutions. The early separatists may be said to have separated from puritanism as well as from the Church of England, for they turned an intolerant face to those puritans (always the overwhelming majority) who remained in the parish churches. Their schism was more painful to the puritans, for whom it represented a rending of meaningful Christian fellowship, than it was to the ecclesiastical authorities, to whom it was merely a wilful defiance of legitimate authority. The main body of puritans quickly became hostile to the separatists, and this doomed the separatist movement to a sterile isolation among the protestant radicals in England. Furthermore, the search for an exclusive and universally binding model of a true Christian church placed upon the tiny separatist congregations a burden impossible to bear. The separatist leaders worked hard and creatively to devise an adequate church order once they had withdrawn from the parish churches; but the very smallest detail of church order and worship became a heavy responsibility when what was at stake was the achievement of a single true Christian model. This afforded opportunities for corrosive strife both within and among separatist congregations. The zeal of these idealists tended to be self-defeating as their internal quarrels were ventilated in print in their own pamphlets and in those of their enemies. Discredited by their rigidity and by their quarrels, the separatist movement lost all momentum inside England, and the exiled separatists turned to the New World. In 1619 most of Francis Johnson's congregation perished in a tragic voyage to Virginia. In 1620 members of Robinson's congregation at Leyden embarked on the *Mayflower*, to sail into history as the Pilgrim Fathers. Of the whole separatist movement there remained behind in London only a leaderless fragment.

The new beginning in the task of organizing successful separate churches has been overlooked in the history of nonconformity. The early separatist experiment took place in a blaze of publicity; Ben Jonson, in his *Alchemist* in 1610, could assume his London audience would be amused at the pastor of the exiled saints Tribulation Wholesome, and his deacon Ananias. The new leaders practised a circumspect secrecy to avoid prosecution as separatists and to minimize contention with puritans who worshipped in the parish churches. As a result they have remained invisible to historians, who have focussed on more visible radicals in the two decades after 1620, the puritans who migrated to Massachusetts or went into exile in the Netherlands. Since these puritans loudly repudiated the doctrinaire separatism of the early separatists even as they physically separated themselves across the seas from the parishes of the Church of England, they contributed nothing to the theory or practice of separate churches within England.

The leaders of the new wave of separate churches within England were left behind to work out an ecclesiastical polity which avoided the isolation of the early separatists while securing the reality of the separate church. Fortunately for them, they benefited from the same circumstance, the rise of the Laudian party in the Church of England, that was driving other puritans overseas; for as the anti-episcopal movement gathered momentum puritans who had no intention of leaving the parish churches became more tolerant of those who did so in a discreet rather than a strident manner. From the beginning, therefore, this new movement stood in an ambivalent relationship with puritan members of the established church. This ambivalence is an essential ingredient both in obscuring this phase of nonconformity and in its success, and as such forms a persistent theme in what follows.

Henry Jacob was the chief architect of the new nonconformity, and the secret congregation he formed in London in 1616 was the focal point for the movement. The most successful of all separate churches in England before the revolution, the Jacob church for twenty-five years served as a recruiting agency and training school for some of the most important sectarian leaders of the coming revolutionary period. It harboured within its membership rigid separatists as well as ordinary Independents, and it accommodated those who had doubts about their baptism without worrying about 'Anabaptist' infection. As groups hived off to organize new churches, the Jacob church became progressively more tolerant of variant forms and by 1642 stood in a parental relationship both to strict separatist and to Baptist congregations. It also became the model for the gathered churches of the Independents as these began to appear during the first civil war in England. The only separate churches to stand entirely outside the influence of the Jacob circle were the General Baptist congregations; these traced their origin back to a division within John Smyth's early separatist congregation in exile, and introduced a genuine Anabaptist element into the sectarian ferment in England. With this exception, treated in chapter 4 below, the first half of this book describes the growth of nonconformity in terms of ever-widening circles from the original Jacob church.

The second part of the book deals with the political results of nonconformity in a period of revolution. The civil war afforded an unprecedented opportunity for gathering churches; by 1646 there were approximately three dozen separate churches in London, organized in a variety of ways. These churches were technically illegal, and in the search for a settlement after the war their existence became increasingly a matter for contention on the victorious parliamentary side. The nonconformists were a tiny minority in society and could scarcely hope to exercise political influence except as part of a larger coalition. But they were also militant and organized, with a foothold in the political institutions of London and a rapidly increasing influence in the middle ranks of the New Model Army. It was therefore a difficult and delicate question whether, in the interests of a permanent political settlement, to attempt to suppress the separate churches and restore ecclesiastical uniformity, or to placate the nonconformist minority by abandoning uniformity. These alternatives were adopted as policies for settlement by competing parliamentary factions, with results that are well known. The radical parliamentary faction, usually described as 'Independents,' by a combination of political tactics and military force outmanoeuvred the rival moderate faction, usually known as 'Presbyterians,' and in the end brought the King to his trial and execution. The political 'Independents' were not necessarily religious Independents at all; but they were the patrons and allies of the nonconformists of the separate churches, without whose assistance the radical coalition could not have achieved its ends.

London forms the stage for this phase of English nonconformity. From 1616, when Henry Jacob returned to London from Middelburg to organize his Independent congregation, or perhaps from 1612 when the Nottinghamshire squire Thomas Helwys moved to London from Amsterdam with his tiny band of General Baptists, London and its suburbs served as a refuge and a magnet for religious radicals, and this vitally important role lasted until the execution of the King symbolized the end of the old persecuting order. It was in London that the members of the separate churches debated the details of their varying church orders while preserving a sense of common purpose; it was in London that they forged links with puritan radicals in the great political coalitions that fought the civil wars; and it was in London that the question of their continued existence as separate churches was decided. These themes give unity and a national significance to the history of the separate churches of London in this period.

A study of the separate churches does not by any means exhaust the subject of religious radicalism in London. The majority of puritans remained loyal to their parish churches. Although I have attempted to define the sometimes ambiguous boundary between a separate gathered church and a reformed parish congregation and to indicate the changing attitudes of parochial puritans to the separate churches, this book does not embody a study of the London parishes; that challenging and important task yet awaits its historian. In another direction, beyond making clear their difference from the separate churches I have not encompassed the amorphous movements of the Antinomians, the Seekers, and the Ranters. For appropriating the term 'saints' to the members of the separate churches I offer these justifications: that these members commonly thought of themselves as saints or 'visible saints'; and that in its ironic or sneering usage the term was perhaps most commonly aimed at the self-selecting aspect of the separate churches. It is true that a man like Oliver Cromwell would think of 'saints' as including parochial Christians, Antinomians, and Seekers as well as members of separate churches; but Cromwell was a man of unusually broad sympathies – this was part of his power. In general I have not found that the term was used for pious puritan gentlemen and merchants who remained loyal to their parish churches, and still less for the Ranters roistering in the taverns.

In 1649 the nonconformist perspective changes fundamentally, and new themes appear which are beyond the scope of this book. Once the English republic was established there was a burgeoning growth of nonconformity across the whole land. The sense of common purpose and common dangers shared by the London churches in the 1640s began to give way in the next decade to a hardening of denominational lines, as groups of churches moved together to define their common ground and to distinguish themselves from other groups. As the regional and national associations of the principal denominations begin to appear in the 1650s, the history of the London churches, although still interesting and important, ceases to occupy centre stage. The Quakers, an important new denomination that succeeded in giving shape and direction to the spiritual turmoil of Seekers and anti-formalists who rejected the denominationalism of the dissenters along with the traditionalism of the parish congregations, were not based in London at all. These larger developments, and not merely the London churches, must be taken into account in tracing the political course of the Interregnum to its final failure.

The Act of Uniformity of 1662, resulting in the ejection of two thousand puritan clergymen from the established church, added the Presbyterians as an involuntary sectarian denomination to the ranks of the nonconformists and substantially reinforced the clerical element in nonconformist leadership. But 1662 is not the central event in the creation of English nonconformity, as the older nonconformist historians implied. The ejections of 1662 were memorialized by Edmund Calamy and shaped into a larger historical perspective by Daniel Neal in his *History of the Puritans*. Historians writing in this tradition organized their histories around the lives of the clergymen. This vision suffers from serious limitations: it ignores the deep and enduring note of anticlericalism in nonconformity, it minimizes the leadership given by laymen, and most serious of all, it casts into the shadows the creative efforts of the men and women who organized the separate churches described in this book. When attention is focussed on the separate churches rather than on the clergymen, these themes appear in a truer light, along with the fundamental truth that nonconformity was part of the puritan revolution in England and not the product of its failure.

I

THE JACOB CHURCH

Henry Jacob

The year 1616 has never been regarded as significant in the history of the puritans in England. The sharp disappointment of the puritan clergy in the early years of the reign of James I lay a decade in the past, although silenced clergymen lingered on across the land. The rise of the Laudians and the bitter conflict of the Thirty Years War that was to make that rise so ominous for puritans, lay some years in the future. The exiled separatists were discredited, by their own quarrels as much as anything else, unless it was by John Smyth turning plain Anabaptist. No one noticed when a puritan clergyman with a reputation for agitation not unlike that of John Field, the great Elizabethan puritan organizer, slipped back into England, probably in disguise, from a decade of lonely exile in Middelburg. He quietly went about visiting old associates from the puritan campaigns of the past, including the famous Walter Travers and John Dod, both silenced. With their tacit or explicit approval he then organized in London a new kind of puritan congregation, separate from the parish churches, on the model later known as Independent. We would not know of this event at all were it not for the church record itself, for no contemporary made a comment that has survived.

This puritan clergyman was Henry Jacob.[1] He was fifty-three years old at the time, nearly twenty years older than the oldest of the early separatist leaders at the time of their separation from the Church of England.[2] The new church was thus not the hasty 'reformation without tarrying' of youth. Jacob had been radical enough in his younger days to consider the separatist alternative, but like John Field before him he found separatism unacceptable, believing that it was wrong to separate from people who 'in simplicity' partook of corrupt traditions but who were 'true Christians nevertheless.'[3] For Jacob, absolute purity of church form was to give way to the consciences of simple believers. This principle served to keep him within the Church of England for many years, but in the long run it was to lead him to an ecclesiastical pluralism.

Jacob was a full-time organizer in the agitation for further reform within the established church at the accession of James I. With 'astonishing industry' he organized the puritan clergy of London and Sussex behind the millenary petition, but he was displeased by the moderation of the puritan spokesmen at the Hampton Court Conference.[4] He was soon taking a more individual and radical line of his own, publishing in mid 1604 a pamphlet advocating a congregational form of government within the parishes of the Church of England and earning thereby several months of imprisonment at the hands of the Bishop of London.[5] By 1606, as Archbishop Bancroft launched his campaign to discipline the puritan clergy, London and indeed all England became too hot for Jacob and he fled into exile at Middelburg. Here he published pamphlets in the name of 'some of the late silenced and deprived ministers,' thus identifying himself with Bancroft's clerical victims rather than with the exiled separatist congregations.[6]

The harsh experience of the puritans in the early years of James's reign led Jacob to think more deeply about his ecclesiastical programme. His deepest conviction was that only the individual congregation could form a true visible church. His book of 1604, anti-episcopal in intent, spelled out the argument in detail in the context of the parish congregations of the Church of England, that each parish congregation was a complete visible church in which the people's consent was required in the election of church officers and in excommunication.[7] Persecution, however, began to loosen this congregational conception from the parish. In 1605 Jacob and others, perhaps imitating a separatist petition of 1604, asked the King for permission 'to assemble together somewhere publicly to the service and worship of God, to use and enjoy peaceably among ourselves alone the whole exercise of God's worship and of church government,' promising also, unlike the separatists, to 'keep brotherly communion with the rest of our English churches as they are now established, according as the French and Dutch churches [in England] do.'[8] Jacob petitioned again from exile in 1609 in the name of the silenced puritan clergy and others for toleration of 'some churches to be gathered by your majesty's special grace in some parts of this kingdom,' exempt from episcopal jurisdiction but under the oversight of 'your subordinate civil magistrates.'[9] Here was the conception of the non-parochial gathered church, existing under the royal supremacy alongside the parish congregations and in communion with them, but it was still implicit that these gathered churches would exist in default of a more fundamental reformation of the parish congregations.

By 1610 the limited and temporary nature of the gathered church began to fade before a more positive conception of the non-parochial gathered church as a true visible church in its own right. This was the result of a shift of emphasis in several aspects of Jacob's congregational theory rather than a conversion to separatism, although the separatists certainly influenced the change. Without denying the magistrate's authority over the church, Jacob began in 1610 to emphasize the kingly office of Christ as the immediate head of each individual congregation.[10] The rule of King Jesus over a worldly kingdom of the saints gathered in their churches was one of the most powerful conceptions of the early separatists.[11] Jacob had been familiar with it earlier, but in discussions with the separatist John Robinson in Leyden in the course of this year he began to grasp the idea in a new light, to see that the kingly office of Christ could serve to liberate the gathered church from its subordination to the magistrate's consent for its very existence.[12] In 1611 Jacob rejected the idea that the congregation under the New Testament was necessarily a parish church or limited to 'any circuit of ground at all.'[13] In his major work on church government in this decade, written in 1612, he argued more insistently that 'Christian people, whether few or many, joined together in a constant society of one ordinary congregation to serve God according to his word, are a true visible church of Christ,' or, more explicitly, that a group of laymen, 'whether they be many, or few,' could join together in a true visible church with 'the power of all the holy things of God, all God's ordinances spiritual.'[14]

The most important change occurred almost imperceptibly. The dominant theme of Jacob's books in this period was that church government must be exercised with the people's free consent; as the gathered church came to occupy the first place in his mind, the idea of consent was extended from acts of church government, such as the election of officers or excommunication, to include the more fundamental issue of church membership, the 'joining by willing consent into a visible church.'[15] Membership in the gathered church was voluntary, in the territorial parish church it was involuntary. Jacob hesitated to incorporate voluntary membership into the definiton of the true visible church in such a way that only the gathered church could be a true church, for he was determined not to cut himself off from Christians in the parish congregations. But he began to speak as if Christians had a legitimate choice of church membership before them, and to exhort them 'to frame the visible church wherein they live to this only true form, or else to betake themselves unto some such church so formed.'[16]

The requirement of the people's consent to acts of church government raised the issue of church membership in another form. Here the question was whether the mixed multitude of the territorial parish was a fit body for such a large responsibility. In 1604 Jacob conceived of this problem in parochial terms, and the solution was the exercise of 'right and true discipline ecclesiastical' within the parish congregation. Since every territorial parishioner was subject to this discipline, the parish congregation might safely be left to conduct its own affairs.[17] Discipline, thus conceived, was parochial and territorial; even under excommunication the weak or scandalous members of the parish were not so much unchurched as under discipline and correction. This was an essentially Presbyterian programme, and it was to lie at the heart of the English Presbyterianism of the 1640s. By 1610 Jacob had abandoned 'discipline,' in favour of 'keeping forth of the malicious and untractable without' the church and of restricting church membership to 'such people as are not ignorant in religion, nor scandalous in their life. For only of such Christ's visible church ought to consist.'[18] In thus choosing what was to become the Independent congregation of 'visible saints', Jacob was again influenced by John Robinson,[19] but he refused to make the separation of the saints from the ungodly the essential definition of a visible church: 'We believe concerning mixtures of the open prophane with some manifest godly Christians, in a visible church, though at once it doth not destroy essentially, nor make void the holiness of that whole assembly, yet truly it putteth that whole assembly into a most dangerous and desperate estate.' This article of the confession of faith issued by Jacob's church in 1616 was full of separatist language ('And who can touch pitch, and not be defiled therewith?') even as it avoided drawing the full separatist conclusion.[20]

The decisive event in Jacob's career was his return to London to gather a church. The principles which inspired the new venture were carefully spelled out in *A Confession and Protestation of the Faith of Certaine Christians* and supported by further arguments in *A Collection of sundry matters*, both published at Middelburg. The *Confession* ended with a petition to the King repeating the request of 1609 for toleration for a gathered church on congregational principles, offering to take the oaths of supremacy and allegiance, and asking the King to 'assign to us some civil magistrate or magistrates qualified with wisdom, learning, and virtue to be...our overseers for our more peaceable, orderly, and dutiful carriage of ourselves, both in our worshipping God, and in all other our affairs.'[21] Having thus established their faith in a Christian magistrate in a Christian commonwealth and avoided the Anabaptist notion of the separation of church and state, Jacob and his colleagues then professed themselves bound 'to obey Christ rather than man' in the matter of Christ's visible church, which was no less than 'the kingdom of Christ upon earth now in the time of the Gospel.'[22]

The kingdom of Christ upon earth looked remarkably like a separatist church. 'Meeting in private for the exercise of our religion,' the members were drawn indiscriminately from the territorial parish churches, where they refused to be 'ordinary and constant members' because they 'dissented' from the public worship of England on twenty-eight grounds, duly listed in the *Confession*.[23] This was not a church within a church, such as the company of select Christians John Cotton later organized within his parish congregation at Boston in Lincolnshire; nor was it, as a Barrowist critic later described it, 'a sequestered meeting from their brethren the [parish] antichristians on part of the day, and to communicate with them the other part of the day.'[24] Instead the Jacob church was a fully developed and completely autonomous rival to the parish churches. Its members held their church membership in this congregation and no other. As a 'free congregation independent' conforming to Christ's prescription for a true visible church, it was endowed with 'the right and power of spiritual administration and government in itself and over itself by the common and free consent of the people, independently and immediately under Christ.'[25]

In the view of the authorities in church and state such a congregation was as separatist, schismatic, and illegal as any Brownist conventicle. The Jacob church therefore shared the dangers of the early separatist congregations, but to a degree at least it escaped the separatist isolation from the main body of puritans within the Church of England. The *Confession* repudiated 'the slander of schism. . .and also of separation' on the ground that the new church recognized the parish churches of England as true churches. Each parish church, although a false church 'in respect of the order of the state' and as it stood 'under and joined to the lord bishops' spiritual dominion,' was nevertheless a true visible church 'in some respect,' insofar as its members professed to serve God 'according to his will in faith and order so far as they know.'[26] Similarly, a parish minister was a 'nullity' in respect of his episcopal ordination and formal appointment to his parish, but this did not make void 'all trueness of ministry in him,' as far as a believing congregation 'consenteth to have him, and useth him for their minister.' Since individual parishes thus contained the seeds of true congregational churches, though overlaid with accretions of false worship and an unwarranted espiscopal jurisdiction, all communion with them could not be severed without schism from Christian fellowship. One article of the *Confession* expressly permitted, and even enjoined, intercommunion in the parishes 'on some weighty occasion,' provided that they testified at the same time that they joined 'only to that which is true in the said [parish] ministry.'[27] That this semi-separatism, as it was known to contemporaries, was not merely a token compromise but a genuinely new approach to the problem of establishing a church apart from the parish churches was to become evident in the subsequent history of the Jacob church.

The Jacob–Lathrop–Jessey church

The Jacob church was the model for the Independent gathered churches of the future. It was also the mother church of a variety of congregations formed by secession, both amicable and contentious. The pressure of circumstances pushed the Jacob church in an ever more radical direction, until the simple dualism of a puritan separate church alongside the parish congregations grew into the pluralism of Independent, separatist, and Baptist congregations competing with the parish churches. The Jacob church stood at the very centre of a new and complex wave of nonconformity that had burst the bounds of puritan orthodoxy long before the revolution had begun in England.

The memory of the executions of Barrow, Greenwood, and Penry and the passage of the act against protestant recusants in 1593 imposed extreme caution upon any separate church that hoped to survive inside England.[28] Most of the evidence relating to the Jacob church is therefore indirect, and the scattered traces, although extensive compared to the record left behind by any similar body, would be difficult to interpret without a key document: in 1641 the third pastor of the church, Henry Jessey, prepared a memorandum which provides a thread of coherence to the previous twenty-five years and permits a more confident assessment of other evidence.* The memorandum has the character of jottings made by Jessey in discussions with older members of the church, probably to serve as an *aide-memoire* when Jessey explained the history of his church to the Independent clergy who were flocking to London in 1641.[29]

The Jessey memorandum states that the church was organized in London after Jacob had consulted with several of the most famous of the silenced puritan clergy, including 'Mr. Travers,' presumably Walter Travers, Thomas Cartwright's associate and an undoubted Presbyterian, John Dod, and Richard Mansell.[30] These men were not

* The Jessey memorandum is part of a collection of original documents which were transcribed in the eighteenth century by Benjamin Stinton, a Baptist pastor in London. Three of the documents, each bearing the character of a memorandum of events written very shortly after they occurred, relate to the history of the Jacob church before 1645: the Jessey memorandum, the Kiffin memorandum, and the Knollys memorandum. These form the basis for the reconstruction given here and in chapter 3.

Independents, and they seem to have approved Jacob's proposal to set up a puritan congregation in communion with the parish churches without realizing how genuinely radical it was. This puritan approval encouraged Jacob to gather his church on the principles laid down in the *Confession*. After a day of fasting and prayer, those instituting the new church joined hands in a ring and each 'made some confession or profession of their faith and repentance; some were longer, some were briefer.' The terms of the church covenant, 'to walk in all God's ways as He had revealed or should make known to them,' directly echoed the covenant adopted by John Smyth and John Robinson at the beginning of their separatist pilgrimage in 1607, 'to walk in all His ways made known, or to be made known unto them.'[31]

In addition to Jacob, who was chosen and ordained as the pastor of the new church within a few days, over a dozen of the early members of the church can be identified. The most important was probably Sabine Staresmore, an energetic young man whose career can be fleetingly glimpsed over three decades. A merchant with extensive contacts in London, he was active in 1618 as an agent for Robinson's church at Leyden in its preliminary negotiations with the Virginia Company in anticipation of the mass migration of the Leyden church to the New World.[32] Richard Browne, a wherryman, in 1610 had rescued the radical puritans William Ames and Robert Parker from their pursuers and conveyed them safely to a ship at Gravesend which took them into exile to Rotterdam; he eventually moved to New England where by 1631 he was the ruling elder of the newly organized church at Watertown.[33] John Bellamie was a member of the Jacob church for a decade after 1616; he was to become a prominent bookseller and a leading lay Presbyterian in London in the 1640s.[34] David Brown, a Scottish writing master who moved to London, appears to have been a member from 1616; he can be traced in radical circles as late as 1652.[35] John Allen of Southwark, identified as a founding member in the Jessey memorandum, was brought before the Court of High Commission with another 'Brownist' in 1636.[36] Other early members can be traced to New England. Robert Lynell, a deacon of the Jacob church who baptized his daughter in his parish church of St Andrew Hubbard in 1623, emigrated with his family to New England sometime after 1634.[37] Yet another unnamed member was admitted to communion, and his child to baptism, in the Salem church in 1630 on the strength of his membership in the Jacob church, much to the alarm of John Cotton, whose own parishioners from England were not recognized as fellow Christians by the Salem church.[38]

The status of the new church as a 'puritan' rather than a 'separatist' congregation created ambiguities from the beginning. According to Bellamie, one of the clergymen who knowingly administered communion to Jacob and his associates in a parish church in the early years was Henry Roborough, a future Presbyterian critic of the Independents.[39] According to a Barrowist critic, all the members of the Jacob church 'went to hearing in the Church of England after the covenant making' as a formal church act in testimony to their principle of remaining in communion with the parish churches.[40] This corporate act, dangerous and also impractical as the church grew in size, was not repeated, and thereafter the settled policy was to leave the practice of intercommunion to the discretion of individual members.[41] Since the members came from widely scattered parishes, this served the very practical purpose of permitting each member to follow his conscience in the matter of attending his own parish church and thus escaping detection as a separatist conventicler. This was particularly relevant in the sensitive matter of baptizing children. Weekly attendance at the parish church was probably of little consequence in the teeming parishes of London, but the failure to produce newly-born children before the parish minister for baptism may have been a source of serious trouble in the parish. Intercommunion with the parish churches could be practised in an appropriately godly parish, but parochial baptisms were performed in the parish where the parents lived, whether godly or not; this was to be a future source of contention within the Jacob church.[42]

The Jacob church was a complete church in itself, offering the sacrament of the Lord's Supper to all members and baptism to those who wished it; we have explicit testimony that Staresmore had his child baptized in the Jacob church.[43] The pastor was supported by voluntary offerings rather than by the compulsory tithes of the parish ministry, and these offerings were also used for the relief of poor members, so that 'all the church's members are givers, or receivers.' One of the most significant of the arrangements of the new church was that 'any understanding member of the church (but women)' might with the church's permission undertake 'the sober, discreet, orderly, and well governed exercise of expounding and applying the Scripture in the congregation.'[44] It was by virtue of this practice that lay members of this church acquired the experience and confidence to become the 'tub-preachers' of a later generation. The Jacob church therefore fulfilled all the needs of Christian worship and fellowship for those members who wished to avoid the parish churches, and from the beginning there were members who were in practice complete separatists. The separatist tendency was reinforced by the aspiration of the church to be 'a free congregation of saints, viz. of visible holy Christians.'[45] It was as a covenanted community of visible saints that the Jacob church announced its institution to the remnant of the old Barrowist congregation in London, intending to practise intercommunion with the separatists as well as with the parish churches. The Barrowist churches in London and Amsterdam, however, refused to associate with the semi-separatists of the Jacob church.[46]

Considering the wide range of opinion and practice among its members, the Jacob church was remarkably free of controversy on the issue of separation. Sabine Staresmore, a strict separatist member, claimed that the members were 'the most part separated,' and John Bellamie, a conservative member, admitted that by 1624 'many of the members' were 'both in judgement and practice against communion' in the parishes.[47] Bellamie's own practice in this respect is interesting. In opinion he was at the opposite pole from Staresmore, identifying himself as a member of a reformed congregation within the Church of England rather than as a separatist; in practice he had withdrawn completely from the parish congregations and was no less a separatist than Staresmore. When Bellamie finally left the church in 1626, it was not over the issue of separation, which he had satisfactorily settled in his own mind, but over the proper manner of ordaining the new pastor, 'that it ought to be performed actually by precedent church officers,' namely by puritan clergymen such as those who had initially given their approval to Jacob's church.[48]

Bellamie's aspiration was to preserve the puritan identity of the congregation, but by 1626 puritan clergy of any stature were less likely to endorse the proceedings of the Jacob church. The breakdown of the role of the Jacob church as a puritan or reformed congregation was implicit in its organization as a voluntary association. This lesson soon came home to puritans who had initially endorsed the enterprise. By 1619 Richard Mansell had turned against the church. His objections went beyond the obvious presence of separatists like Staresmore in the church to include the 'matter of prophecy,' that is, the right extended to laymen to 'exercise' or preach within the Jacob church. The most interesting charge was against 'our indiscretion, for taking in so many that want [lack] houses for our meeting, and women without their husbands, and servants without their masters' consent.' This suggests that Jacob's puritan supporters had envisaged an undertaking cautiously limited to householders who could accommodate the meetings of the church in rotation. But as Staresmore pointed out, scriptural duties stood 'notwithstanding the opposition of any creature,' and a voluntary congregation explicitly based upon the free choice of its members could not easily be regulated to suit the ideas of its most cautious followers.[49]

The Jacob church early demonstrated the socially explosive nature of the gathered church: it could cut through social barriers and through institutions like the family to pose a threat to the whole social order. Mansell's reaction foreshadowed that of many puritans who were initially sympathetic to the gathered church only to recoil as they saw the practical social results of voluntary associations.

Mansell's views were shared by some members within the church. Jacob's ministry, Staresmore said, was made unprofitable to some, 'and divers of the brethren are of late so shaken by you [Mansell], that I fear their sincerities, and some have also turned back upon us, yea head against us.'[50] It was perhaps these difficulties with the puritan or conservative wing of the church that led Jessey to sum up Jacob's pastorate with the remark that 'in the time of his service much trouble attended that state and people, within and without.' Jacob found his position sufficiently difficult that he secured his formal dismissal from the church to go to Virginia in 1622, where he died in 1624.[51]

The Jacob church was not yet radical enough to elect a layman to the pastoral office, but for two years lay members edified 'one another in the best manner they could according to their gifts.' In 1624 a former clergyman joined the congregation and was soon elected pastor in Jacob's place. John Lathrop was a Cambridge graduate who had been a humble curate at Egerton in Kent until, at the age of forty, he renounced his ordination in the Church of England and moved to London to join the Jacob church. Described in the Jessey memorandum as 'a man of tender heart and a humble and meek spirit,' Lathrop restored stability to the congregation by carefully following Jacob's latitudinarian policy.[52]

During Lathrop's pastorate external circumstances reinforced the internal drift of the congregation in a separatist direction. The rise of William Laud to a position of influence and power within the Church of England, which sent some puritans to the New World, sent others into the Jacob church and greatly strengthened strict separatist tendencies inside the church. Matters came to a head in 1630, when separatists within the congregation challenged the policy that permitted other members to practise intercommunion with the parish churches; the precipitating incident was the baptism of the child of one of the members in a parish church, which angered the strict separatist minority. The controversy was acute enough for the Jacob church to decide to renew the church covenant. John Duppa, the leader of the separatist faction, urged his fellow members 'to detest and protest against the parish churches' in the new covenant, but others were unwilling to be bound in the covenant either to protest against or to pronounce in favour of the parishes, 'not knowing what in time to come God might further manifest to them thereabout.' The latitudinarians were in the majority, but they were willing to compromise with the separatists by adding to the previous covenant an undertaking 'to forsake all false ways.' For the moment peace was restored, but when the latitudinarians interpreted the new covenant in the old semi-separatist sense, the separatist minority withdrew from the church.[53]

The 1630 secession led by Duppa was the first major division of the Jacob church since its foundation, and it deprived the church of some of its most influential members. Among the dozen dissidents who can be identified were Sabine Staresmore, who had been a practising separatist from the beginning, Daniel Chidley 'the elder', possibly one of the elders of the Jacob church, David Brown the Scottish writing master, and John Jerrow, a glover from Tewkesbury in Gloucestershire.[54] The schismatics proceeded to organize their own church, grafting on to Jacob's conception of the Independent gathered church the requirement of strict separation from the parishes of the Church of England.

The defection of the Duppa group does not seem to have materially weakened the Lathrop church, for its morale was high enough to withstand the next serious crisis. In April 1632 the whole church was detected and arrested by Tomlinson, the Bishop of London's pursuivant. Most of the members were brought before the Court of High Commission, which made a major effort to deal decisively with the stubborn problem of these separatists by imprisoning them all for a long time. In the proceedings against them, Bishop Laud several times expressed his horror and disgust at these 'dangerous men' who formed a 'scattered company sown in all the city' and outlying parishes, 'all of different places.'[55] The members of the church were released from prison about eighteen months later,[56] but the leaders were singled out for special treatment. Lathrop and Samuel Eaton were released on bail after two years of imprisonment, and Ralph Grafton, an upholsterer of Cornhill who was described as a 'rich man' and a 'principal ringleader', was fined two hundred pounds as well as being imprisoned for an indefinite period.[57] Although none of the congregation recanted, Lathrop and thirty others decided that the wilderness of New England was preferable to the threat of imprisonment in London.[58]

The next major division of the Jacob church occurred when most of the members were released from prison in September 1633. Recent events had given a strong impetus to strict separatist sentiment in the congregation; at least one member, Samuel How, left the church immediately upon his release from prison to join a strict separatist church formerly led by John Canne.[59] Of the ten people who initiated the 1633 division, at least five had been in prison. Samuel Eaton, who had been unconcerned about the practice of attending parish churches in 1632, joined the new separatist church as its pastor as soon as he was released from prison early in 1634, and seven other members of the Jacob church soon joined the original ten. The three reasons given in the Jessey memorandum for this division – it was not a schism – reveal the drift of the parent church itself towards a separatist position. First, the dissidents denied the 'truth of the parish churches,' as Duppa and his followers had done earlier. Second, the church was now so large that 'it might be prejudicial', a phrase referring to the needs of concealment as well as the ease of assembly for a scattered membership. Third, there was a desire to 'further the communion of those churches in order amongst themselves,' which can be interpreted as a desire to enter into communion with the strict separatist societies of Duppa and How. These demands were met by the parent church; Eaton's new separatist Independent church was held in fraternal fellowship by the Jacob church.[60]

The growth and vitality of the Jacob church is indicated by its capacity to withstand sizeable withdrawals between 1630 and 1634. Eleven members are named in the 1630 secession, thirty members went to New England with Lathrop, a further eighteen withdrew to form Eaton's church, and undoubtedly other members were drawn away to the strict separatist societies.

With Lathrop's departure the Jacob church remained without a pastor until 1637 when Henry Jessey was offered the position. Jessey was a clergyman with a wide range of contacts among influential and radical puritans. For several years after his graduation from Cambridge, he had been chaplain to Brampton Gurdon at Assington, Suffolk, where he was a close neighbour and good friend of the Winthrop family at Groton. He remained in touch with the Winthrops after their departure for New England and emigration was never far from his mind during the 1630s, but he was to follow a different road to the New Jerusalem. His appointment to a living at Aughton in Yorkshire in 1633 was followed within months by his ejection for nonconformity. He found refuge in the household of Sir Matthew Boynton, who considered moving to New England in 1636 with his household, including Jessey, but abandoned the plan. Since his passage to New England with Boynton had not materialized, Jessey moved to London in the summer of 1637 and soon afterwards accepted the pastoral charge of the Jacob church which had been urged on him for some time; he was to hold this position until his death in 1663.[61] His appointment widened the circle of the church's contacts. In November 1639

Jessey was sent by the congregation to assist in the formation of a congregational church at Llanvaches in South Wales under William Wroth and Walter Cradock. This church was explicitly based on the model of the Jacob church; the men associated with it were to transform the religious life of Wales within the next generation, and they remained on intimate terms with the London churches, both Baptist and Independent, that grew out of the Jacob church.[62]

The final division of the original Jacob church in the pre-revolutionary period occurred on 18 May 1640. The congregation 'became two by mutual consent, just half being with Mr. P. Barbone, and the other half with Mr. H. Jessey'. The reason for the division was 'prudence': the growth of the church had complicated the problem of concealment, and geographical convenience may have been the most significant criterion in the division. Praise-God Barbone met with his church, when safety permitted, at his premises in Fleet Street beyond the western boundary of the City, while Jessey at this period lived in the Liberty of the Tower in the east.[63] Each half of the original congregation renewed the church covenant and elected its own officers, and both of the new churches stood in direct line of succession from the original Jacob church of 1616. The issue of separatism, which had divided the church in 1630 and 1633, was now dead. Thus when Samuel Eaton's separatist church broke up after his death in 1639, most of its strict separatist members rejoined Jessey's church and many remained with him at the 1640 division.[64] Barbone's church was equally separatist, and Praise-God Barbone, the 'reverend unlearned leatherseller,' was the prime model for the tub-preachers and lay pastors of the puritan revolution.

New Donatists: offshoots of the Jacob church

To explore the history of the offshoots of the Jacob church is to enter the obscurity of the puritan underworld where the sectarian explosion of the 1640s was prepared. The government's efforts to suppress conventicles after 1632 had the opposite result of stimulating their growth in size and numbers and of driving their members to take up more radical attitudes. This phenomenon, involving hundreds of people in the Jacob circle alone, has been little studied, partly because of sparse evidence that is difficult to interpret, and also because of anachronistic denominational perspectives. Yet each of the churches in the Jacob circle was developing along individual lines in this decade, for they were as yet free of that internal uniformity and external differentiation implied in a modern denominationalism. They must be studied church by church, as they grappled with a whole series of practical and

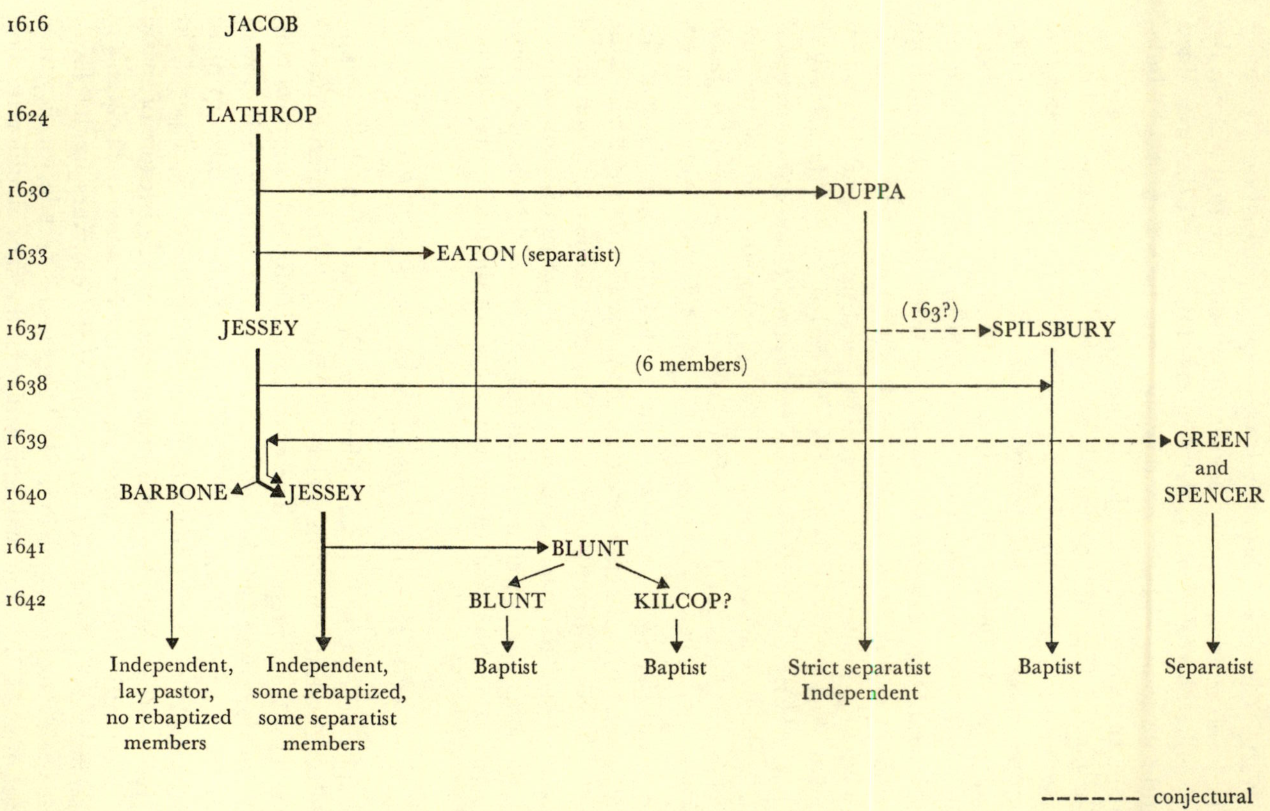

TABLE 1 *The Jacob Church and its offshoots*

theoretical problems: the institution of a lay pastorate; whether separation from the parish churches required a new separatist baptism; whether to baptize believers instead of infants; whether to practise intercommunion with other, differing, separate churches, or with the parish churches, or with those who practised intercommunion with the parish churches; and whether individual members were free to differ without forfeiting their church membership.

The Duppa church, the earliest of the secessions from the Jacob church, was ferociously separatist. Its members refused even to enter the parish church buildings where 'idolatrous' services had been performed, and they bitterly condemned Independents who did so.[65] The church, however, had been deeply influenced by Jacob's congregationalism and identified itself wholeheartedly with the developing Independent tradition rather than with the separatism of the past. This is evident in the most remarkable book ever written by a member of this church, Mrs Katherine Chidley's *Justification of the Independent Churches of Christ*, published in 1641 in answer to Thomas Edwards' first blast against the Independents. Although she did not gloss over the distinction between 'separates' and 'semi-separates,' Mrs. Chidley was primarily concerned to defend Independent church government as such rather than strict separatism; in the circumstances of 1641 she was confident that the triumph of Independency among 'all the Lord's people' would be the triumph of strict separatism.[66]

The members of the Duppa church were already experienced separatists when they organized their new church, but one problem demanded and received an original solution. The early separatist churches had for the most part chosen former clergymen as pastors, and the Jacob church had continued this tradition. The Duppa church had little prospect of attracting a convenient former clergyman, and in any case it was too small and too poor to support a full-time pastor. It was therefore forced to face squarely the problems of a lay pastorate, and it may have been the first of the separate churches to do so. This involved two aspects: first, the congregation's right to choose and ordain to the pastoral office a lay member of the church rather than a former clergyman or trained theological graduate; second (and this departed from the principles of the Jacob church), the pastor's right (or duty) to work to maintain himself rather than to live on the church's offerings. Mrs Chidley defended both of these positions against Edwards, and it is clear that the church had given them careful thought.[67]

Unfortunately it is not possible to identify conclusively the pastor of this church, but it may have been John Duppa, the separatist spokesman inside the Jacob church before the secession; he was described as

'Duper a cow-keeper' in a list of tub-preachers in 1647.[68] There were a number of other qualified members, some of whom represented the church publicly on occasion: Daniel Chidley 'the elder,' whose son Samuel was to become pastor twenty years later; Sabine Staresmore, a man of long separatist experience when he returned from the Netherlands to join this church in the early 1630s; Benjamin Wilkins, listed as a tub-preacher along with Duppa in 1647 as 'Wilkins the meal-man'; Rice Boy of Coleman Street, who was already a notorious puritan radical in Wiltshire and Gloucestershire when he moved to London to join this church;[69] and a shadowy dish merchant of Cheapside named Knight who, according to John Taylor the water-poet, was sent in 1640 by 'the brethren' on an evangelical tour of Suffolk where he was caught, only to escape to Amsterdam.[70] Probably the strongest personality in the church was the formidable Katherine Chidley, barred by her sex from church office; she was still a potent political force in London in 1653 in defending the Leveller John Lilburne in the twilight of his career.[71] David Brown was successful enough in London at teaching adults to write that he could afford to have a summer house at Greenwich.[72] Few additional identifications can be added for the 1640s, but they include Colonel Thomas Pride of Pride's Purge, and Captain William Goodson, a future Cromwellian vice-admiral, either of whom might have joined the church earlier.[73]

The second separatist Independent church of the Jacob circle in London was formed when members of the parent church were released from their imprisonment in September 1633 convinced that a strict separatism was henceforth necessary. Samuel Eaton was chosen pastor of the new church after his own release from prison in the spring of 1634, and during the next five years the church flourished, attracting into the separatist movement such recruits as the young William Kiffin.[74] But Eaton was always under the shadow of the Court of High Commission, and in August 1638 he was suddenly arrested again on a warrant from Archbishop Laud and taken to Newgate. He died there a year later, a martyr and hero among the separatists; two hundred 'Brownists and Anabaptists' accompanied his body to the churchyard, where an officious grave-digger who said he must fetch a minister was told that 'he might spare his labour.'[75]

The first firm evidence of a crisis over baptism among the London separatists relates to Eaton's church: in reporting the 1633 secession from the Jacob church, the Jessey memorandum added the words, 'Mr. Eaton with some others receiving a further baptism.' The problem of baptism was unavoidable for separatists determined to separate completely from a false church, for this brought into question their own baptism received in infancy in the Church of England. To baptize anew all their members, as the Donatists had done in ancient Africa, brought the separatists face to face with the dread prospect of Anabaptism. For most Englishmen the simple act of rebaptism, not its motive, constituted the essence of the Anabaptist offence. Thus Joseph Hall, the future Bishop of Exeter, had observed to the separatist John Robinson in 1611 that 'either you must go forward to Anabaptism, or come back to us'; and many clergymen were to use this argument against separatists in the future in the confident expectation that the spectre of Anabaptism would serve as a deterrent to separation.[76] The early separatists were frightened of this issue. Preoccupied as they were with separation from a false church, they seem to have identified Anabaptism as involving a rebaptism made necessary because the baptism of the church of Rome was false. In this light, Henry Barrow in 1590 diligently discussed whether the baptism of Rome was valid for that generation who had become members of the Church of England in maturity in the English Reformation, and it is at least open to question whether he ever fully grasped that the fundamental Anabaptist tenet was believer's baptism. Nearly twenty years later the separatist Francis Johnson watched John Smyth's progress into a true Anabaptism from close quarters in Amsterdam, and although he grasped intellectually that the issue was believer's baptism he nevertheless remained more emotionally involved with the problem of the baptism of false churches; his argument with Smyth was 'oddly tangential,' in the opinion of the most recent authority.[77]

The leaders of the new wave of separatism in London in the 1630s had to face this problem all over again. Since they were not university graduates thoroughly drilled to respond to the Anabaptist bogeyman as presented in the writings of the continental protestant divines, the act of rebaptism as the solution to the problem of complete separation from a false church may have held fewer terrors for them. For some this opened the possibility of an ultra-separatist rebaptism, necessarily administered to adults in the first instance to correct the inadequacy of the baptism of a false church; but this was not believer's baptism in principle, for the children of the separated faithful could thereafter receive a true baptism in a true church in the normal manner of infant baptism. This seems to have been the practice of Eaton and some of the members of his church.* Most separatists remained loyal to the views of the early separatists and condemned any act of rebaptism as a particularly indecent and disorderly act that brought the infamy of 'Anabaptism' upon the whole separatist community. This division of

* See Appendix A.

the separatists of the 1630s over separatist rebaptism left a detectable residue in the attitudes of the opponents of rebaptism in works published in the early 1640s. Thus Praise-God Barbone, a steadfast opponent of the act of rebaptism, was far better prepared in 1642 to refute ultra-separatist arguments by defending the baptism of the Church of England than he was to refute Baptists by defending infant baptism, even although he knew that it was believer's baptism that was at stake among his opponents by that date.[78] This purely separatist level of the baptism controversy which engulfed the Jacob circle of churches was soon lost sight of because it was so quickly superseded, as far as the rebaptizers went, by believer's baptism.

The first appearance among the separatists of true Baptists, practising believer's baptism, is an obscure topic that will probably never be entirely freed from conjecture. The only firm fact is that in 1638 six members left the Jacob church to join the church of John Spilsbury because they were 'convinced that baptism was not for infants, but professed believers.' Since this express statement of the motivation of the six dissidents is given in the Kiffin memorandum, a retrospective view by a Baptist fully familiar with the issues involved, we may accept as certain that in 1638 there was in London a congregation under Spilsbury's leadership practising believer's baptism.[79] A verse of John Taylor the water-poet in 1641 reported that 'one Spilsbury rose up of late' and 'rebaptized in Anabaptist fashion one Eaton (of the new found separation).'[80] Taylor's gossip is not necessarily reliable, but his verse suggests that Eaton may have secured his ultra-separatist rebaptism from Spilsbury, in which case Spilsbury had passed through an ultra-separatist phase himself before becoming a true Baptist. Spilsbury would thus appear to be the pioneer of ultra-separatist rebaptism as well as of believer's baptism among the London separatists. There is an indirect confirmation of Spilsbury's separatist phase in his later writings where he continued to argue that the baptism of a false church was invalid, a point most Baptists omitted because it was superfluous to their contention that infant baptism was unwarranted in the New Testament. An even surer indication of this separatist phase was Spilsbury's insistence throughout his mature Baptist career that a true church must be based upon a covenant even when all of its members had undergone believer's baptism; on this he differed from his fellow Baptists.[81] This points to a separatist origin for Spilsbury's church, and it is perhaps an echo of anxious debates in which the early members had reassured one another that a covenanted congregation had full authority from Christ to institute ordinances in isolation from all other churches. There is a parallel here with the congregationalism expressed by Mrs Chidley which enabled the Duppa church to choose and ordain a layman as their pastor.

One problem remains unresolved: where had Spilsbury's church come from? There is at least a possibility that it had originated by withdrawal from the Duppa church over the issue of ultra-separatist rebaptism, probably some years before 1638. As a schismatic secession from the Duppa church, Spilsbury's congregation would be well known to both the Eaton and Jacob churches but not immediately related to them, thus accounting for mere references to Spilsbury in the Jessey and Kiffin memorandums. This would account, too, for Spilsbury's convinced congregationalism and his refusal to abandon the church covenant. There is no direct evidence for this suggestion, but the behaviour of the Duppa church is consonant with a past division over the issue of ultra-separatist rebaptism; it resolutely rejected such a course and would not tolerate rebaptized members in the congregation. Also, in 1641, Samuel Chidley of this church prepared a set of arguments against believer's baptism and sent them in manuscript to Spilsbury. He subsequently refrained from publishing the manuscript for ten years, although he showed no such reticence in publishing vigorous refutations of other Baptists in the early 1640s.[82] This suggests an early association between the two men, and no comparable link can be found between Spilsbury's church and any other separatist church in London. The Spilsbury church can perhaps also be included in the Jacob circle of churches in London.

By 1638 the issues of separatism and baptism had considerably complicated the relationships of the Jacob circle of churches. The parent church under Jessey's leadership had remained faithful to its original latitudinarianism and had even extended it by giving a friendly dismissal to the strict separatists of 1633 and to the six Baptist dissidents of 1638. The Duppa church of 1630 pursued a strict separatist policy of refusing communion with the parish churches and with the semi-separatists of the Jacob church; but they also refused to tolerate rebaptized members in the church. The Spilsbury church at first probably required ultra-separatist rebaptism of all members, but by 1638 had been converted to believer's baptism for all members. The Eaton church, although a strict separatist church, remained in communion with the Jacob church and included among its membership both those who had received an ultra-separatist rebaptism and those who had not; there is no substantial reason to believe it ever contained advocates of believer's baptism.

The situation was further complicated by the dissolution of Eaton's church after his death in 1639, when most of the members, including those with an ultra-separatist rebaptism, probably rejoined the parent church under Jessey's leadership.[83] Other members may have been involved in the organization of a new separatist church in London in 1639 which, like Duppa's church, did not tolerate rebaptized members. The leaders of the new church were John Green, a feltmaker, and John Spencer, once the coachman of the puritan Lord Brooke. If Green was identical with the unnamed 'hatmaker' who was one of the original members of the 1633 congregation, then this new church also had a connection with the Jacob church.[84] Upon the division of the parent Jacob church in May 1640, the rebaptized members of Eaton's church presumably remained with Jessey's half of the church, while Barbone's refused to tolerate rebaptism among its members.

The next crisis which overtook Jessey's branch of the Jacob church also involved baptism, but in a new aspect. The initiative came from Richard Blunt, a member of Eaton's church who had rejoined the parent Jacob church in 1639 and remained with Jessey in the 1640 division. Sometime after this Blunt became convinced that baptism was for believers alone, and that it 'ought to be by dipping the body into the water, resembling burial and rising again.' Altogether he won fifty-two people to his point of view. This success led to another massive withdrawal from Jessey's church sometime in 1641, but this time the secession did not lead immediately to the formation of a new church. Blunt and his followers were uncertain how to initiate the practice of immersing believers. They could not turn to Spilsbury, since he practised believer's baptism by sprinkling rather than by total immersion; furthermore, some of Blunt's followers objected to Spilsbury's adherence to a church covenant, insisting that believer's baptism was the proper entrance into the church. The group decided to meet in 'two companies,' which were not yet properly constituted churches, until the procedure for instituting believer's baptism was settled. Blunt, who spoke Dutch, was sent to Holland to learn what he could from the Anabaptist Collegiants near Leyden who practised immersion.

At the beginning of January 1642 the two companies met together to undergo believer's baptism by immersion. Blunt baptized Samuel Blacklock who 'was a teacher amongst them,' and after Blacklock had baptized Blunt in turn the two men baptized the thirty-nine others present. A few days later twelve more people were baptized. Little is known about the organization of the two Particular Baptist churches that emerged from this great immersion ceremony, although Richard Blunt became the pastor of one, and Thomas Kilcop of the other.[85] Spilsbury soon afterward also adopted immersion as the proper mode of baptism for believers, but he may have rejected as a disorderly practice the necessity of baptizing for a third time the original members of his church who were already sprinkled as believers.[86] By 1642 there were thus three separate churches in London which required believer's baptism of all members.

Baptist principles continued to spread within Jessey's church as well. Sometime in 1642 William Kiffin was convinced of believer's baptism and probably rebaptised; on 17 October 1642 he launched his career as a Baptist spokesman by engaging in a famous dispute on baptism with Dr Daniel Featley. Kiffin, a former member of Eaton's church which had tolerated a mixed membership, was not yet persuaded that a true church could be formed by believer's baptism alone. He therefore remained a member of Jessey's church until late 1643 or early 1644, and Jessey, with his customary tolerance, was prepared to accommodate such differences in judgement within his congregation.[87] There can be no clearer indication of the powerful influence of the latitudinarianism that had always characterized the Jacob church.

On the eve of the civil war in England in 1642, the puritan congregation founded by Henry Jacob had not only survived and flourished for twenty-five years, it had also given rise directly to no fewer than six separate churches in London and indirectly to two more. The congregations of Jessey and Barbone were the immediate successors of the original church, and the former especially occupied a highly ambiguous position in the developing Independent tradition. The Duppa church was the prototype for separatist Independents, and the Eaton church, although it did not survive the Laudian decade, had in its half dozen years of existence recruited such people as William Kiffin into the sectarian movement. The two Baptist congregations of January 1642 formed the foundation for subsequent Particular Baptist development. Less intimately connected with the Jacob church but probably owing their existence as organized societies to men who had been trained in one or other of its offshoots were the Baptist congregation of Spilsbury and the separatist congregation of Green and Spencer.

The seven surviving churches of the Jacob circle in 1642 (that is, all but Eaton's church) were to have an impact out of all proportion to their numbers in shaping the radical sectarian developments of the revolutionary decade ahead. Their influence was to be exerted in directions and in institutions that Henry Jacob could not have foreseen and perhaps would not have welcomed when he founded his church in 1616. It was as a result of their experience over a quarter of a century as separate churches that the influence of the Jacob circle was to be thrown so decisively on the side of sectarian organization. The full measure of their institutional impact will become evident in a review of the larger context of this period.

2

'THESE BROKEN TIMES'* LONDON SEPARATISM ON THE EVE OF THE REVOLUTION

Quasi-separatism

In the generation before the puritan revolution the disaffection of Englishmen with the ceremonies and organization of the established church reached the proportions of a vast flood spreading over the parishes of England. Almost invisible beneath the flat surface of the flood waters ran the narrow channels of the separate churches which, when the waters receded with the passing of the revolution, were to leave the parishes permanently scarred with nonconformist congregations. In order to trace these faint channels it is necessary to distinguish them from other forms of activity which might be described as quasi-separatist, that is, unofficial meetings for religious purposes outside regular parish worship and usually of an inter-parochial character, but lacking the essential conviction that they were churches.

A first example illustrates the typical nature of such quasi-separatism. In 1632 the young apprentice William Kiffin, seventeen years old, had passed through the initial stages of his conversion and had become a zealous follower of puritan sermons. Coming to know several other apprentices of similar interests, he began to meet with them regularly every Sunday. They went together to a morning lecture at six o'clock, but met first an hour before 'to spend it in prayer, and in communicating to each other what experience we had received from the Lord; or else to repeat some sermon which we had heard before'. As time went on, they grew a little bolder: 'we also read some portion of Scripture, and spake from it what it pleased God to enable us.'[1] These gatherings took place outside the constituted order of the Church of England, those who attended came from several parishes, and the participants grew increasingly bolder in what amounted to lay preaching. Had this

* Laud, *Works*, v, 598.

group of apprentices come to the notice of the authorities, it would have been regarded as a Brownist conventicle, but it was not in any sense a separatist church with a definite membership and rules of internal order. When Kiffin finally joined Samuel Eaton's church, he moved from an ephemeral association of like-minded people into an institution with fully articulated principles of organization and worship.[2]

A second example illustrates how difficult it was for such groups to achieve the full stature of a separate church. The example is borrowed from Bristol, where for twenty years preceding the formation of the Broadmead Independent church a group of people had been engaged in quasi-separatist activities on a large scale. Here, 'awakened souls and honest minded people' flocked to hear the minister of St Philip's parish, Mr Yeamans, 'and sat under his light near 20 years.' His admirers kept 'many fast days together in private houses,' where 'they kept many days of prayer together, as a company of good people, sensible of the sins and snares of their day.' As they grew 'somewhat numerous in that work,' the company attracted to themselves the same reproaches made against more organized separatist congregations: it was said that 'they met together in the night to be unclean,' and that 'they had women preachers among them, because there were many good women. . .that, when they should upon occasion be speaking with the world about the things thereof, in their buying or selling, they would speak very heavenly.'[3] In 1640 five members of the group decided to separate from the corrupt worship of the Church of England; the difficulty is revealed in the terms used to describe this event in the church records: 'These persons went out from hearing Common Prayer, not knowing whither they went.' Their practice at this time was to absent themselves from the parish service while the Prayer Book was in use, but to enter the church in time for the sermon by the puritan minister, who was the husband of one of the separatists. On Sunday afternoon the five separatists met by themselves, 'and so built up one another.' It was only at Easter the following year that they took the first tentative step towards a separatist organization when the separatist John Canne, 'a man skilful in Gospel order,' on a visit to Bristol instructed them in 'the order of God's house,' showing them 'how they should join together, and take in members.' Canne was, however, a little too radical for the Bristol separatists, and his advice that they should hire a barn to meet in was not well received.[4] By the summer of 1642 there were a hundred and sixty members, but it was not until the autumn of that year that they enjoyed their first communion together as a church. Even this advance was possible only because many members of the Llanvaches Independent church had taken refuge in Bristol from the Royalists, bringing with them their pastor Walter Cradock, who administered the Lord's Supper in the Bristol church. The following year the capture of Bristol by the Royalists forced the church to flee to London, where it continued to meet with the Llanvaches church. Not until 1645 did the Broadmead church have its own pastor, an ordained clergyman.[5] Thus even after twenty years of meetings as radical puritans it took another five years to organize separatist worship on a regular basis in the Broadmead church.

A third example illustrates the view the authorities took of such quasi-separatist practices. In 1640 and 1641 one of the most notorious cases of lay preaching in London involved Roger Quatermayne, a Southwark solicitor. Quatermayne appeared before the Court of High Commission several times in 1640 and was eventually brought before the Privy Council, one of whom remarked that 'you are a Separatist, an Anabaptist, a Brownist, a Familist, and you are preacher to them all'. Archbishop Laud considered him 'the ring-leader of all the Separatists'.[6] He was none of these, but a radical puritan layman who was in regular communion with the Church of England, as duly attested by Dr Daniel Featley.[7] His offence was to organize 'conferences' of godly people both in Southwark and at his old home in Berkshire. During his appearance before the Privy Council on 25 October 1640 he was asked what they did at these meetings:

Quatermayne: My Lord, thus; we pray, and we read the Scriptures, and as well as we are able find out the meaning of the Holy Ghost therein, and what we understand from the word, we impart to our company.
A Lord: So, said one of the Lords, and is not this preaching?
Quatermayne: No, my Lord, I do not understand it so, it is nothing but godly conference, which every Christian man is bound to do and perform; for it is our duty to edify and build up one another in our most holy faith, which we cannot do, except it be opened unto us.
Archbishop: Then said the Archbishop, this is his constant practice in city and country, to draw people together, and to make conventicles.
Quatermayne: My Lord, I want information in my judgement, I understand not what you mean by *conventicle*, I did always think that public duties did not make void private, but that both might stand with a Christian.
Archbishop: No more it doth not, said the Archbishop, but your conventicles are not private.
Quatermayne: My Lord, I am sure they are not public; I pray, my Lord, inform my judgement what a conventicle is.
Archbishop: Why, this is a conventicle, said the Archbishop, when ten or twelve or more or less meet together, to pray, read, preach, expound, this is a conventicle.
Quatermayne: My Lord, I do not so understand it.[8]

However repugnant they were to the authorities, Quatermayne's activities were not truly separatist.

These quasi-separatist activities were as old as puritanism itself. Dr Patrick Collinson has vividly described the exercises and 'night conventicles' of the late Elizabethan period among ever widening circles of laymen.[9] Archbishop Laud's policies within the Church of England and his attempt to stamp out these irregularities served only to give them added impetus. Oliver Cromwell in 1638 was associated with a quasi-separatist society at Ely not unlike the earlier stages of the Bristol group, and Sir Henry Vane the younger met with a similar group at Barnard Castle.[10] John Bunyan's 'poor company' at Bedford had passed through the same long evolutionary process as the Bristol group, and the historian of the Bedford church echoed the Bristol historian in his description of the godly people who 'even while they remained without all form and order as to visible church communion according to the testament of Christ were very zealous according to their light, not only to edify themselves, but also to propagate the Gospel.'[11] Quasi-separatism could occasionally lead spontaneously to separatist organization, but without experienced and determined leadership the results could be unfortunate, as in the case related by Peter Cole, the London bookseller, to Thomas Edwards one day in December 1644. Cole had known 'a church of Brownists within these few years' to which he had 'once thought of all other churches to have joined himself a member'; but this church now denied the Scriptures to be the word of God 'because there were untruths contained in them,' and when Cole had visited them on a fast day recently he 'found them playing at tables.'[12] On the other hand, many of those engaged in quasi-separatist activity loathed separatism in principle; here the spectre of Brownism could act as a deterrent to fully separatist organization, as in the case of John Cotton's covenanted group of godly persons in St Botolph's parish in Boston, Lincolnshire, where the quasi-separatists formed virtually a select congregation within a regular parochial congregation.[13]

The phenomenon of quasi-separatism was of great importance for its powerful effect as a solvent of the parish community. The overwhelming majority of such groups seem to have been inter-parochial, as like-minded Christians from a wide area gathered around a favourite preacher or met to encourage one another in the face of the ignorant multitude. But such meetings were inherently unstable in membership and necessarily limited in function. The typical attitude of participants was expressed by John Bellamie when, speaking of his experience as a conservative puritan, he said, 'Truly, I bless God, I have often met with sundry select companies of godly Christians in holy duties, and been willing, according to the best of my abilities, to do or receive any good to or from them.'[14] 'Select companies' were fluid in their membership, as opposed to the closed and secretive membership of the separate church; they were 'sundry' within the experience of the individual, rather than exclusive as was membership in a covenanted congregation; and their purpose was 'holy duties' (the recapitulation of sermons, the study of the Bible, and the building up of one another's faith), not 'ordinances' (the exercise of worship and the administration of the sacraments). These associations must therefore be clearly distinguished from separate churches, such as the Jacob circle of churches, which stood forth as fully developed rivals to the traditional parish churches of England.

The greater spiritual importance of the family after the protestant reformation encouraged such quasi-separatism in the development of family prayers and 'holy duties' supplementary to the regular weekly worship in the parish church. This 'spiritualization of the household,' as it has been described by Christopher Hill, was ambivalent in its effect.[15] Family prayers tended to reinforce patriarchal authority in the household, which could thus become a subordinate unit in the parochial system of spiritual discipline desired by conservative puritans. The household, however, was a less stable institution than the territorial parish, for children grew up and the turnover of domestic servants, apprentices, or resident journeymen was usually rapid. The spiritual household was important less for the preservation of patriarchal forms of discipline than for the spiritualization of some of its individual members, accustoming them as individuals to seek religious associations outside the parish church.[16] In the Laudian period such 'private duties' became for many a necessary supplement to the unpopular ritualistic emphasis of the parish services. In such circumstances the family circle easily broke open to include sympathetic neighbours. This can be illustrated in the case of Quatermayne whose family, consisting only of himself and his wife, he thought too narrow a circle for adequate spiritual refreshment; on the day before each of his many appearances before the Court of High Commission and the Privy Council, 'therefore I must call in my neighbours to help me.' In a similar vein he defended his keeping of 'conventicles' in the country by saying that he was visiting 'friends' in his birthplace; in his own mind these quasi-separatist activities that so frightened the authorities were simply fulfilling the prescription of family prayers.[17] Although Dr Hill has suggested that 'we can see the independent congregation in process of formation here: as an extension of household prayers,' this was not the case.[18] Even in its most extreme form, in the households of noblemen or greater gentry possessing a resident chaplain who was a congregationalist by conviction, such extended household worship did not tend to become a separate church but remained simply a quasi-separatist group.[19]

There were changes too in the institutions of the parish where, Dr Hill has pointed out, 'economic facts. . .were creating before 1640 a kind of *de facto* voluntaryism in many parishes,' especially through the puritan device of providing voluntary augmentations for parish ministers and lecturers.[20] Professor Haller suggested that 'every Puritan group which at any time joined together to engage a lecturer tended to become a "gathered church," centred in its preaching minister and self-limited in membership to his convinced personal followers.'[21] No such case of a gathered church is known, and the effect of these developments is more indirect than Dr Hill or Professor Haller allow. The institutional development was in the direction of a parochial congregationalism in which interested lay members of the parish exercised increasing influence over the institutions of the parish; the culmination of this tendency in the revolutionary period was the parochial presbytery, not the gathered church. On the other hand, the self-selecting aspect of this growing voluntaryism undermined the solidarity of the Christian community of the territorial parish. The lectures especially acted as a solvent of older and narrower loyalties, for while it was illegal to attend church services outside the parish where one resided, lectures could be attended anywhere. Such great puritan lectureships as St Antholin's in London were deliberately aimed at the community as a whole to supply the deficiency in preaching that existed in many urban parishes.[22]

The cumulative effect of quasi-separatism, household prayers, and puritan lectureships was to diminish the importance of the services of the parish church and to provide a fluid and unstable environment in which individuals grew accustomed to voluntary associations and to the exercise of choice in religiously meaningful activity. The important result was an increase in religious individualism. Participation in these activities could predispose individuals to join a separate church when the opportunity arose; but these activities did not in themselves culminate in separate churches, because the separate church was not a quasi-separatist supplement to parish worship but a complete alternative. Those puritans who engaged in quasi-separatism were clear in their own minds about the difference between a separatist or Brownist church and the parish church, and about their own relations with either one of these institutions. The ecclesiastical authorities, on the other hand, blurred these distinctions because in their perspective there was no essential difference between a quasi-separatist puritan group meeting illegally and an outwardly similar group claiming to be a church. In this sense, puritans engaged in quasi-separatism were psychologically prepared to make the distinction and thus to accept the reality of the separate churches, and their perception of these matters differed significantly from that of the Laudian hierarchy. Puritan radicalism which was not in itself separatist in intent contributed in this way to the intellectual climate that permitted the separate churches to grow.

Beyond the Jacob circle

Other separate churches in London beyond the Jacob circle are difficult to trace. Two such churches, which had a continuous existence for decades, were the tiny General Baptist congregations described in chapter 4; but there is no sign of them in the contemporary records of the 1630s. There were complaints of heretics and of lay preachers, but as with the quasi-separatists the evidence must be carefully weighed before we can be sure that we are dealing with true separate churches. Even when all the difficulties of the evidence are taken into account, however, the Jacob circle, although it had no monopoly, appears to have accounted for most of the organized separatist activity in London before the revolution.

The wholesale approach to religious deviance adopted by the authorities in the Laudian period makes it difficult to form a critical assessment of the evidence for heresy in London. The general warrant under which the Court of High Commission pursued Prynne, Bastwick, and Burton in 1636 announced that

> credible information has been given that there are at present in London and many other parts, sundry sorts of separatists and sectaries, as namely, Brownists, Anabaptists, Arians, Thraskists, Familists, Sensualists, Antinomians, and others, who refuse on Sundays...to come to their parish churches, but meet together in great numbers...in private houses and places, and there keep conventicles and exercises of religion, by the laws of the realm prohibited.[23]

The credibility of this sinister list of heresies is suspect when a quasi-separatist like Quatermayne could be described as 'a Separatist, an Anabaptist, a Brownist, a Familist.' Among the High Commission papers of Sir John Lambe was one from the later 1630s describing several groups in London under the designations of the Families of the Mount and of the Valley, the Sensualists, and the Antinomians, and naming nearly fifty people in four overlapping groups.[24] The dominant personality was the mystic Dr John Everard, living a fugitive life in London after the deprivation of his living in 1636, and the dominant tradition was one of continental mysticism, shaped by the writings of Henry Niclaes and by the *Theologica Germanica.* This tradition certainly had a leavening effect upon the religious radicalism of the revolutionary period, but it is doubtful if these groups had much institutional impact; their meetings may have had only a quasi-separatist character.[25] Another such eccentric group existed for a while around John Trask, who believed that the Jewish sabbath, and perhaps even the Jewish law, were still in force. His wife remained loyal to these ideas and lived out her life in prison, but Trask recanted and ended his life in the bosom of the Jacob church, or at least in the house of one of the members.[26] Trask's sabbatarianism, like Everard's mysticism, had lingering echoes through the rest of the century, but it left no significant institutional survival at this period.

As the machinery of ecclesiastical regulation broke down with the meeting of the Long Parliament there was an outburst of lay preaching in London, but this too does not necessarily indicate the massive organization of separatist congregations. The most detailed list of lay preachers published in London in 1641 named seventeen lay preachers, describing them in enough detail to carry conviction, but Green and Spencer, 'the two arch-separatists,' are the only familiar names on the list. While several men are said to have preached every week, as might be expected in a separatist church, others preached once a fortnight, or on the first day of each month, or even twice a week.[27] This suggests that the author has indiscriminately listed quasi-separatists and eccentric individuals preaching to casually assembled groups of their fellow citizens, while he has missed the better organized and better concealed separate churches. John Green and John Spencer became notorious as lay preachers not because they were pastors of a separate church but because they sought every opportunity to preach to the general public. Thomas Edwards later wrote of Green that he was 'one of the first mechanicks that presently upon the first sitting of this Parliament preached in our [parish] churches publicly, as at Aldgate and elsewhere.'[28] The lay preaching of 1641 was offensive because it was public, not because it was separatist; most separatist lay preachers continued to preach secretly in their congregations, thus remaining as invisible to contemporaries as to historians.

True separate churches can be identified only after all of these distinctions have been made. The surviving evidence suggests that outside the Jacob circle of churches there were few others before the puritan revolution. The ancient Barrowist church, first organized in Elizabeth's reign, lingered on to 1632, when it was detected by the authorities and two of its members were imprisoned with members of the Jacob church;

it does not appear to have survived this final disaster.[29] Another separate church, first organized in London in 1621 by a Mr Hubbard, flourished in the 1630s, but it owed its success to a pastor recruited from the Jacob church, Samuel How. A semi-separatist member of the Jacob church when this church was detected and imprisoned in 1632, the experience made him an outright separatist; as soon as he was released from prison in 1633 he joined the separatist congregation originally organized by Hubbard. This church had survived a dozen years only with difficulty, but it revived under How's leadership.[30] 'How the cobbler' was the most famous lay preacher of the Laudian decade. He owed his notoriety to a sermon preached in January 1639 in the Nag's Head Tavern in the parish of St Stephen Coleman Street before a hundred people, including the vicar of the parish, John Goodwin.[31] The sermon, immediately printed as *The Sufficiency of the Spirits Teaching*, challenged the monopoly of university-educated preachers and defended the right of laymen to preach.[32] When How died in September 1640, the institutional future of the church was assured; the deacon, Stephen More, a cloth merchant in Philpot Lane, was chosen pastor in his place.

In the rising excitement of the latter part of the Laudian decade new separatist congregations may have been organized, but they are virtually impossible to trace. The most important possibility is the separatist church of Edmund Rosier, a London clothier, which was certainly in existence in the early 1640s when its most prominent member was John Lilburne.[33] The origin of this church is unknown, but Lilburne's early career offers a glimpse of separatist and quasi-separatist associations at work in pre-revolutionary London. He was a young apprentice in the puritan household of Thomas Hewson, a clothier at London Stone who was a friend of the Winthrop family, of Henry Jessey, and of Rosier. Rosier took Lilburne with him to visit Dr John Bastwick in the Gatehouse prison in 1636, thus launching Lilburne on his career as a radical puritan polemicist.[34] Lilburne was arrested in December 1637 for his role in printing and importing into England Dr Bastwick's satiric attack on the bishops, the *Letany*. The principal evidence against him in the Court of Star Chamber was the confession of Edmund Chillenden, a member of How's church caught distributing seditious literature, who secured his own release from Newgate by implicating Lilburne. About this time too, Lilburne knew Samuel Chidley of Duppa's church, and William Kiffin, who assisted Lilburne in the publication of his pamphlets in 1641.[35] Despite these contacts with three well established separatist congregations, Lilburne was no more than a quasi-separatist in 1638, 'being never yet in any of their [separatist] congregations in England.'[36] In prison, just as Eaton and How had done before him, the young Lilburne cast away all scruples and became a complete separatist. In September 1638 he wrote a pamphlet advocating rigid separation which was smuggled to Amsterdam where it was printed by John Canne.[37] Until his release from prison in 1641, however, Lilburne had no opportunity to join a separate church, and it was perhaps only at this time that Rosier's church was organized.

Other possible churches at this period are considerably more shadowy. Richard Rogers, a glover near Whitecross Street, who had been implicated in the distribution of pamphlets against the bishops in 1637, was said in one pamplet in 1641 to have a 'congregation as he terms it,' and in another, to be a preacher at a Brownist conventicle meeting at Mr Porter's house in nearby Goat Alley.[38] These charges are unusually specific; but there is no further trace of Rogers and no way of identifying his church. There is also the case of Adam or Alan Banks, a hosier of Coleman Street who appeared at the bar of the House of Commons in June 1641 as a notorious lay preacher. Banks can be linked with John Bolton, a goldsmith of Foster Lane, who is later visible as a prominent radical in London; these men may have been the leaders of their own church at this time.[39]

Separatism remained an unpopular alternative with the mass of puritans, whose discontents did not extend as far as abandoning the uniform and universal national church in principle. The separate churches were limited in size by the need for meeting secretly in private houses, and even in 1641 only the largest congregations had more than a hundred members.[40] Thus the total membership of the London separatist congregations on the eve of the revolution was perhaps one thousand or so, a negligible number in a metropolitan centre of more than a quarter of a million people. The separatists were also intensely unpopular with the public in general. An 'overthwart neighbour' betrayed one meeting of the Jessey church to the authorities in 1638, and the most common cause for the discovery of the separate churches was the presence of a spontaneous mob at their meeting places.[41] The weekly meetings of the churches were moved from house to house to avoid detection, and Samuel How was said to have conducted meetings 'up and down in fields and woods.' The meetings often lasted all day; during 'the heat of the bishops' severities,' William Kiffin said, speaking of his experience in Eaton's church, 'we were forced to meet very early in the morning, and to continue together till night.' Mrs Chidley of Duppa's church said that some members wore periwigs 'to blind the eyes of the bishop's bloodhounds when they have come to take them,' and on one occasion Jessey's identity as a clergyman and pastor of his congregation was successfully concealed from his captors.[42] When in

December 1641 Praise-God Barbone opened the meeting of his church to the general public, the result was a tumult involving thousands of people.[43] After this experience the separate churches generally continued the custom of private and more or less secret meetings well into the revolutionary period. As Mrs Chidley remarked to the puritan Thomas Edwards in 1641, separatist meetings were sometimes dangerous to their lives and always dangerous to their liberty, 'for though we meet never so privately and peaceably, yet such cattle as yourself are always bleating in the ears of your parish officers and constables.'[44]

From anti-episcopacy to anti-clericalism

It is already evident that the near monopoly of the Jacob circle of churches before 1640 did not mean that these churches were uniform in church order. Their common conviction of the congregational nature of the true Christian church permitted each of these groups to convince itself that it was truly a church; charitably interpreted, this congregationalism also enabled them to agree to differ about questions of church order. The tremendous vitality of the Jacob circle in these years was due to this diversity. But the development of these churches moved in directions which could scarcely have been imagined when the Jacob church was founded in 1616. The most important change was the appearance of a lay pastorate, with a concomitant growth among these churches of a rabid anti-clericalism that was not typical of puritanism in general.

Jacob's intention, when he founded his congregation, was that the puritan gathered church, like the parish congregation, should have a professional minister. The three successive pastors of the parent church, Jacob, Lathrop, and Jessey, were supported by the congregation, and they were, furthermore, former clergymen of the national church. The determination of the Jacob church to enjoy a professional ministry is evident in the long intervals they were prepared to wait without a pastor in order to secure the services of an appropriately trained candidate, an interval of two years between Jacob and Lathrop, and three years between Lathrop and Jessey. Independent gathered churches of the revolutionary period also preserved a professional ministry recruited among former clergymen of the national church, but these later Independent pastors generally held lectureships in the national church, thus easing considerably the financial burden of their congregations in supporting them. This possibility did not exist for the smaller Jacob church during its first quarter century of furtive existence. Their willingness to meet the cost of a professional ministry and their evident care in the selection of a pastor suggest that for the members of the Jacob church a professionally trained and full time pastor was necessary to their sense of identity as a church apart from the parish congregations.

By the end of the 1630s the leaders of the separate churches in London, except Jessey, were tradesmen who supported themselves: John Duppa was 'a cow-keeper,' Samuel Eaton a button-maker, Samuel How and John Spilsbury, cobblers, Praise-God Barbone a leather seller, John Green a hat maker, and John Spencer a 'horse-rubber.'[45] The development of such self-supporting ministers, although beyond Jacob's intention, was nevertheless due to his decision to permit private members of his church to 'exercise' before the congregation, for this practice destroyed the preaching monopoly of a professional ministry. Once laymen became accustomed to preach it was a short step to a lay pastorate. The step was taken by the Duppa church. After their long experience as members of the Jacob church, the founders of this new separatist church were secure in their sense of identity as a church, and several of their members were experienced preachers. Samuel How's famous sermon at the Nag's Head Tavern in 1639 in defence of lay preaching provided a formal justification for an already widely prevalent practice, but the unspoken implication was that the lay preacher was qualified to exercise the pastoral office within the separate church. From this point onwards we can distinguish two types of separate churches, those with a professional ministry and those with a lay pastorate.

The diversity of the Jacob circle of churches was made possible by the lay pastorate. Separate churches were freed of a considerable financial burden when their lay pastors supported themselves. This permitted smaller and less affluent groups to band together to form a church whenever a serious conflict arose over church order, and, as we have seen, this happened several times in the Jacob church and its offshoots in the 1630s. The separate churches were freed in this way from dependence upon wealthy puritan sponsors, and their membership was composed overwhelmingly of what Christopher Hill has characterized as 'the industrious sort of people.'[46] The court records of the separatists list glovers, cobblers, bakers, haberdashers, leather dressers, gunmakers, last makers, cord-wainers, weavers, tailors, feltmakers, clothmakers, and an occasional merchant. These were not people who undertook the dangerous step of separation from the Church of England with nothing to lose, nor the disorderly rabble depicted in the anti-sectarian literature of the period. Established in trades and usually with young families to maintain, they underwent real hardship if they were imprisoned for separatism. Most of them must have been relatively poor, but this is not always the case. Samuel Eames, a citizen and clothworker rebaptized by

Richard Blunt in 1642, could afford to invest one hundred pounds in the Irish Adventurers, and Blunt himself was wealthy enough to undertake a trip to the Netherlands in 1641 on behalf of his Baptist associates.[47]

The upkeep of a professional minister was beyond the resources of a congregation of tradesmen. There is some evidence, admittedly conjectural, that the Jacob church contained members who were substantially wealthier than this. In 1638, lists of house valuations were prepared for most London parishes for the purpose of assessing tithes; the lists preserve in most cases the names of householders and the 'moderated rent,' that is, the true annual rent reduced by one fourth for the purpose of the assessment. The premises of Alderman Sir Thomas Soames in Soper Lane, which may serve to establish a standard, were assessed at a moderated rent of seventy pounds; Soames was one of the wealthiest merchants of London, and although he was a puritan member for the City in the Long Parliament, he was no friend of the separatists.[48] By comparison, Ralph Grafton, the wealthy upholsterer who was singled out among Lathrop's congregation in 1632 as a 'rich man,' was assessed twenty-three pounds for his house in Cornhill.[49] Stephen More, in 1638 the deacon of How's congregation and later its pastor, was said by the historian of the church to have been 'a citizen of good worth, and possessed of some estate'; his house near Philpot Lane was rated at a true annual rent of ten pounds.[50] The General Baptist Edward Barber, who described himself proudly in his pamphlets as a citizen and merchant tailor of London, was assessed at eight pounds for his house in Threadneedle Street.[51] These were all leading men in their respective congregations and can be identified conclusively in the tithe records. Among the quasi-separatists of the Laudian decade, John Lilburne's friend Edmund Rosier the clothier was assessed at twenty pounds for his premises in Ironmonger Lane.[52]

In August 1641 a section of Jessey's church meeting at 'our Brother Golding's' house was discovered by a constable who summoned Sir Thomas Soames to deal with them.[53] If it may be inferred from this that the meeting took place in the vicinity of Soames' house in Soper Lane, a tentative identification in the 1638 tithes records of several of those involved can be ventured. They were men of considerable substance. Peter Golding's house in the parish of St Thomas the Apostle, where the meeting was discovered, was rated at a moderated rent of twenty-six pounds annually, and John Stonard in the neighbouring parish of St Mary le Bow was assessed at fifty pounds for his premises. William Shambrook was rated at twenty-four pounds for his house in St Mary Colechurch parish, just north of Soper Lane.[54] Shambrook's later career is fully in accord with his status as reflected in these records.

In 1644 his house was the scene of an important meeting of the leading separatists and Independents in London. By 1647 he was a lieutenant-colonel of the London militia and a key figure in the controversy between the Presbyterians and the Independents for control of the London militia in that year. He was killed in the Second Civil War in 1648 a few weeks after he had been promoted to colonel of the Tower regiment.[55] A fourth man, Mr Puckle, who was captured with Shambrook and the others in 1641, does not appear in the tithe records, but it is perhaps more than a coincidence that in 1659 William Puckle was also a lieutenant-colonel of the London militia and a supporter of the radical faction in the London militia committee.[56] The presence of such men in the Jacob church would explain the ability of this church to preserve a professional ministry.

The other principal financial obligation of the separate church was that of supporting poor members and widows. The Jacob church had decided in 1616, as a practical aspect of their separation from the parish system of the Church of England, that the church should support its own poor, and according to Mrs Chidley this was the general custom of the separatist churches in 1641. She went on to complain that the separatists were also forced to support the poor of the parish, as was well known to 'all landlords that do let them houses, for if they know them to be Separates, and that they will not have to do with the priests in the payment of that they call "dues", they make their tenant pay the more rent, for if the tenant will not, the landlord must.'[57] Mrs Chidley also gave classic expression to the economic grievances of the poor against the parish clergy. Compulsory tithes were 'sore against the people's will,' but even more annoying were the multitudes of special fees that bore heavily on the poor in their every encounter with the clergy. Even the birth of a dead child was expensive, as the clergy must be paid 'for reading a dirge' over the body and for the churching of the mother. To bury a child in the churchyard of one of the 'great parishes' which was supposed to be free to the poor, even the poorest parent had to lay out seven or eight shillings. At Bedlam, which was 'the cheapest place' Mrs Chidley knew, apart from fees for bearers, diggers, and the burial plot, there must be 'a twelvepenny priest to say something over the grave, and he will grudge if he have not more than a shilling, though he say but a few words without the book.' If a poor man were forced to work upon 'one of their Saints-days,' he must pay a groat to the paritor who summoned him to court, and if he failed to pay the fees for his offence he was excommunicated and must pay at least a noble to be reinstated in the church. If he died excommunicate, his friends must pay five pounds to have him posthumously absolved so that he could be buried in consecrated ground. The clergy therefore were a worse plague than the locusts of Egypt, for where the locusts ate the green things of the land the clergy ate up 'both green and dry.'[58]

No work gave better expression than Mrs Chidley's to the profound anti-clericalism of the London separatist community in 1641. They had come a long way from the situation at the founding of Henry Jacob's church in 1616, which had been more anti-episcopal than anti-clerical. The custom of lay preaching, incipient in the 1616 congregation, had flowered into a fully elaborated lay pastorate by the beginning of the revolution. The bitterness created by the persecutions of the Court of High Commission had driven semi-separatists and quasi-separatists like Eaton, How, and Lilburne into complete separation, and the whole separatist movement became deeply infused with hatred for the 'black-coats.' This anti-clericalism was given added force by the economic grievances of 'the industrious sort of people' and the poor against an institution whose spiritual authority was completely discredited. The separatist churches undoubtedly drew upon a widespread popular anti-clericalism, but they also transformed it by channelling a vague and diffused discontent into institutions that challenged the very existence of the traditional church.[59]

There was an important limitation to the radicalism of the separatists. What they were separating from was not the moral evil of the world at large but the false worship of the Church of England. What they aspired to was purity of worship rather than the creation of a holy community of moral perfection separated from the unregenerate world. There was a vast gulf between the English separatists, with their endless preoccupations over the form and matter of the visible church, and such radical Anabaptist groups on the Continent as the Hutterites, who sought to create a perfect Christian community in this world. English separatists were too thoroughly imbued with the Calvinist teachings of their puritan mentors to be 'perfectionists.' They knew the distinction between the visible and the invisible church, and they knew the world to be so hopelessly fallen that the elect could only be saved through grace, and not through an impossible moral perfection.[60] They claimed instead that the New Testament provided a standard for Christian worship and church organization to which the established church scarcely bothered to aspire and which it was the responsibility of Christians to achieve.

The growth of Independency

Even as circumstances pushed the Jacob church ever deeper into the sectarian world, it continued in its highly ambiguous and fruitful role as a puritan congregation; for those same circumstances made semi-separatist principles more attractive to radical puritans. As tensions increased within the Church of England, radical puritans mingled more freely with the Jacob circle, and the parent Jacob church became the model for the formation of other Independent gathered churches.

The overwhelming majority of the puritan clergy and most puritan laymen abhorred separatism as a policy and were fearful of separatists. The sensational mass arrest of the Jacob church in 1632, however, aroused uneasiness among puritans, whose minds were increasingly divided between sympathy for persecuted saints and distaste at the prospect of separatism. John Davenport, the vicar of St Stephen Coleman Street, preached publicly against such separation, but he was apparently attempting to stifle his own growing doubts about the Church of England. The Jessey memorandum smugly records that he was sent 'a large answer' by those in prison, which so moved him that he reputedly never took communion in the Church of England again, but fled first to Holland and afterwards to New England where 'he now preacheth the same truth that these do here, though there without such persecution.'[61] For their part the separatists had always identified themselves with the puritan tradition and reproached puritans only for their failure to live up to their own principles. The inner religious life of the separatist saint, as described in William Kiffin's autobiographical account of his conversion in the 1630s, was entirely conventional in puritan terms, ranging from his providential attendance at a St Antholin's lecture on the duty of servants to masters at the very moment when he had decided, at the age of fifteen, to run away from his own master, through diligent attendance at puritan sermons, to the culminating religious crisis of his life which left him, at seventeen, with a mature understanding of the workings of grace in the human heart. It was only when this conversion was complete that Kiffin turned his attention to questions of church order and, influenced by the sermons of Jose Glover and Jeremiah Burroughes, entered on the path that led into Samuel Eaton's separatist congregation before 1638.[62]

If Kiffin's discontent took him into a separatist congregation, that of other puritans took them into exile or to the remote wilderness of Massachusetts. Exile and emigration were also forms of separation, of withdrawal from the parish churches and episcopal jurisdiction of the Church of England, even if those who thus left England loudly professed their rejection of separatism in principle. This diversity of *de facto* separation served to blur the issue of separatism, and the influence of the separate churches on radical puritans became more extensive as London became a place of refuge for fugitive and displaced clergymen and a marshalling point for puritans going abroad. In January 1638 Samuel Eaton, Mr Glover, and other outsiders attended an important meeting of the Jacob church.[63] Jose Glover, the son of a successful London merchant, had been suspended from his living at Sutton in Surrey in 1634 for refusing to read the Book of Sports. He moved back to London, where Kiffin was influenced by his preaching in favour of Independency. Glover's separation was to take the form of emigration, and he died on a ship bound for Massachusetts.[64] Another clergyman, Hanserd Knollys, who resigned his living in Lincolnshire, 'tarried long' in London about 1637 waiting for a passage to New England; he knew Kiffin at this period and joined the Jacob church under Jessey after his return to England in 1641.[65] Kiffin heard Jeremiah Burroughes preach in the late 1630s when the latter visited London after his deprivation by the notorious Bishop Wren of Norwich and before he left England to accept office in the exiled English church at Rotterdam.[66] William Carter, who resigned his rectory at St John Zachary in 1630, and Thomas Goodwin, who resigned his lectureship in Cambridge in 1634, both lived obscurely in London where they may have had contacts with members of the Jacob circle of churches.[67] Such clergymen added to the radical ferment by preaching furtively whenever they could; as Kiffin's case makes clear, their preaching served to win recruits for the separate churches even if the preachers thought primarily in terms of exile or emigration.

The central figure connecting the Jacob church with the developing Independent wing of puritanism was Henry Jessey. A Yorkshireman, Jessey made a wide circle of contacts in the south while he was chaplain to the Gurdon family at Assington in Suffolk. His close friendship with the neighbouring Winthrop family probably provided his first links with London puritans, for John Winthrop worked in London for many years prior to his departure for Massachusetts in 1630. Through the Winthrops Jessey came to know Thomas Hewson, the puritan clothier living at London Stone who was soon to be John Lilburne's master. Jessey's mailing address for his correspondence with his New England friends in the 1630s was the bookshop of Henry Overton in Pope's Head Alley; a decade later Overton was a prominent member of a gathered church and the principal publisher of the Independents.[68] His return to Yorkshire in 1633 brought Jessey into contact with a group of radical Yorkshiremen, one of whom, Sir Matthew Boynton, made Jessey his chaplain after the deprivation of his Yorkshire living. In mid 1636 Boynton moved to within twenty miles of London, to a place five miles distant from the parish church, so that under Jessey's chaplaincy the Boynton household became a quasi-separatist conventicle.[69] Boynton at this time was deeply involved in the negotiations for the Saybrook project of emigration to Connecticut under the sponsorship of Lord Saye and Sele and Lord Brooke. As a member of Boynton's household Jessey must have been familiar with the principals in the project: his own personal friend John Winthrop the younger, Boynton's Yorkshire friends Sir William Constable and Sir Richard Saltonstall, Oliver Cromwell's Huntingdonshire landlord Henry Lawrence, and the clergyman Philip Nye.[70] Sometime after Jessey's move to London, these men (except Winthrop) moved to Arnhem, where Philip Nye and Thomas Goodwin became the pastors of a gathered church. Jessey's deepest identification throughout his life was with this group of Independents; even after the Restoration he continued to meet regularly with the Congregational leaders Thomas Goodwin and John Owen.[71]

Jessey's decision to join the Jacob church as its pastor must have been well known in this circle of future Independent patrons and leaders, and in this way they would become familiar with the semi-separatist ecclesiastical policy worked out by Henry Jacob. As their discontent with the Laudian church deepened, they may have decided to gather a church in England on the Jacob model prior to their departure for the Netherlands. The merest hint of this comes from the bitter puritan enemy of the Independents, Thomas Edwards, who suggested that a church was gathered at Missenden in Buckinghamshire, not far from London, just before the migration.[72] There is a further hint in *The Apologeticall Narration* published by the Independent clergy in 1643, in which the authors remarked, in a context suggesting they did this before their exile, that 'some of us after we actually were in this way of communion baptized our children in parishional congregations,' just as many of the semi-separatists of the Jacob church had done.[73] The separatist implications of the newly gathered church were disguised, perhaps even for some of the participants, by the *de facto* separation of exile, where the principle of separation ceased to be an urgent problem.

The separatists of the Jacob circle of churches identified themselves with radical puritanism as it was beginning to take shape as the Independent wing of the larger puritan movement, and this must have been an important source of the self-confidence and courage which enabled these small congregations to defy the Laudian regime. Their range of contacts can be glimpsed again in 1614, when controls on the press in London broke down. Kiffin, now a member of Jessey's church, undertook the publication of a second edition of John Lilburne's *Christian Mans Triall* and of a sermon of Thomas Goodwin, *A Glimpse of Syons Glory,*[74] preached at the gathering of a church in the Netherlands in 1641, both with signed prefaces by Kiffin. These pamphlets were published by the separatist bookseller William Larner, who also handled Katherine Chidley's *Justification of the Independent Churches of Christ*. On the eve of the revolution quasi-separatists, semi-separatists, strict separatists and Independents had acquired a sense of community and of common enterprise.

The anti-episcopal alliance

Reviewing his career while sitting in the Tower awaiting trial in the next decade, Archbishop Laud was inclined to blame the 'Brownists' as the chief cause of his downfall. He believed they sought his destruction with every means at their command because he had hindered and punished them for 'their conventicles and separation from the Church of England,' that they had combined with the celebrated trio of puritans, William Prynne, John Bastwick, and Henry Burton, to render him odious throughout England.[75] Laud's judgement on this point was paradoxical because he was destroyed, as he knew very well, by noble lords, great squires, and rich merchants, through the instrumentality of the Long Parliament where the influence of the separatists was negligible. The truth of his judgement rested upon his identification of the separatists as the militant spearhead of the main body of puritanism; that is, the separatists were no longer isolated. If many of their new Independent friends left England for Massachusetts or the Netherlands, more conservative puritans who remained behind were increasingly inclined to work with separatists against the bishops. This was the result of Laud's failure to distinguish between separate churches and puritan 'conventicles.' By 1641 many puritans must have concluded with Lord Brooke that it was the 'bishops' commotions' that made separatists: 'They [the bishops] cry out of schism, schism, sects and schisms; and well they may: they make them, and it is strange they should not know them.'[76]

The collaboration between conservative puritans and separatists in an anti-episcopal alliance was established by 1637. Prynne, Bastwick, and Burton were heroes among the London separatists even although Prynne and Bastwick decried separatism in any form. John Lilburne and Edmund Chillenden were implicated in the printing, importation, and distribution of Bastwick's most effective attack on the bishops, the *Letany*. Chillenden, Henry Wallis, and Stephen More, all of How's church, and Rice Boy of Duppa's, were involved in a network that distributed Prynne's *News from Ipswich* and his *Divine Tragedie* as far as Norwich, at modest profits to themselves.[77] In the comprehensive indictment prepared by the Attorney-General, which launched the prosecution of Prynne, Bastwick, and Burton before the Court of Star Chamber in 1637, this collaboration between separatists and puritans was fully evident. Among the twenty-one persons named in the indictment were Chillenden of How's church, and Chillenden's master, George Kendall, Rice Boy of Duppa's church, Samuel Richardson of Spilsbury's, the separatist Richard Rogers, and two men, Edward Manning and Thomas Jackson, who may be tentatively identified with the Jacob church. There may have been other separatists among those on the list who cannot be further identified.[78]

The London separatist community also contributed significantly to the sensation caused by the punishment of the three puritan martyrs in New Palace Yard on 30 June 1637. Probably most of the separatists in London were present in the huge sympathetic crowd which witnessed the punishment and comprised the first great popular demonstration in London against the regime. David Brown of Duppa's church claimed to have been present, and Henry Jessey, who moved to London a few weeks later to take over the pastorate of the Jacob church, collected eye witness accounts to send to the Winthrops in New England. The transfer of the martyrs to their distant prisons, according to Jessey, became triumphal marches as the resources of organized separatism and puritanism were drawn upon to give the whole affair nation-wide publicity. Jessey also said that as a result of this episode the bishops had lost the 'poor credit they had with the vulgar' and that every 'wretch, and swearing and drunken beast almost, is ready on the least speech, to cry out on them.'[79] The events of 1637 made such a deep impression on the separatists that they almost forgot their own very real isolation in the euphoria of belonging to a powerful national coalition in opposition to the bishops. They became more overtly and aggressively anti-episcopal. For weeks after the punishment of the puritans, Laud said, handbills were scattered through the streets and pasted up on posts to denounce 'the Arch-wolf of Canterbury' for 'persecuting the saints, and shedding the blood of the martyrs.' In prison in 1638 Samuel Eaton 'railed' against the bishops and against Laud personally.[80] At the punishment of John Lilburne by the Star Chamber in 1638, the sympathies of the crowd were clearly on Lilburne's side against the bishops.[81]

The government was increasingly nonplussed by the separatists. At the beginning of 1637 the Privy Council had considered reviving the Elizabethan statute against the separatists to force their leaders to abjure the kingdom, but they drew back from this extreme step because they doubted its effectiveness.[82] By 1640 it was apparent that they had failed to break the will and the organization of the separatists, and as the difficulties of the government increased, particularly with Scotland, separatists grew bolder. During the Short Parliament members of the Jacob church fasted for the success of the Parliament. On 22 October 1640, just before the meeting of the Long Parliament, a mob of two thousand 'Brownists' took advantage of a meeting of the Court of High Commission at St Paul's in the City to raise a 'foul clamour' which quickly ended the session; as the Commissioners left the convocation house 'the people followed hooting as birds at an owl,' and soon benches and cushions were flying into the street.[83] This riot occurred in the first week of the Court's Michaelmas term, when William Shambrook and several other members of Jessey's church, Thomas Lambe and several General Baptists, and the quasi-separatist Roger Quatermayne of Southwark, were bound by bond to reappear before the Court.[84] A few days later another mob ransacked St Paul's looking for the records of the Court of High Commission. 'I like not this preface to the Parliament,' wrote Laud.[85]

The anti-episcopal alliance of 1637 was reconstituted in 1641 after the triumphal return to London of Prynne, Bastwick, and Burton, and the release from the Fleet of John Lilburne on Oliver Cromwell's motion in the House of Commons. It is impossible to identify the part played by separatists in the popular demonstrations in London in 1641, but it was probably an important one. They were militant, organized, articulate, and in individual cases, reckless. At the height of the riots against the bishops in late December 1641, John Lilburne ('with my sword in my hand') was in the front rank of those who fought with Colonel Lunsford at Westminster Hall.[86] On such occasions the separatists would be merely part of much larger popular demonstrations, but they may also have initiated smaller episodes. In May 1642 about a hundred 'fanatic and fantastic schismatics' gathered at St Olave's in the Old Jewry, in Coleman Street ward not far from the Windmill Tavern, to shout at the Bishop of Chichester when he arrived to preach before the Lord Mayor, 'A Pope, a Pope.'[87]

The collaboration between separatists, the more determined puritans and the more radical parliamentarians can be established in several episodes. In late 1641 the future Presbyterian and Independent clergymen of London made a formal agreement to refrain from public controversy in order to forward the anti-episcopal cause. One of the terms of the agreement was that since 'the preaching of some laymen, tradesmen and mechanics in the public congregations was a great stone of offence in the building of the Temple,' presumably by bringing discredit upon the whole anti-episcopal movement, the Independent clergy (or at least those 'judged to be most gracious and powerful with them') undertook to dissuade the lay preachers from appearing in public pulpits 'especially at that time.'[88] The implicit assumption that the separatist preachers were amenable to puritan control in the interests of getting rid of the bishops was borne out by the virtual end of lay preaching in public in 1642, although it continued of course within the separate churches. There were other contacts as well. When Hanserd Knollys arrived penniless in London from New England in December 1641, John Bastwick sent him twenty shillings. William Kiffin, imprisoned for lay preaching in Southwark early in 1642, turned to Lord Brooke for assistance. David Brown of Duppa's church visited Cromwell and Lord Brooke at the beginning of the Long Parliament when they both lived in Holborn to give them 'some papers very fit for those times,' probably exhortations to separation.[89] Cromwell's motion in the Commons to secure Lilburne's release from the Fleet prison was not merely a casual act of goodwill; it was undoubtedly prearranged with Lilburne's friends. On 28 March 1642 Brown appeared with his family and servants at the bar of the House of Commons to give the House its first information about the Kentish petition drawn up at the Maidstone assizes in which the gentry began to rally to the King and which decried lay preachers, seditious pamphlets, and disobedient clergymen. It was S. R. Gardiner's judgement that 'if any one moment can be selected as that in which the Civil War became inevitable, it is that of the vote of March 28, by which the Kentish petitioners were treated as criminals.'[90] It is difficult to believe that Brown's act in reporting to the House of Commons had not been concerted with Lord Brooke and Oliver Cromwell.[91]

The most important of the separatist leaders of the 1640s in London were permanently influenced by their participation in the broader anti-episcopal coalition between 1637 and 1642. When Prynne and Bastwick later turned on the sects Lilburne took it as a personal betrayal, and his career as a Leveller polemicist began in 1645 with his pamphlets against Prynne. This sense of betrayal by former anti-episcopal allies haunted the separatist element in the Leveller movement. On the other hand, not all of the separatist community was to be as deeply committed to the Leveller movement as Lilburne. Others, of whom William Kiffin was to be the most influential, saw the only hope of securing the liberty of the sects to lie in preserving the anti-episcopal coalition rather than in dividing it. This view, as deeply rooted in the pre-revolutionary period as Lilburne's own, was to contribute to the collapse of the Leveller movement in 1649.

3
PARTICULAR BAPTISTS AND SEPARATISTS

Believer's baptism

The divisions that we make for purposes of analysis among the separate churches of the 1640s are rough and ready; they do not yet follow denominational lines. This chapter studies separate churches practising believer's baptism or possessing lay pastors; separate churches with clergymen as pastors, the Independent gathered churches, are described in chapter 5. The whole of the Jacob circle of churches is dealt with in this chapter, for the parent church under Jessey's pastorate also came to practise believer's baptism on a latitudinarian basis; but the Jessey church could with equal justification be grouped as a normal example with the Independent gathered churches.

The dispute over believer's baptism also served to blur lines of division, for it extended beyond Baptist congregations to influence people who remained in the parish congregations. The Baptists initiated the literary dispute as soon as the machinery of censorship collapsed; the controversy developed into one of the most substantial of the revolutionary period, commanding an audience far beyond the separate churches. Many puritans came to doubt the scriptural foundations of infant baptism without having any intention of undergoing a rebaptism or entering a separate church. This wide public interest served to defuse the attempt of conservative puritan clergy to brand the Baptists as 'Anabaptists.'

What makes 'so many differences of religion amongst those that seem to be guided by the Word,' asked Thomas Kilcop in the first published Particular Baptist pamphlet in 1642, 'but their holding of points by consequences; for the Word is one and the same.'[1] Sharing fully in the bibliolatry of puritanism, the Baptists argued that believer's baptism was the only baptism for which there was an express command from Christ in the New Testament, citing Mark 16.16: 'He that believeth and is baptized shall be saved'; and Matthew 28.19: 'Go ye therefore, and teach all nations, baptizing them in the name of the Father, and of the Son, and of the Holy Ghost.' They demanded of the defenders of infant baptism an express warrant in the New Testament for the baptism of children or a single explicit example to show that infant baptism was practised by the primitive Christian communities. Their challenge thrust the burden of proof onto the shoulders of their opponents, and during the next decades the conventional clergy expended massive scholarship to demonstrate that there may have been children in the households of the jailor (Acts 16.33), or of Lydia (Acts 16.15), or of Stephanas (1 Cor. 1.16), or in the church at Colossae (Col. 3.20). But to no avail. The Baptist demand for an express warrant or an explicit example was not met to their satisfaction, and their contention that believer's baptism alone was justified by 'God's naked truth' won adherents even outside organized Baptist churches.

Since precept and example in the New Testament were at best ambiguous, the conventional clergy did indeed resort to 'consequences' in their defence of infant baptism. The 'necessary' proof from Scripture for infant baptism, according to Dr Daniel Featley, was the analogy with circumcision, the seal of the covenant with Abraham administered to infants.[2] The implications were profound, for infant baptism on the analogy of circumcision became the binding symbol of the unity of church and state as dual aspects of an integral Christian commonwealth in which every member, irrespective of his individual inner spiritual life, had outward responsibilities both as a Christian and as a citizen. By denying the validity of the analogy, the Baptists attached to their principle of believer's baptism a set of contrary 'consequences' which centred around the conception of a gathered church composed exclusively of believers and completely autonomous in its spiritual authority. Having in this way laid the foundations in principle for the complete separation of church and state, the Baptists refused to face the necessity of finding secular political principles to guide the life of the citizen in the state. Since the Baptists were not quietists but active participants in the English civil war and its aftermath, their failure to recognize the secular nature of the state was to have important consequences in the course of the revolution.

The Independents were caught in a conflict of contradictory loyalties on the baptism issue. Strict separatist Independents were hard pressed by the Baptists to justify their retention of the baptism they had received in the Church of England while separating in all other respects. Semi-separatist Independents were in a yet more awkward position, as they had to reconcile their ideal of a gathered church of visible saints with their still deep attachment to the traditional view of the Christian commonwealth in which the magistrate acted as a 'nursing father' to the church, and with their lingering contacts with puritans within the Church of England. Still more intricate problems arose for all Independents from their practice of administering baptism to the natural seed of believers, children of church members who on the analogy with circumcision were within the legitimate range of the seals of the covenant. For the infants grew up, without necessarily becoming the visible saints to whom church membership was in theory restricted, and it became a problem whether baptism should be extended in turn to their children although at maturity they had qualified neither for full membership in the church of their parents nor for dismissal on grounds of conduct. In the end, the Half-Way Covenant of the New England churches in 1662 preserved neither the purity of the church nor the purity of baptism as limited to the seed of believers.[3]

Believer's baptism solved many of these problems at a stroke. By providing a new, adult baptism it snapped the last link connecting separatists with the traditional church; and by asserting the complete discontinuity between the old covenant sealed by circumcision and the new sealed by believer's baptism, the Baptist arguments simply swept aside the varied and intricate arguments about the role of the magistrate in a Christian society which lingered on among conservative Independents. In the face of the complex problems present in the Independent position, believer's baptism exercised a potent appeal and as a result was adopted spontaneously, without the direct intervention of Baptist missionaries, among radical groups already inclined to separatism or to the limitation of church membership to visible saints. In New England, Roger Williams, always sensitive to the extreme implications of his position, took up the practice in 1639.[4] The conviction that believer's baptism was alone justified by the New Testament came to Thomas Patience as he walked 'in the woods in that wilderness' of Massachusetts, where for 'three days one after another' the Lord broke into his soul with pertinent scriptures and 'sealing manifestations of his love.'[5] The principle also swept through the English churches in the Netherlands in the 1640s. Joseph Symonds, the pastor of the important English church at Rotterdam, complained that his church was overgrown with Anabaptists, and the church at Arnhem, according to Thomas Edwards, went over in a body to Anabaptism just before its return to England in 1646.[6] Among these converts was an elder of the Arnhem congregation, Henry Lawrence, the most influentially placed of all Baptists in the revolutionary period; in 1646 he published anonymously at Rotterdam the longest defence of believer's baptism written by a layman in this period.[7]

The case for believer's baptism was strong enough to raise doubts about infant baptism in the minds of men well removed from the ranks of the organized Independents. 'When I was first called forth to the sacred ministerial work,' said Richard Baxter, 'I began to have some doubts about the lawfulness of infant baptism.' He forebore the practice while he studied the matter thoroughly, and although he was soon convinced that there was 'more probability for infant baptism than was against it,' yet because 'the Scripture spoke so sparingly to the point' he dared not 'adventure upon a full pastoral charge, but to preach only as a lecturer, till I was fully resolved.'[8] His last doubts about infant baptism disappeared only when he saw the practical sectarian results of believer's baptism in the revolutionary period. John Tombes, the vicar of Leominster in Herefordshire, was convinced as early as 1627, when he was at Magdalen Hall, Oxford, that the analogy with circumcision was not a sufficient warrant for infant baptism; he baptized the children of his parish, as he expressly told his parishioners, upon the warrant of 1 Corinthians 7.14: 'For the unbelieving husband is sanctified by the wife, and the unbelieving wife is sanctified by the husband: else were your children unclean; but now are they holy.' Forced to move to Bristol by the outbreak of the civil war in 1642, Tombes was convinced by an unnamed anti-paedobaptist that this text was not sufficient warrant for infant baptism, whereupon he gave up the practice entirely and became the literary champion of believer's baptism in England.[9]

A conviction that only the baptism of believers was warranted by the New Testament did not necessarily lead to the creation of Baptist institutions. Lucy Hutchinson, the wife and biographer of Colonel John Hutchinson, the governor of Nottingham, decided about 1646 that infant baptism was unjustifiable. Being 'young and modest,' she kept her peace until her pregnancy in the following year led her to broach the matter with her husband. After first searching the Scriptures, then reading 'all the eminent treatises on both sides, which at that time came thick from the presses,' and finally consulting the local clergy, the Colonel decided infant baptism was unwarranted, and the child, when it was born, was not baptized. Neither the Colonel nor his wife, however, manifested any inclination to undergo rebaptism themselves, and they continued to attend the 'national assemblies' where they were 'often glanced at in their public sermons' as 'fanatics and anabaptists.'[10] The practice of discontinuing infant baptism without proceeding to the further step of rebaptism was perhaps widespread among the Independent congregations of the 1640s. Thomas Edwards charged that 'the best Independent churches and congregations are mixed assemblies and medlies, consisting of persons whereof some are Anabaptists,' to form a 'linsey wolsey compounded religion.'[11] To reject infant baptism was one thing; positively to adopt believer's baptism and undergo rebaptism was another. Particular Baptist institutions developed from the *practice* of believer's baptism, including rebaptism, and this involved more than the mere substitution of adult for infant baptism.

The case against implementing believer's baptism was stated by Praise-God Barbone, who published a pamphlet vigorously attacking those involved in Richard Blunt's immersion ceremony in January 1642. Barbone's primary objection was that there was no authority for the institution of baptism by one who was himself unbaptized, thus raising the question of a 'succession' of baptism. To reject the validity of the baptism of the traditional churches through the ages when they were overgrown with error was to enter 'into an endless labyrinth'; for if there was no succession of baptism from the time of the Apostles through the traditional churches, then a true baptism could be restored only by an administrator having an extraordinary commission such as John the Baptist had.[12] This argument proved to have an explosive force among the London separatists, for it could be combined with the principle – not the practice – of believer's baptism to produce the characteristic Seeker conclusion that all Christian ordinances had been lost by the apostasy of the churches and could be restored only by those who, like John the Baptist and the Apostles, had a special commission to do so. Until such qualified administrators appeared there could be no true Christian ordinances and therefore no true churches at all. Within weeks of his rebaptism at Providence in 1639 Roger Williams had with characteristic impetuosity reached precisely this conclusion.[13] These Seeker views wrecked Richard Blunt's own congregation soon after it was organized. Thomas Edwards reported that this church, 'one of the first and prime churches of Anabaptists now in these latter times, [broke] into pieces, and some went one way, some another, divers fell off to no church at all.'[14]

In their earliest published pamphlets, the Particular Baptist leaders sought to counter the doubts raised by Barbone's argument. Thomas Kilcop and Robert Barrow argued that there was in the New Testament an ordinary commission to believers to institute baptism.[15] John Spilsbury agreed with them but added that for the sake of order baptism should be instituted by believers who were already covenanted together in a church.[16] Although these arguments were able to forestall the collapse of other Baptist churches, individual Baptists in significant numbers came to doubt the authority for their believer's baptism, while many Independents were inhibited by Seeker principles from the practice of believer's baptism. The foundation of Particular Baptist churches thus required, in addition to the principle of believer's baptism, a conviction that ordinary Christians could implement baptism without either a 'succession' or an extraordinary commission. By 1646, when Spilsbury, Kilcop, and Barrow each returned in major works to the refutation of the Seekers, it was necessary to add arguments to prove that the believer's baptism of the New Testament was the baptism of water and not the baptism of fire or of the Spirit.[17]

The Seven Churches of London

Baptist losses to the Seekers were negligible when compared with their gains from the separatists. When the Particular Baptists of London issued their public *Confession of Faith* in October 1644, it was signed by the representatives of seven congregations whose members had been recruited from nearly every important separatist church in London.[18] The formative stages of several of the seven congregations are unknown, but the Knollys memorandum, a document relating to the Jacob church under Jessey's leadership and culminating in Jessey's own conversion to believer's baptism in June 1645, makes it possible to trace in some detail the most significant developments that led to the publication of the *Confession* in 1644.[19]

The baptism controversy was no novelty in Jessey's church at the beginning of 1644. William Kiffin had been a Baptist since 1642, but Jessey's tolerance and Kiffin's own view of his baptism as a personal rather than a church matter had permitted him to remain a member of Jessey's church. This uneasy equilibrium was upset early in 1644 by a controversy that arose within the congregation about the baptism of a child of one of the members, Hanserd Knollys. After an interval with Manchester's army, Knollys had returned to London late in 1643 for the birth of a child to his wife. Jessey's urging that the child be brought to the church for baptism failed to satisfy Knollys' growing doubts about the legitimacy of infant baptism.[20] From mid January into March there were weekly meetings of the congregation to discuss the issue. Kiffin argued cogently against infant baptism and many of the members were 'staggered,' at least sixteen of them deciding against the practice. The immediate outcome of this stage of the controversy was Kiffin's decision to withdraw from Jessey's church with some of those who supported him, on the ground that a true church must be formed by believer's baptism. This was a serious blow to the parent church not because those who withdrew advocated believer's baptism, which in Kiffin's case had been tolerated for well over a year, but because they were schismatics, rending a true Christian fellowship. The church held a series of fasts over the matter in March and April, and since opinion was divided whether the schismatics should be excommunicated or not, it was decided to consult with the leaders of the Independent churches of London.[21]

The conference took place at William Shambrook's house towards the end of May. The attendance is revealing of the inner structure of puritan radicalism in London at this time, and of the Particular Baptist relationship with it. The most important men there were four of the authors of the *Apologeticall Narration*, Thomas Goodwin, Philip Nye, Jeremiah Burroughes, and Sidrach Simpson, the unofficial leaders of Independency in England. Representatives of three of the leading separatist Independent congregations, Praise-God Barbone, Sabine Staresmore, and Edmund Rosier, were there. So were William Erbury – at some undetermined stage of his radical career – and two prominent Independent laymen, Dr Parker and the lawyer John Cook. These men, representing the whole spectrum of organized radicalism in London at this date apart from the General Baptists, decided that Kiffin and his associates were motivated by 'tender conscience and holiness' rather than obstinacy, and that they should not be excommunicated or admonished. They also advised that the Jessey church should regard the dissidents still as members and 'desire conversing together so far as their principles permit them,' unless they grow 'giddy and scandalous.'[22] William Kiffin's Particular Baptist congregation thus came into existence with the blessings of separatist and Independent leaders alike.

Hanserd Knollys did not participate in the new venture. During the summer of 1644 he preached openly against infant baptism from the pulpit of St Mary le Bow Cheapside, which led to complaints to the Westminster Assembly and to his imprisonment for a period by order of the House of Commons. He was also impeded by the doubts of his wife about whether there was an authorized administrator for believer's baptism.[23] As a result, his name did not appear among the subscribers to the Particular Baptist *Confession* in October.

The Confession of Faith of those Churches which are commonly (though falsely) called Anabaptists was picked up from the London bookstalls by George Thomason the book collector on 16 October. A revealing passage in the preface reflected the growth of a denominational outlook among the London Particular Baptists:

And because it may be conceived, that what is here published, may be but the judgement of some one particular congregation, more refined than the rest; we do therefore here subscribe it, some of each body in the name and by the appointment of seven congregations, who though we be distinct in respect of our particular bodies, for conveniency sake, being as many as can well meet together in one place, yet are all one in communion, holding Jesus Christ to be our head and Lord.

Although the seven churches were 'one in communion,' the purpose of the *Confession* was not to lay down a binding rule of faith but to demonstrate to the world at large that the errors of the 'Anabaptists' were falsely laid to their charge. The Baptists were vulnerable to an extremely effective form of attack. Simply by adopting believer's baptism they had passed, in the view of conservatives, from an unstable but comprehensible position on the fringes of puritanism into the alien abyss of 'Anabaptism,' whose notorious errors they were presumed to share. Stephen Marshall, perhaps the most prominent of all puritan clergymen, expressed precisely this point of view at Westminster Abbey in a morning lecture intended to counter the effects of Knollys' sermons in the parish churches.[24] This opinion of the Baptists was echoed in the mob, encouraging the worldly, according to the preface of the *Confession*, 'if they can find the place of our meeting, to get together in clusters to stone us, as looking upon us as a people holding such things as that we are not worthy to live.'[25]

The articles of the *Confession* relating to the church established the normal pattern for most, though not all, subsequent Particular Baptist churches in England. A true visible church was 'a company of visible saints, called and separated from the world' (article 33), gathered by believer's baptism by immersion (39, 40), choosing its own officers (36), and exercising its own discipline through the ultimate sanction of excommunication (42). Authority was vested in the general body of the church. Ministers were to be supported by the voluntary offerings of the church, and tithes were not 'by constraint to be compelled from the people by a forced law' (38). Gifted members of the church not in office might by the appointment of the church exercise their gifts (45). Following the model of the Barrowist confession of 1596, the authors eschewed any claim to perfection in the visible church (46). The threat of the Seekers was met by an article that explicitly stated the ordinary commission of a 'preaching disciple' to institute the ordinance of baptism (41). The typical Particular Baptist church, therefore, was to be thoroughly separatist and lay in character, and restricted to members who had undergone believer's baptism.

The separatist origin of the seven congregations was evident from the list of subscribers to the *Confession*.[26] The first signature was that of William Kiffin, whose extreme sensitivity throughout his career to the charge of holding Anabaptist errors suggests that he may have been the initiator and perhaps the principal author of the *Confession*. His associate was Thomas Patience, recently returned from New England,

TABLE 2 *Subscribers to the London Particular Baptist* Confession.

1644 edition	1646 edition
William Kiffin	Thomas Gunne
Thomas Patience	John Mabbitt
John Spilsbery	John Spilsberry
George Tipping	Samuel Richardson
Samuel Richardson	Paul Hobson
Thomas Skippard	Thomas Goare
Thomas Munday	Benjamin Cockes
Thomas Gunne	Thomas Kilikop
John Mabbatt	Thomas Munden
John Webb	George Tipping
Thomas Killcop	William Kiffin
Paul Hobson	Thomas Patient
Thomas Goare	Hanserd Knollys
Joseph Phelpes	Thomas Holms
Edward Heath	Denis le Barbier
	Christoph le Durer

and the church they represented had come into being since March, around the nucleus of those who had withdrawn at that time from Jessey's church. The second church was Spilsbury's, represented by Spilsbury, George Tipping, and Samuel Richardson. Spilsbury endorsed the *Confession* although he had not changed his opinion about the necessity of a church covenant preceding baptism; he now supported baptism by immersion, but he did not believe that those who had undergone believer's baptism by sprinkling were under the necessity of repeating their baptism by immersion.[27]

The third church was represented by Thomas Shepard and Thomas Munden, both of whom had been baptized by Blunt in January 1642.[28] It is possible that this was the remnant of Richard Blunt's own congregation, reorganized under new leadership after the disruption of the original church. The second church organized at the time of the original immersion ceremony was probably identical with the fifth church in the *Confession*, represented by Thomas Kilcop, who had been baptized by Blunt, and John Webb, who was recruited from Samuel

How's church now under the pastorate of Stephen More.[29] Kilcop's prompt reply to Barbone's criticisms of the immersion ceremony suggests both his early prominence among the Baptists and his confidence in his baptism. His association with Webb indicates that this church was recruiting members from other separatist churches. The fourth church listed in the confession, represented by Thomas Gunne and John Mabbatt, probably came into existence by separation from More's separatist church, which was 'not without their troubles within by schism' during this period.[30] The sixth church, represented by Paul Hobson and Thomas Goare, came from Green and Spencer's church.[31] The seventh church, represented by Joseph Phelpes and Edward Heath, cannot be further identified, nor was it represented in the second edition of the *Confession* fifteen months later.

Important changes took place among the London Baptists in the interval before the second edition of the *Confession* was published in January 1646.[32] The most significant were connected with Jessey's church, where the baptism issue continued to trouble the congregation after the withdrawal of Kiffin in March 1644. About three dozen members were convinced of believer's baptism in the following months, but their conversion did not immediately lead either to rebaptism or to withdrawal from Jessey's church; they were restrained by doubts as to whether there was an authorized administrator for believer's baptism. Among this group was Henry Jessey himself, who decided about the middle of 1644 that baptism was for believers alone. The problem of the administrator was not easily resolved. A further series of conferences with the Independents was organized, this time 'about what is requisite to the restoring of ordinances, if lost.'[33] The outcome was inconclusive, and only the appearance of the *Confession* of the seven churches in October encouraged some of the waverers to conclude that 'such disciples as are gifted to teach and evangelize may also baptize.' One of those so convinced was Knollys' wife, and this cleared the way for Knollys to set up his own Baptist congregation about the end of the year. Finally, on 29 June 1645, Jessey himself was rebaptized by Knollys after deciding that the practice of believer's baptism was legitimate.[34]

Henry Jessey was perhaps the most important convert won by the Particular Baptists in this decade. The majority of his congregation refused to follow his example in undergoing believer's baptism, and his church became a mixed communion congregation including Baptists and non-Baptists, based upon the church covenant. Eventually most members were rebaptized, but at Jessey's death in 1663 there were still some who had not adopted Baptist practices.[35] Jessey scrupulously refused to impose uniformity in the congregation and he skilfully avoided further disputes or schisms during the rest of his pastorate. This was a considerable personal achievement, and its results were important; for 'Baptized Independent' congregations were eventually organized on Jessey's principles in various parts of England, including the Broadmead church at Bristol and John Bunyan's church at Bedford. Because he did not require uniformity of baptism within the congregation, Jessey never subscribed to the successive editions of the *Confession* of the London churches; but he remained on intimate terms with the stricter London Baptists, so many of whom had at one time or another passed through his congregation.

Other changes recorded in the second edition of the *Confession* in January 1646 were relatively slight. The church of Phelpes and Heath had disappeared, and that of Hanserd Knollys and Thomas Holms took its place as one of the seven churches. George Tipping moved from Spilsbury's church to Thomas Munden's to replace Thomas Shepard, who was probably absent in the service of the Parliamentary armies.[36] John Webb had also joined the Army,[37] and Kilcop's new colleague was Benjamin Cox, a former clergyman who had already been active as a Baptist evangelist outside London. An eighth church, formed in 1643 by separation from the French Reformed congregation in London over the baptism issue, was represented by two men, but its subsequent history is obscure.[38]

The further history of the Baptist congregations is as hidden as that of other separate churches in London. Thomas Edwards knew of the meetings of Knollys' church, which were held for a time next door to the parish church of St Helen Bishopsgate; according to the neighbours as many as a thousand people came on Sundays, which may explain why Knollys' landlord asked him to move. He appeared next at Finsbury Fields where he made 'a great meeting house by breaking one room into another.'[39] It is unlikely that Knollys had a thousand members in his church. The explanation of Edwards' information is probably that the meetings of Knollys' church, unlike those of other Baptist congregations, were open to the general public, who would be less disturbed by the ministry of a former clergyman than by a lay pastor and preacher. Paul Hobson, when he returned to London from the Army, preached at 'Moorfields or thereabouts,' and his church had perhaps already settled at Petty France, near Moorfields. On Wednesday afternoons Hobson preached at Chequer Alley in Finsbury Fields, probably at Knollys' church, in what appears to have been an imitation of the conventional weekday puritan lectures.[40] Henry Jessey, a bachelor, had lodgings in Swan Alley, Coleman Street, and his congregation met in the neighbourhood and shared its premises with

William Carter's Independent gathered church.[41] In the latter part of the decade new Baptist leaders appeared, including Edward Drapes, John Fountain, William Conset, Mr Tomlins, and Mr Wade 'the schoolmaster,' but very little is known about them at this time; they were all apparently members of the original seven churches.[42]

The campaign against the 'Anabaptists,' and the second Confession

A second edition of the *Confession* was made necessary by the continuing campaign against the 'Anabaptists' and by the failure of the first edition to convince any but already sympathetic Independents of the doctrinal orthodoxy and social responsibility of the Baptists. Thomas Edwards' thunder against the sects in his lectures at Christ Church provoked the usually cautious Kiffin in November 1645 to publish and distribute a handbill challenging Edwards to permit his victims to talk back at the end of his lectures.[43] Daniel Featley sought to curry favour with Parliament by publishing an account of his dispute at Southwark in 1642 with Kiffin and other Baptists; *The Dippers Dipt* was an enormous success, passing through three editions before the end of 1645. The Baptists were deeply disturbed, and Samuel Richardson immediately published a semi-official reply, denying the spectrum of Anabaptist errors attributed to the Baptists by Featley and challenging him to produce a single English illustration of his charges.[44] Most provoking of all to the Baptists was an episode that occurred towards the end of 1645, when a projected public disputation between six Baptists and six of the most prominent Presbyterian clergymen in London was forbidden at the last moment by the Lord Mayor on the ground that 'there may be hazard of the disturbance of the public peace.'[45]

Two of the Baptist spokesmen in the projected disputation were former clergymen, Hanserd Knollys and Benjamin Cox. Before the civil war Cox had a living at Bideford in Devon, but in 1642 he was endeavouring to gather a separatist church in or near Barnstaple. By late 1643 or early 1644 he appeared as a Baptist evangelist in Coventry where Richard Baxter encountered him; according to Baxter, Cox, 'an ancient minister of competent parts and learning,' had been sent from London to organize the Baptists of Coventry, and this is the first suggestion of Cox's connection with the London Baptists.[46] His name did not appear on the first London *Confession*, but in the second edition he appeared with Thomas Kilcop representing one of the oldest Baptist congregations in London. His influence was important in securing changes in the direction of a more conservative Calvinism in the revised *Confession*.[47]

Additional intellectual depth was given to the Baptist defence of believer's baptism by the activity of John Tombes, who envisaged a Reformed or Presbyterian national church practising believer's baptism. Attracted to London in 1643 by the prospect of winning members of the Westminster Assembly to his views, Tombes was first assigned the parish church of Fenchurch; when his position at Fenchurch became untenable, he applied for the position of preacher at the Temple, an appointment particularly suitable since it involved no baptisms. He was awarded it in January 1645 only after a private interview with Stephen Marshall in which he undertook not to preach his opinions in that pulpit unless provoked by someone preaching there what he 'conceived to be an error.' Before the year was out Tombes had published against infant baptism and his appointment at the Temple was not renewed.[48]

The baptism controversy entered a new stage with the publication of Tombes' arguments against infant baptism. He was promptly answered by a number of the conservative clergy who had simply ignored the publications of the Baptists themselves.[49] Tombes in turn answered all of his critics in detail and at length, and eventually his controversial work was to assume monumental proportions. The argument went on over the heads of the Baptists; Tombes' opponents sought to deal with Parliament for effective laws against Anabaptists. Tombes increasingly the Baptists not by direct controversial encounters but by appealing to found himself in the position of defending the Baptists. He welcomed their *Confession of Faith* as an accurate expression of their views and considered the campaign against the 'Anabaptists' as 'artifices serving only to prevent impartial discussing of things which is necessary that truth may appear.'[50]

If the sermons and writings of these clergymen served to give Baptist arguments a degree of respectability, the preaching and writing of some of the lay pastors undermined this. As these earnest Baptist pastors sought to understand and explain for their followers the great Christian doctrines of the past, they inevitably burst through the narrow bounds of that Calvinist orthodoxy they were so anxious to claim for themselves. When Samuel Richardson published a popularization of Calvinist doctrine for his fellow Baptists he was promptly answered by another pastor of long standing, Thomas Kilcop. Kilcop had come under the influence of the writings of the millenarian Robert Maton, and he interpreted the doctrinal problem in a millenarian perspective: 'That justification is by Christ alone, I grant, and that he shall take away and utterly destroy the sins of his people, and present his people holy, and without spot, I affirm; but that he hath done thus already, I deny; for they are not spotless, till Christ's appearing.' The redemption of the elect had not occurred in the past, at the historic moment of Christ's sacrifice, but would occur in the future at the historic moment of the second coming, and this moment would be marked by such signs as the restoration of the Jews to their own land. Kilcop recommended Maton's book to his readers, but he made no attempt to place the second coming in the immediate future.[51]

Yet another vein of more mystical radicalism is found in the pamphlets of Paul Hobson. A moderate Calvinist who signed both editions of the London confession, Hobson was concerned more that the Gospel should be preached to all men without limit than that the doctrine of election and reprobation should be taught correctly.[52] In three works published between 1645 and 1647, he propounded a view of religious experience that continually hovered on the verge of mystical exaltation:

> You see no man can live in the bosom of Christ, and in the glory of Christ, but he is made one with Christ. Saints, they are not only made perfect hereafter, as most professors run away with that; but they are admitted and have some entrance into heaven here; they live as saints, they walk as saints, they trade as saints, they live with Christ; they walk up and down in loves, love compasses them round about, they are swallowed up of loves; they live in loving, and love in living; ordinances are but shells; but saints while they are cracking the shell to others, they are eating the kernel themselves, and live thereby.[53]

The grace of the New Testament conferred upon the saints an inward bliss by which Hobson anticipated that there would be a continual purification of churches, 'congregations picked out of congregations' until the time would come 'that there will be a people who kiss and embrace one another in spirit, and shall live in loving and enjoying one another far more than ever yet our eyes have seen.'[54] In *A Garden Inclosed* in 1647 he described the believer to whom baptism was offered in the New Testament as 'a soul who from the enjoyment of a Christ within, is made able to believe a Christ without.'[55]

On 29 January 1646, Samuel Richardson and Benjamin Cox stood outside the door of the House of Commons to hand copies of the second edition of the *Confession* of the seven churches to Members as they entered the House.[56] It had been revised with great care. Featley had confessed of the first edition, after remarking that 'they cover a little rats-bane in a great quantity of sugar,' that among the fifty-three articles 'there are not above six but may pass with a fair construction.'[57] Featley's criticisms were met by revising the offending articles in accordance with the express words of Scripture. In response to the rapid growth of the Arminian General Baptists, the doctrinal articles were rephrased in a stricter Calvinist sense, and a harmless phrase asserting that the Gospel was to be preached to all men, which was intended to strengthen the ordinary commission of 'preaching disciples' against the objections of the Seekers, was removed from the article on election.[58] Finally, care had been taken to have the pamphlet duly licensed by John Downam. The House of Commons proved unsympathetic; it sent the Serjeant-at-arms to seize the pamphlets and to bring Richardson and Cox to the bar of the House, and it ordered the Stationers' Company to suppress the *Confession.*

The reaction of the clergy was one of frank scepticism that the *Confession* represented the real beliefs of the 'Anabaptists' in England. In the first part of *Gangraena* a few weeks later, Edwards declared that the published opinions and the practices of some of the very men who subscribed it did not accord with what the *Confession* professed; as for the *Confession* itself, he said only that some points were expressed 'generally and doubtfully,' and not as they were held in the reformed churches.[59] Robert Baillie, one of the Scottish commissioners to the Westminster Assembly, agreed with Edwards and went on to ask why only seven of 'some hundreds' of Anabaptist congregations in England endorsed the *Confession.* Believing that Thomas Lambe's General Baptist church was in communion with the seven that signed the *Confession*, he argued that the confession involved a deliberate misrepresentation of the opinions held in the London congregations.[60] More serious than either of these was the reaction of Stephen Marshall. A moderate Presbyterian, Marshall was working strenuously to arrive at an accommodation in church government with the Erastians and the Independents, efforts that were watched by Baillie with a suspicion scarcely less than that which he directed at the Baptists. Marshall was precisely the kind of man whom the Baptists hoped to convince of their orthodoxy and respectability. The stakes were high, for the toleration of the Baptists in England appeared at this point to hinge on winning over such men. Marshall's comment on the *Confession* was that

> I acknowledge it the most orthodox of any Anabaptists' confession that ever I read (although there are sundry heterodox opinions in it) and such an one as I believe thousands of our new Anabaptists will be far from owning, as any man may be able to say without a spirit of divination, knowing that their received and usual doctrines do much more agree with the Anabaptists in Germany, than with this handful who made this confession here in London.[61]

The ingrained suspicion of puritan clergymen, schooled through a lifetime of study in the works of the continental divines on the errors of the Anabaptists, were not easily to be overcome.

The Baptist *Confession* nevertheless embarrassed the clergy by forcing them to resort to extraneous evidence to justify the vehemence of their condemnation, whether it was the other publications and reputed acts of English Baptists, or the confusion with the General Baptists, or, most commonly, the identification of English Baptists with continental Anabaptists. The clerical campaign against the English Anabaptists in pulpit and press did not slacken pace, but it was becoming less convincing. An 'eminent Parliament man,' although he was 'no broacher of these opinions,' was reported in the summer of 1646 to have remarked that the 'Anabaptists were not heretics, but only schismatics at the worst; and that he thought the baptizing of children could not be proved out of the word of God.'[62]

The survival of the separatists

The history of the separate churches under lay pastors, which we will designate simply as separatist churches, is of an almost impenetrable obscurity at this period. In addition to the sizeable inroads on their membership made by the Baptists, they also had to survive the powerful competition of the many Independent gathered churches organized in London in the mid 1640s, for these churches tolerated among their membership the profession and practice of a strict separatism. Yet these churches did manage to survive through the 1640s, and the lay pastors had an important role to play in the course of the revolution even if they failed to establish a distinctive denomination.[63]

Praise-God Barbone's church is an excellent example. Barbone himself was an important London politician of the 1650s who has given his name to the Nominated Parliament of 1653.[64] His church is visible at its inception in 1640 when the Jacob church was divided into two. A public meeting of the church in Barbone's shop in Fleet Street in 1641 gave the church a brief notoriety, but it then becomes invisible until a number of the members signed the London Fifth Monarchy *Declaration* of 1654. Nothing more is known of the church. From its origin it might be inferred that its practices were semi-separatist; this may have had a practical significance in permitting members to participate in the affairs of the vestries in their home parishes and to enter the political life of the City through this channel.[65] The strict separatists of the Duppa church, on the other hand, probably eschewed vestry politics as another aspect of the antichristian life of the parishes of the established church. Colonel Thomas Pride, that other eponymous hero of the Puritan Revolution, belonged to the Duppa church, whose existence is the best documented of all among the London separatist congregations.[66] The church was well known among radicals in London;

Henry Burton remarked in the course of a quarrel with them that his own more recent Independent congregation was 'not bound to make account to any other church or people in the world, although never so famous.'[67]

The Duppa church had been strict separatists from the beginning in 1630, and in 1641 Mrs Chidley was confident that the Independents would come to share their separatism. As the Independent gathered churches with clerical pastors grew in number, however, it was evident that the Independents remained true to the semi-separatism of the Jacob tradition. The Duppa church watched this development with dismay, and they turned increasingly to the older Barrowist tradition for support in their strict separatism. In 1645 Mrs Chidley vigorously defended Barrow against Thomas Edwards, and her remark that the execution of Barrow and Greenwood in 1593 'was done without the Queen's knowledge, the grief whereof (by relation of those who were near her) she carried to her death,' suggests that she was in touch with the folk-tradition of the old London Barrowist community.[68] The Duppa church found its chief support in another Barrowist principle, that parish church buildings were idolatrous places entirely prohibited to members of true Christian churches.[69] In her advocacy of this position against William Greenhill at Stepney in the summer of 1645, Mrs Chidley drew away 'some persons to Brownism' from Greenhill's gathered church. Their insistence upon this point led to formal conferences between the Duppa church and the gathered churches of Henry Burton and John Goodwin in 1645 and 1648, and although the Independent congregations were willing to practise intercommunion, the separatists would not agree as long as the Independents continued to enter parish church buildings. In the end this principle proved to be little more than an eccentricity that served to isolate this church from other separate churches. By 1656 Samuel Chidley conceded that his opponents counted his published arguments on this matter 'a work of madness.'[70]

The bare existence of several such separatist churches is all that can be demonstrated. Stephen More's church had a troubled existence in the mid 1640s (perhaps caused by Baptists and Seekers), but it renewed its covenant in May 1648, when the pastor and twelve members signed the new covenant in the name of the church.[71] Edmund Rosier, Lilburne's friend from the days of Laudian tyranny, is visible as a London radical after 1648; it is only from Lilburne's testimony that we know he was the pastor of a church in which Lilburne 'walked many years in fellowship' in the 1640s.[72] Another of the early churches whose history remains hidden from us is that of Green and Spencer; it is not certain that this church survived the defections of the Baptists. According to Edwards, 'Green the felt-maker' went with Colonel Homstead on an expedition to the Earl of Warwick's projected plantation in Trinidad about 1643. By 1646 he was back in London,

> and now preaches in an alley in Coleman Street, once on the Lord's day, and once on the week day, where there is great resort and flocking to him, that yards, rooms and house are all full, so that he causes his neighbours' conventicles as Cretensis's [John Goodwin's] and others to be oft times very thin, and Independents to preach to bare walls and empty seats in comparison of this great rabbi. [73]

Edwards implies that Green and Spencer continued as prominent 'sectaries' in London, but nothing more is known of this church. Although the existence of Samuel Highland's Southwark congregation cannot be proved before 1654 when members of this church signed the Fifth Monarchy *Declaration*, Highland was active in the Leveller movement in the 1640s, one member had been in prison as long ago as 1636 as a Brownist, and there were semi-separatists in Southwark in 1642 who cannot otherwise be accounted for. The most important of these, Ambrose Andrews, was appointed along with Highland to the radical Southwark militia committee in September 1647.[74]

The existence of the churches of Barbone, Duppa, More, Green and Spencer, Rosier, and Highland, three of them at least surviving over decades, is sufficient to establish the significance of this category of churches. Further examples in the 1640s are conjectural. An extensive list of 'tub-preachers' in 1647 included twenty names, eleven of whom were well known sectarian pastors. The remaining nine may have been preachers in known churches, or pastors of unknown churches, or possibly preachers without regular churches at all.[75] There were undoubtedly groups of people in London who aspired without permanent success to an organized church relationship, such as the 'church of Brownists' known to the bookseller Peter Cole.[76] Churches that certainly existed in the 1650s may have been organized earlier without leaving recognizable traces. One such possibility was the church of Lieutenant-Colonel John Fenton, several of whose members signed the Fifth Monarchy *Declaration* of 1654; Fenton was a leading London radical by the end of the 1640s.[77] Some known radicals may have belonged to still other churches, if they were not members of churches already listed. The most important such case is that of John Bolton, a goldsmith of Foster Lane who, with Alan Banks and two others, had provided bail for a group of General Baptists in January 1641; a few months later Banks himself was brought before the House of Commons, for lay preaching.[78] In 1645 Mr Bolton and Mr Jackson attended the conferences over the baptism controversy in Jessey's church along with a number of prominent Independents; this attests to Bolton's importance in a well established London congregation.[79] Finally, Bolton appeared as one of the radical leaders in the London Common Council by the end of the decade, along with such familiar names as Pride, Barbone, Rosier, Eames, and Fenton.[80]

There is scarcely a basis for conjecture as to the size of these separatist congregations, but they must have been small churches composed primarily of tradesmen. They did not have a great future before them as separate churches; perhaps one or two survived the Restoration in 1660. But the lay pastors and the lay preachers associated with them in these churches profited from their experience of leadership to gain a wider political leadership in London in the revolutionary turmoil of the late 1640s, both in the organized Leveller movement and on the London Common Council. Historians have generally counted these men as Baptists. They were not Baptists, and were therefore perhaps less inhibited in their political radicalism. But there is this truth in the identification, that separatist and Baptist churches were variants of the same institution, separatist congregations under lay pastors.

4

ANABAPTISTS: THE GENERAL BAPTISTS

Anabaptist origins

An important group of separate churches in London stood aloof from all the others and at a greater remove from the common puritan background. They were eventually known as General Baptists because they believed in general redemption; throughout the period of this book they were called 'Anabaptists' and were hopelessly confused by contemporaries with the Particular Baptists. But where the Particular Baptists scarcely understood the errors attributed to them as 'Anabaptists,' the General Baptists had been profoundly shaped by the continental Anabaptist tradition and came closest of all the sectaries in England to being true Anabaptists. Like the Particular Baptists, the General Baptists repudiated the name of 'Anabaptists,' but they did so because they rejected several specifically Anabaptist beliefs, notably the Anabaptist assertion of the unchristian and unredeemable nature of all magistracy.

The formation of the General Baptist sect came in the early pre-Jacob phase of English separatism, and indeed the General Baptists were the only significant survivors in England of the early separatist tradition.[1] The initial move towards the Anabaptists arose from an old dilemma of the early English separatists: if the Church of England was a false church whose ordination and communion must be totally abandoned, then on what grounds could they retain the baptism received in infancy? 'Good in substance, but bad in form will not salve this sore,' acknowledged the separatist Henry Barrow in 1590; yet he and other English separatists urgently sought to avoid 'falling up on the shelves and quicksands of Anabaptistry' and concluded therefore that baptism 'ought not unto such to be repeated as afterward forsake the false church and join unto the church of God.'[2] For John Smyth, the pastor of the Gainsborough separatists who fled to Amsterdam in 1608, this spectre of Anabaptism held no terrors, and as he came to doubt the validity of his baptism he and others of his congregation approached the important Waterlander Mennonite church in Amsterdam. Here they were quickly convinced that their baptism was false because administered to infants who were incapable of saving faith instead of to believers who alone were eligible for the seal of the covenant of the New Testament. Smyth reconstituted his church by rebaptizing first himself and then the rest of his company. With Waterlander help, Smyth's church worked out the implications of believer's baptism to arrive at a new understanding of the church as consisting of believers only. It could not be a national church, and it involved therefore the complete separation of church and state. More profoundly, it involved the insight that the liberty of the individual conscience was not to be forced, and that religious persecution was both wrong and futile. Waterlander influence was decisive also in converting Smyth's church from the orthodox predestinarian doctrine of the puritans to the Anabaptist doctrine that attributed responsibility to man in the matter of his salvation, the doctrine of general redemption. Thus far his church was united, but Smyth himself was troubled by his precipitate act of self-baptism, and increasingly inclined to go forward to a full union with the Waterlanders; this raised the issue of still other Anabaptist beliefs which began to divide the church. The leader of the opposition was an elder of the church, Thomas Helwys, a member of the minor gentry of Nottinghamshire and a leading organizer of the migration of the Scrooby–Gainsborough separatists.

Helwys is the true founder of the General Baptists, a remarkable achievement for a layman. With the support of a minority of the congregation, he excommunicated Smyth and the majority because they applied for union with the Waterlanders. Helwys objected fundamentally to the claim of the Waterlanders that they alone administered a true baptism and that only their elders could ordain elders; this 'succession,' he said, was contrary to the liberty of the gospel. But he also rejected other characteristic Anabaptist beliefs which Smyth and his followers were being asked to accept. The Anabaptist doctrine of the celestial flesh of Christ was completely alien to the English radical tradition and was rejected out of hand. The Anabaptist position on magistracy, that because he bore the sword the magistrate could not belong to the church even in a private capacity, and that to swear oaths, bear arms, or undertake other magisterial functions was unlawful to the Christian, was more strenuously opposed. Probably no Englishman of his generation had as profound a dedication to the separation of church and state as Helwys, but he refused to go on to the Anabaptist conclusion that magistracy was inherently evil, or repugnant to the Christian. Finally, in 1612, Helwys decided that it was wrong for

Christians when persecuted to fly into exile, and his tiny church prepared to return to England. It was a courageous decision which established the future General Baptist denomination in England, and the conviction that exile was wrong was to be characteristic of the sect.

Life in Amsterdam had become very difficult for Helwys and his church. They were isolated from English separatists and Dutch Anabaptists alike; even the most zealous 'consume that they have and fall under hard conditions, and little by little lose their first love also.'[3] Conditions in England were worse, at least for the leaders, although there was more opportunity for evangelism. Helwys was dead before 1616, possibly as early as 1613, when he was still a middle-aged man – he was born sometime after 1570. His successor in the leadership of the congregation, which settled in London, was John Murton, a Gainsborough furrier who was himself only twenty-one years old when the separatists left Gainsborough for exile in Amsterdam. Murton in his turn was dead by 1626, before reaching middle age; both men were undoubtedly victims of prison life. These laymen gave their sect superb and self-confident leadership which beyond everything else asserted the spiritual autonomy of simple men; that no man was saved by the faith of others was the constant theme of their writings. More than other leaders of the early separatists in England they foreshadowed the aggressive lay evangelism of the revolutionary period.

By 1625 there were five congregations with at least one hundred and fifty members in England, at London, Lincoln, Sarum, Coventry, and Tiverton, as well as a schismatic group of sixteen in Southwark which was excommunicated by the others because it was harbouring Socinians. The harsh conditions of their life, however, had left the congregations largely leaderless by this date, and this led to renewed negotiations for union with the Waterlanders. Once again the unwillingness of the English congregations to condemn magistracy as inherently evil led to the breakdown of negotiations, and the General Baptists in England failed to become Anabaptists in the continental sense. Little is known of their history between 1630 and 1640, but the arrival of a trickle of refugees in Amsterdam, including John Murton's widow by 1630, is an indication that this decade was the most difficult of all for the General Baptist congregations. There are traces of their existence at Salisbury, Tiverton, Lincoln, and London; and in 1639 and 1640 several important future General Baptist leaders can be identified among the prisoners of the Court of High Commission, including Edward Barber and Thomas Lambe of London, John Garbrand of Southwark, and Henoch Howet of Lincoln.[4] From these tiny and tenacious groups an important and distinctive movement was to spring.

The General Baptists

By 1641 the General Baptists had adapted Anabaptist principles to their English requirements so thoroughly that they emphatically rejected the name of 'Anabaptists' and had lost even the memory of dependence upon the Waterlander teachings, but their tradition was to be permanently marked in a number of ways. The most important manifestation of this past contact with genuine Anabaptists that above all others gave the sect its distinctive identity in England was the doctrine of general redemption.

The usual theme of General Baptist preachers, according to their critics, was 'Christ's dying for all,' the doctrine of general redemption from which they eventually derived their denominational designation. This rather than believer's baptism was their fundamental tenet, and as a result General Baptists had no sense of common purpose with the Particular Baptists and their Calvinist predestinarian orthodoxy. Indeed the Particular Baptist Benjamin Cox, who had himself once been tempted by the Arminian 'errors,' said that the General Baptists refused to recognize the Particular Baptists as fellow Christians but called them 'the gates of Hell, their common enemy.'[5] When converts were made from the Particular Baptists, as they were in Kent at least, they were frequently required to undergo yet another baptism into the General Baptist faith.[6] This doctrinal rivalry might have been more acute than it was if it had not been mitigated in the larger perspective by a common involvement on the parliamentary side in the civil war; in the same spirit John Goodwin's Arminianism was excused by puritans eager for allies in their life-and-death struggle to eliminate episcopal authority from England.

The most elaborate published statement of General Baptist doctrine in this period was *The Fountain of Free Grace Opened*, published in 1645 and reprinted in 1648 in the name of 'the congregation of Christ in London, constituted by baptism upon the profession of faith, falsely called Anabaptists.' The pamphlet, almost certainly written by Thomas Lambe, embodied a cautious statement of the Arminian criticism of orthodox Calvinism, and it made its points with a conciseness and theological subtlety astonishing in a humble soap-boiler.[7] Lambe was anxious to avoid the heresy of free will, but he was equally opposed to a doctrine which, in asserting that Christ had died only for the predestined elect, would appear to leave God directly responsible for the damnation of others. Only the doctrine that Christ had died in atonement for the sins of all mankind could assure the believer absolutely and sustain his faith. There was a circumscribed area of human responsibility in which the 'opposing, despising or neglecting' of this message of general redemption was 'wholly man's evil work,' and the whole blame and punishment for failing to believe therefore rested upon the individual, just as the 'receiving, esteeming or improving' of grace proceeded 'from the covenant [of grace] itself, and not from man.'[8] This negative description of the refusal of grace offered to all was strikingly parallel to the later Quaker description of refusing to recognize the inner light immanent in all men; the Quaker doctrine of the inner light was derived in part from General Baptist teaching of general redemption.[9] But the General Baptists, unlike the Quakers, were biblicists with a severely practical moralistic outlook characteristic of modern fundamentalist sects. Their doctrine of general redemption, by placing a heavy emphasis upon individual responsibility in the matter of salvation, appealed to those who were repelled by the extreme antinomian consequences of the Calvinist doctrine of double predestination.[10]

The doctrine of general redemption appealed to a deeply rooted native English tendency towards what Patrick Collinson has called 'rustic Pelagianism.'[11] In the long run the General Baptist sect rested firmly upon this rural base, but in the early years of the revolutionary period its appeal was no less successful among the lower classes of London. This urban Pelagianism ran a different course from its rural counterpart. More intense and more closely linked with a class base than was perhaps possible in rural society, it became deeply involved in the political movement of the Levellers and experienced a sharp defeat with the collapse of that movement. Thereafter the initiative in the sect shifted decisively into the hands of the provincial leaders, and the predominant tone became increasingly quietistic. The whole range of this experience – rural Pelagianism, urban radicalism, and increasing quietism – lay beyond the more limited and conventional experience of the Particular Baptist sect.

The General Baptists were in no sense Independents, and this also served to isolate them from other sectarians who had been deeply influenced by the idea of congregational independency. Their strict separatism and their profound anti-clericalism reinforced their lack of a congregational theory to make the General Baptists the most remote of all the sects from the religious Independents with their powerful clerical leadership. Church authority was understood not to arise from the covenanted congregation but to flow directly from the Bible and to operate above the level of the individual congregation. Consequently the early itinerant evangelists exercised a real if at first ill-defined authority as officers of what they called the 'Church of Christ' rather than as officers of their individual congregations. As a result of these peculiarities in doctrine and organization, the General Baptists were able to recruit members directly from the parish churches more easily than did the Particular Baptists, whose appeal was more apt to attract those already involved in intermediate stages of separatist worship.

The fundamental factor in the explosive General Baptist evangelism after 1640, however, was to be found in the prevailing excitement and exaltation at the prospect of a national reformation which infected the whole spectrum of puritanism. The degree to which the General Baptists, despite the alien element in their background, could identify themselves with this national aspiration was revealed in the preface of Edward Barber's small pamphlet on baptism early in 1642. He began by expressing his wonder that God should 'raise up me, a poor tradesman, to devulge this glorious truth' of believer's baptism by immersion, but this modesty must be weighed against his proud description of himself as a 'citizen and merchant tailor of London.' He measured the reformation in national rather than in narrowly sectarian terms, and his heroes were laymen. After speaking of the 'great cause we have to admire the goodness and love of God to this nation, in King Edward the Sixth's days, for the great light that then brake forth,' he indicted the clergy without reserve for changing their religion between the reigns of Henry VIII and Elizabeth; as a profession they were forever discredited as unfit for religious leadership. The bishops had recently been brought to their knees by 'divers gentlemen, laymen as they call them,' in Parliament, not by the puritan clergy who in Laud's days 'were gone beyond the seas or hid themselves when, if ever, the kingdom stood in need.' Now that light was 'springing forth in such abundance' outside the ranks of the clergy, and now that God had opened the ear of Parliament 'to hear whatever by any shall be spoken for God's glory, and the good of this state,' Barber believed it was the duty of men like himself to speak what the Lord had vouchsafed them.[12] In the same spirit, a year later he asked Parliament, who he still hoped would take the part of God's 'poor despised saints against their antichristian great opposers,' to arrange a debate between some of the Brownists and Anabaptists and the divines of the Westminster Assembly.[13] For a decade the leaders of the General Baptists were to be sustained by the identification of their cause with the prospect of a national reformation, until the disillusionment of the 1650s revived the pessimistic and quietistic outlook that had characterized the sect in the 1620s.

The London churches

The opening event in the General Baptist evangelical campaign in London appears to have been a public assembly of all their adherents at a house in Whitechapel on 10 January 1641. The meeting attracted the attention of a great crowd which was divided in its sympathies, some breaking into the house where the meeting was held, others fighting the constables who soon appeared on the scene. Many of the General Baptists were sent to the New Prison as separatists, and five days later nine of them secured their release on bail. On 19 January the General Baptists remaining in prison petitioned the House of Lords for relief, charging violence and wrongful imprisonment against the magistrate who had committed them, but the Lords ordered that they be left to the ordinary course of the law.[14]

The Whitechapel meeting and its attendant riot, which preceded by eleven months the comparable riot outside Barbone's shop in Fleet Street, must have burst on the London scene like a bombshell. During the previous year individual General Baptists had appeared before the Court of High Commission, but there is no clue in the court records to the organizations to which they belonged and probably the authorities themselves had no idea of the kind of movement they were dealing with. The Whitechapel meeting was attended by members of what appear to be three distinct congregations, since among those released on bail on 15 January were Thomas Lambe, Mark Whitelocke, who was a constant associate of Edward Barber at this period, and two Southwark General Baptists, John Garbrand and Thomas Seales. The relationship between Lambe and Barber at this time is difficult to determine, but they were probably already leaders of separate societies in London.[15] The presence of Garbrand and Seales from Southwark strengthens the impression that the Whitechapel meeting involved more than a single congregation. Garbrand, a silk-dyer who had appeared before the Court of High Commission in the previous June along with his wife and Elizabeth Staines, a widow, probably belonged to the congregation organized by Elias Tookey in 1624. Daniel Featley complained in 1644 that the Anabaptists had been active near his residence in Southwark 'for more than twenty years,' and under John Clayton's leadership this was to be the most important General Baptist congregation in Southwark for a generation to come.[16] The congregations of Lambe, Barber, and Garbrand are soon readily distinguishable; the presence of these men at Whitechapel in circumstances that produced a riot suggests that this meeting was one of unusual scope embracing more than a single congregation. If this was the case, then the General Baptists were much more securely established in London at the beginning of the Long Parliament than other surviving records indicate.

The host congregation in Whitechapel seems to have been Thomas Lambe's. This church can be briefly glimpsed again two years later when a Royalist denounced 'one of our chief divines, namely Nicholas Tew the girdler at the Exchange, who teacheth at Whitechapel in a chamber every Sabbath day.'[17] By the end of 1644 Tew had moved to Coleman Street, where he and Richard Overton had a secret press. Thomas Lambe 'an oilman' was named to the House of Lords in January 1645 as one of those responsible for distributing a small sheet from this press attacking Essex and Manchester for their leadership of the parliamentary armies.[18] About this same time, too, the church met regularly in Bell Alley, Coleman Street, until it moved to Spitalfields late in 1645. Tew remains a shadowy figure, but Overton was to become a leading propagandist and organizer in the Leveller movement in London. The career of Thomas Lambe, the pastor of the congregation, was fully as remarkable as that of the better known Overton. Usually described as a soapboiler, Lambe spent so much of his time in evangelical activity that he may have received at least part of his living from his congregation. A man of dynamic energy, he developed unique evangelical techniques among the first generation of sectarian leaders. His roving missionary tours through large areas of the English countryside were unmatched until the development of the great Quaker itinerants of the next decade, and his appreciation of the benefits of publicity was rivalled only by the Levellers. He welcomed public disputes with the ordained clergy, and by regarding himself as the lawfully ordained pastor of a true Christian congregation he claimed the right to preach in the pulpits of parish churches; his sermon at St Bennet Gracechurch on 5 November 1644 was said to have drawn 'a mighty great audience.'[19] Under his leadership his congregation became the base for an explosive evangelical campaign in London and throughout southern England.

Lambe's church was easily the most visible and notorious of all sectarian congregations in London up to the end of the first civil war. It was unique among the non-parochial congregations in that its meetings were regularly open to the public, and no congregation looms larger in the pages of Edwards' *Gangraena*. It rivalled the theatre in its capacity to draw crowds, 'especially young youths and wenches,' and on Sundays 'many people, some of other separate churches, and some of our [parish] churches, will go to this Lambe's church for novelty, because of the disputes and wranglings that will be there upon questions, all kinds of things started and vented almost, and several companies in the same room, some speaking in one part, some in another.' It was the custom of the congregation for two or three men to preach successively, and 'when one hath done, there's sometimes difference in the church who shall exercise next, 'tis put to the vote, some for one, some for another. . .and strangers who come thither will make a cry, and cry out for whom they like best as well as the church.' Nor were the preachers left to deliver their messages undisturbed; for it was 'usual and lawful, not only for the company to stand up and object against the doctrine delivered when the exerciser of his gifts hath made an end, but in the midst of it, so that sometimes upon some standing up and objecting, there's *pro* and *con* for almost an hour, and falling out among themselves before the man can have finished his discourse.' Sometimes the meeting broke apart in sections, and there was 'such a confusion and noise, as if it were at a play; and some will be speaking here, some there.'[20]

Lambe's church was the base for an extensive evangelical campaign throughout southern England. The itinerant evangelist was a distinctive feature of the General Baptists during the 1640s. As early as 1642 Lambe described himself in a letter as a 'messenger of Jesus Christ, put apart to teach the Gospel-grace'; in the next decade the 'messenger' became a permanent supra-congregational officer of the General Baptist denomination.[21] Lambe's church attracted and trained some of the most effective sectarian evangelists of the revolutionary period: Henry Denne, a former clergyman, Samuel Oates, a weaver of Norwich, and Jeremiah Ives, a cheesemonger and boxmaker of London. All were baptized by Lambe, and they remained closely connected with his church, preaching there regularly whenever they were in London. Other permanent members of the church, Edward Tench and Timothy Batt, a physician, both well known as preachers, occasionally accompanied the evangelists on their tours.

Lambe himself was the most active evangelist in his church. Between 1641 and 1646 he can be traced, usually with a companion, in Gloucestershire (with Clement Wrighter, who was briefly a member of Lambe's church before achieving notoriety as one of the leading sceptics of London), in Norfolk, in Essex (with Timothy Batt), in Surrey and Hampshire (with Samuel Oates), in Kent (with Henry Denne), and in Wiltshire (with Jeremiah Ives).[22] Of his associates, Denne was the most important. A Cambridge graduate, he held a living at Eltisley in Cambridgeshire, the family home of John Desborough, since 1636 a brother-in-law of Oliver Cromwell. Denne was rebaptized by Thomas Lambe in 1644 and became a member of Lambe's church, but he did not spend much time in London, being sent by the church to evangelize in Cambridgeshire and the surrounding counties. Thomas Edwards was shocked that Denne continued to preach in the parish church at Eltisley, but by December 1645 he had heard a report that Denne was driving a cart on the highway to London in the conviction that 'ministers must work with their hands, and follow some worldly calling.'[23] However shocking Denne's behaviour to his fellow clergymen, it was sedate when compared with that of Samuel Oates, the most flamboyant of the itinerants connected with Lambe's church. A weaver of Norwich, Oates was a member of a General Baptist church that may have been organized there as early as Lambe's visit in 1642.[24] In 1645 Oates came to London where he preached in Lambe's church, and he accompanied Lambe through Surrey and Hampshire to Portsmouth. His apprenticeship finished, he launched a great evangelical tour which for the next three years the parish clergy universally condemned as the progress of a disorderly rabble. Sometimes accompanied by other members of Lambe's church, Oates moved slowly through Essex, Lincolnshire, Northamptonshire, and Leicestershire until in 1648 he finally settled briefly in Rutland. Everywhere he went there were tumults and riots; an attempt was made to convict him for the murder of a woman who died shortly after Oates had rebaptised her in March 'in a very cold season,' but Oates was acquitted. The magistrates were nervous of Oates; one of Edwards' informants wrote from Essex that 'no magistrate in the country dare meddle with him, for they say they have hunted these out of the country into their dens in London, and imprisoned some, and they are released and sent like decoy ducks into the country to fetch in more.'[25]

Edward Barber's congregation stands in complete contrast to Lambe's. Barber himself avoided the publicity that Lambe sought out, and the only recorded public fracas of his career occurred as late as 1648 when he challenged Edmund Calamy to a dispute in his parish church and had to be rescued by a constable from the pummelling of an excited mob.[26] Barber was well known to Edwards as an Anabaptist leader, but the heresiographer received only one description of this church, and that from a member of the congregation. His account of the meeting of the church at a 'great house' in Bishopsgate Street near Threadneedle Street on 12 November 1645 is of exceptional interest:

When the company was met together they began with prayer; after prayer, every one of the company kneeled down apart; and Barber, with another of their way, went to each of them one after another, and laid both their hands upon every particular head, women as well as men, and either in a way of prayer, prayed they might receive the Holy Ghost; or else barely to every one of them used these words, *Receive the Holy Ghost.*

After this ceremony was finished, the meeting sat down to supper 'which was dressed for them by a cook.' When the meal was over and before the cloth was removed, the Lord's Supper was administered to the congregation. Thereafter a question was proposed, whether Christ died for all men, and the meeting was still discussing this when Edwards' informant left them at eleven o'clock in the evening. The ceremony at the beginning of the meeting, the laying on of hands on all baptized believers, marked a new departure in this congregation; hitherto laying on of hands had been restricted to the ordination of church officers. Edwards' informant, who was uncertain about the significance of the new practice, learned from other members that 'such persons who now after the laying on of these hands shall have gifts, must be sent to preach into the countries, yea into the streets openly and publicly, yea to the doors of the Parliament House.' The restraint that characterized this congregation was reflected in their decision 'to forbear a while from sending them into the streets publicly, and to the Parliament to preach, till they should see how things would go.'[27]

Edwards' account of the inauguration of the laying on of hands in Barber's church ended with the information that 'the like had been done in another church of the Anabaptists before'; and here, in Lambe's church, the new practice early demonstrated its future capacity for disrupting General Baptist congregations. The idea was first broached in Lambe's church by Francis Cornewell, a former clergyman who was in 1645 a member of a General Baptist congregation meeting at Orpington in Kent. It was adopted enthusiastically by a minority of the congregation led by a physician, John Griffith; the majority of the church agreed to permit the practice if Griffith and his followers promised a 'peaceable demeanour' in the congregation.[28] This appears to have occurred shortly before the ceremony in Barber's church and was undoubtedly Barber's inspiration. The success in Barber's church in turn encouraged the minority in Lambe's church to advance their claim that the laying on of hands was a foundation principle of the Christian religion and that communion was unlawful with those who refused the new ordinance. Early in 1646, therefore, Griffith and his followers 'made a rent and a separation' from Lambe's church to establish a new General Baptist congregation which required laying on of hands on all members. The new church, which met under Griffith's pastoral charge in an alley not far from the parent church, lived for several years in obscurity, but as the new practice was gradually adopted by the majority of General Baptist congregations in England its importance increased until Griffith became one of the most influential and successful of the General Baptist pastors in London.[29] Lambe himself and the evangelists associated with his church steadfastly opposed laying on of hands and in the long run found themselves isolated and without influence in the denomination they had done so much to advance.

Two other General Baptist congregations in London can scarcely be traced before 1649, although they were undoubtedly important. About all that can be said of the Southwark congregation represented at the Whitechapel meeting by Garbrand and Seales is that it did not adopt the practice of laying on of hands in this decade. Edwards heard in 1646 of a feltmaker of Southwark named Crab, 'a dipper and a preacher,' who was perhaps a member of the congregation.[30] The only one of Crab's converts identified by Edwards was Samuel Fulcher, 'an egg man' who was later a member of the second church under discussion, the congregation of Samuel Loveday meeting on Tower Hill. The origin of this church is entirely obscure, but it was already well established in 1650 when Loveday described himself on the title page of a small book on doctrine as the 'Servant of the Church of Christ.'[31] Its later history indicates that it was closely akin to Barber's in spirit and practice, and it adopted both the laying on of hands and the practice of communion after a congregational supper.

The early General Baptist congregations in London lacked the cohesion of the seven Particular Baptist churches, and they were isolated from the network that linked Particular Baptists with the separatists and the Independents. Thoroughly separatist and entirely lay in leadership, the General Baptists recruited their members from a lower social level than did other separate churches. Lambe, Barber, Griffith and Loveday were able and articulate men, but they shared the leadership of their congregations with Andrew Debman, 'a cooper by trade, a sorry fellow, that can neither write nor read,' who was nevertheless, according to Edwards, 'a great preacher among the sectaries.'[32] This was a far cry from such men among the Particular Baptists as William Kiffin, an eminently successful merchant who was appointed a parliamentary assessor of taxes for Middlesex in 1647, and Samuel Richardson, who in the same year laid out one thousand pounds to buy up soldiers' arrears of pay and soon afterwards lost to Royalist privateers a ship in which he had a half interest.[33] Lack of evidence precludes even an informed guess about the extent of the General Baptist success among the masses of London, but the impression of vitality that may be gathered from Edwards' pages is borne out by the consistent General Baptist support for the Leveller movement.

The sectarian fringes

The General Baptists stood at the edge of organized sectarianism. Although the congregations of the sect possessed the same basic institutional stability as other separate churches, they were looser in organization, more radical in outlook, and more fluid in membership. The genuine Anabaptist element in their tradition accounts for beliefs and practices that went beyond those of other separate churches. The heresiographers reported that there were groups of Anabaptists at this period who refused to take oaths before magistrates, that Lambe's church refused to permit the marriage of members with unbelievers and perhaps sanctioned the divorce of the faithful from the unbeliever, and that members of this church worked at their trades on Sunday. Edwards heard of a woman preacher in Lincolnshire, of whom it was 'reported also she baptizeth, but that's not so certain.' The latter was in fact unlikely, for ordinances were administered only by pastors or elders, and these were always men in General Baptist churches. If women were permitted to preach, it was probably as private members of the congregation exercising their gifts among other women; thus Edwards heard of a woman near Brasted in Kent, an Anabaptist, who preached to women.[34]

This happened also in Thomas Lambe's church where Mrs Attaway, the most notorious woman preacher in London, began her career. She and one or two of her 'Sisters' began their exercise among 'some of their own sex,' but they soon decided 'to admit of all that pleased to come' and late in 1645 instituted a public weekday lecture, on Tuesday afternoons, in imitation of the conventional puritan lectures. The Tuesday lecture was an immediate success and attracted 'a world of people, to the number of a thousand first and last to Bell Alley,' Coleman Street, so that the lecture had to be moved to more spacious premises. The audience at first treated the women with respect, but the invitation to discuss matters handled in the lectures soon introduced controversies and led to 'such laughing, confusion and disorder at the meeting' that Edwards' informant, a minister, 'professed he never saw the like.' The transformation of private exercises among the women members of Lambe's church into the Tuesday lectures took place without the formal approval of the congregation; one of the female members of the church stood up in the lecture to tell Mrs Attaway 'she ought not to preach to the world' and complained that she could not speak freely as a church member before the multitude attending the lecture. Mrs Attaway, however, was rapidly passing out of the orbit of the General Baptist congregation. In January 1646 she told her audience that 'for her part she was in the wilderness, waiting for the pouring out of the Spirit'; she denied that she was preaching and said that she was exercising her gifts, for she could not be convinced 'that any in the world this day living, had any commission to preach.' By the end of February it was reported that Mrs Attaway had run away with another woman's husband to Jerusalem.[35]

A common accusation against individual General Baptists was that they held the mortalist heresy, that 'the soul of man was created mortal, and dies or sleeps with the body.'[36] Edwards published an account of a public disputation in January 1646 in Thomas Lambe's church in its new location at Spitalfields, on the proposition that 'God made man, and every part of man of the dust of the earth; and therefore man and every part of man must return to the dust again.' The protagonists were both members of the congregation, Batty defending the mortalist position and Lambe himself refuting it. Edwards' report is particularly valuable in that it identifies the moderator on Batty's side as Richard Overton, soon to become notorious as the ablest of the Leveller polemicists.[37] Overton had already published anonymously *Mans Mortalitie*, a pamphlet ranked by the House of Commons with John Milton's tract on divorce and Roger Williams' *Bloody Tenet of Persecution* as among the most scandalous yet seen in England. Certainly his mortalism was a Christian heresy rather than a novel materialism; the doctrine was sustained by a literal belief in a day of resurrection for all mankind.[38] Mortalism was never adopted as an official tenet of the sect, but it became common enough that accusations of mortalism against individuals may be taken as presumptive evidence of membership in a General Baptist church.

The position of the General Baptists on the frontiers of organized sectarianism exercised a powerful attraction for enthusiasts who in their search for religious fulfilment passed from church to church and from sect to sect. The classic pattern of 'falling off' was described by Edwards in the case of Clement Wrighter, Lambe's associate on the Gloucestershire tour in 1641:

> There is one Clement Wrighter in London, but anciently belonging to Worcester, sometimes a professor of religion, and judged to have been godly, who is now an arch heretic and fearful apostate, an old wolf, and a subtle man. . .This man about 7 or 8 years ago, fell off from the communion of our churches, to Independency and Brownism, and was much taken with Mr. Robinson's books, as that of the Justification of Separation; from that he fell to Anabaptism and Arminianism, and to mortalism, holding the soul mortal. . .After that he fell to be a Seeker, and is now an Antiscripturist, a Questionist and Sceptic, and I fear an Atheist.[39]

No longer a member of an organized congregation, he continued active in London, distributing papers and questions among those 'whom he thinks he may corrupt, and that will be faithful to him.' Among his friends was the merchant William Walwyn, already busy establishing his credit among the sects by his activity on behalf of religious toleration but soon suspected of sharing Wrighter's scepticism. Like Walwyn,

Wrighter seems to have retained the friendship of some of the leading sectaries of London on the strength of his dedication to toleration; 'he comes into public meetings of the sectaries upon occasions of meeting to draw up petitions for the Parliament or other businesses.'[40] Wrighter's experience was not uncommon, and it illuminates one of the roots of the rationalism and secularism of the Leveller movement.

Another and more inward view of the process of 'falling off' is provided by Luke Howard's brief spiritual autobiography written in 1687. After an early experience as a quasi-separatist, Howard first joined a fully organized separatist worship among the Particular Baptists in Kent.[41] His falling off to the General Baptists was one of the major religious experiences of his life, as he left the 'dark stuff' of predestination for the doctrine of general redemption. But his uneasiness about a new baptism and about 'the bad lives of some called Brothers and Sisters' prepared the way for his next insight, which came upon him suddenly 'in a meeting,' that the baptism of the gospel was the baptism of the Spirit. 'This visitation and convincement of the Lord was so great. . .that it brought me clear down to the earth, where I saw all carnal ordinances lay,' and Howard gave himself up 'to a seeking state again, and became dead to all forms.'[42] Howard's description of his experience after this point affords an exceptional insight into those 'notions' which, by a conventional formula, were said to follow the seeking state.[43] At first he was 'ready to think that there was nothing in religion to be known more than I had found'; this led him to the temptation of 'madness and folly,' undoubtedly shared by many notionists, that 'if ever thou wilt know greater things than thou dost, thou must commit some great evil first.' In some this notion led to the excesses of the Ranters, in Howard it led to nothing more serious than 'company keeping' and gaming, but 'the end of all my madness was sorrow.' A stage of desolation followed, when 'I mourned in secret with tears, in the brokenness of my heart,' which was eventually succeeded by one of cynicism, 'to take my fill of the world, with all I could enjoy thereof. Then I said within myself, I will now be as proud and as fine in apparel as I can possibly be, and as time-serving with all manner of eloquences, and compliments, and flattering titles, as I can possibly learn.' It was as a prosperous and popular tradesman that, in London on business, he went one Sunday to hear 'one Cordwell in Lombard Street, a mystery man so called,' where the young Quaker William Caton stood up to speak. Howard remarked to his companion, 'come let us be gone to dinner. . .for I know as much as he can tell me, or more than I or he either can live in'; but he was close to his final illumination, which occurred when Caton soon afterwards appeared in Dover.[44]

By the later 1640s, London abounded in mystery men and their audiences – Seekers, Familists, Antinomians, and Ranters. For the most part these people were individualists, and it is very difficult to detect among them more than a rudimentary network of personal contacts. Lawrence Clarkson spoke of his association with the Antinomians of London in these terms: 'in this sect I continued a certain time, for church it was none, in that it was but part form, and part none.'[45] People who had rejected the 'legalism' of the traditional parish worship were not always satisfied with the alternative presented by the separate churches, especially as the latter began to settle into specific forms strenuously defended. The Quaker movement, which was to provide a spiritual home for much of this *malaise*, still lay in the future. In the late 1640s, the Leveller movement perhaps absorbed the energies of some of these people, but as we shall see the Levellers failed to create an autonomous secular political organization that could substitute for the institutional strength and stability of the separate churches.

One of the important facts of this period is that so many of these radical individualists had passed through the separate churches in their search for spiritual or worldly satisfaction. Their subsequent 'radicalism' was a far less fearsome thing for the saints of the separate churches than for the respectable classes of society in general. Clement Wrighter, although an 'anti-scripturist' and a known sceptic, continued to collaborate with the saints in the struggle for religious toleration, and the saints knew from the beginning that the price of toleration must be freedom for the scepticism of Wrighter as well as for the separate churches. It was a price they were prepared to pay.

5

KING JESUS AND THE GATHERING OF INDEPENDENT CHURCHES IN LONDON

King Jesus in 1641

The gathering of the Independent churches was sustained by the deeply held conviction that the act of entering a congregation of visible saints was to enter Christ's 'kingdom' not in a metaphorical but in a literal sense. William Kiffin described it as 'this great truth, Christ the king of his church,' in his preface to Thomas Goodwin's sermon in 1641, *A Glimpse of Syons Glory*, itself concerned with developing the idea in a particular millenial direction.[1] Henry Burton in 1641 spoke of Jesus as 'the sole anointed King of his church' and as 'the one and only King of saints.'[2] This was perhaps the most compelling conviction of the Independents of the 1640s; an irritated critic in 1646 expressed it exactly in describing an Independent preacher who proclaimed 'Christ a king, and every new-moulded congregation his kingdom.'[3] By transferring the headship or kingly office of Christ from the mystical body of the universal church to the immediate local congregation of saints on earth, the Independents eliminated all intermediaries – whether the royal supremacy or the papal, episcopal, or presbyterian hierarchies – between Christ as head of the church and the individual saint. The saint could thus enter Christ's kingdom immediately, and on this earth, not in a future life or in a future millennial age; and he could do so without worrying unduly about those details of church order which preoccupied the clergy. Further, he was advancing Christ's kingdom on earth by swelling its ranks, and thus playing a part in the divine plan for human history. By investing the act of entering a gathered church of visible saints with this cosmic significance, the idea of Christ's kingly office provided a substantial emotional justification for the step, which must have been nearly always inwardly disturbing, of leaving the traditional parish churches.

Christ's kingly office in this sense had the further advantage that although it placed Christ's kingdom on this earth and brought the saints literally within the scope of the divine plan for human history, it could be flexibly linked with almost any vision of what that plan was. It was not necessarily a millenarian idea. The early Barrowists, who used it to justify their own separatist church order, were not millenarians, nor was Henry Jacob, who used it to transform his conception of the gathered church from a temporary expedient into an autonomous true visible church.[4] By 1641, however, the Independent clergy gave it a distinctly millenarian twist by grafting on the idea of a coming age in which Christ would rule the world through his saints. This new conception of the rule of the saints was carefully limited by the Independent preachers to a millennium which had not yet arrived or to the second coming of Christ which had not yet occurred; they were not advocating the immediate rule of the saints but rather the immediate gathering of the saints into churches, quite a different matter. By raising the prospect of the millennium, however, this Independent preaching served to accentuate the providential significance of contemporary actions and to heighten among their listeners the awareness of being God's instruments on earth. The millenarian fancy strengthened its hold on the Independent congregations as the decade wore on, enhancing their sense of acting as God's instruments and in the end nerving their arms to strike off the King's head, even although the proper conditions for the rule of the saints, the coming of the millennium or the second coming of Christ, were not fulfilled.

Thomas Goodwin's sermon preached in Holland early in 1641 demonstrates how the kingly office of Christ could be expressed in millenial and apocalyptic language. *A Glimpse of Syons Glory* is a superb expression of exuberant optimism that Babylon is falling and the reign of Christ approaching; it can still vividly convey to readers the intense excitement sweeping through the communities of English exiles at the news of the first weeks of the Long Parliament in England. The central conception is the gathered church (indeed the sermon was preached at the inauguration of a newly gathered church) which the preacher presented in a context leading directly to the personal reign of Christ on earth, suggesting on the basis of the calculations of Thomas Brightman that the events leading to Christ's reign would begin in 1650 and come to a head forty-five years later. However, the main burden of the sermon relates not to the rule of the saints but to the security of the saints in the gathered church, 'that it shall be delivered from all the enemies of it, and from all molesting troubles, and so be in a most blessed safety and security.' Thus could people 'of the meaner rank, common people,' by entering into Christ's kingdom in a gathered church, participate personally in the divine drama.[5]

Millenarianism was a pronounced characteristic of the Independents of the early 1640s. Dr John F. Wilson has demonstrated the strength of millenarian ideas among the Independents who preached before the House of Commons.[6] John Archer, whose *Personalle Raigne of Christ upon Earth* was published in London in 1641, was an Independent associated with Thomas Goodwin and Philip Nye in the Arnhem congregation.[7] Several of Thomas Goodwin's sermons on the Fifth Monarchy, preached in London in the early 1640s, were published a decade later by some of the Fifth Monarchy men.[8] Most of the prominent Independent clergymen, Henry Burton, Jeremiah Burroughes, Nathaniel Homes, William Bridge, Joseph Symonds, Nicholas Lockyer, and Henry Jessey, expressed millenarian ideas in sermons or pamphlets.[9] It was in the Independent congregations that these ideas were most strongly developed, and it was the Independents John Rogers, Christopher Feake, John Simpson, and Vavasor Powell who were to give leadership to the Fifth Monarchy movement of the next decade. Millenarianism spilled over from the Independents to the 'sects,' especially the Particular Baptists, but even here it was strongest among those who were closest to the Independents, the former clergymen Henry Jessey and Hanserd Knollys; the eventual conversion of John Simpson and Vavasor Powell to Baptist practices had the effect of moderating their millenarian enthusiasm.[10]

The millenarianism of the Independents must be qualified in two important respects. In the first place, the kingdom of Christ in the gathered churches must be distinguished from millenarianism and the idea of the rule of the saints.[11] The Independents of the early 1640s sought to convey the meaning and importance of the kingdom of Christ in his gathered churches of visible saints, which had a concrete existence in this world, by using an imagery relating to God's ultimate and apocalyptic purposes in human history. The fundamental convictions of the Independents centred in the concrete experience of Christ's kingdom in the gathered church, not in the extended imagery of the millennium. As they grew more secure in their gathered churches, the 'respectable' Independent clergy abandoned the language of the millennium, but not before they had created a context in which a more literal-minded generation of Fifth Monarchy enthusiasts began to conceive of the millennium in concrete terms as the rule of the saints. There is a difference of a whole generation between these two stages; the earlier Independents expressed in millenarian language their triumph over Laud as the saints gathered in their churches; the Fifth Monarchy men expressed in millenarian language their despair at the failure of the rule of the saints in the world to materialize. The Independent clergy of the early 1640s also found in millenarianism an esoteric language which conveyed a hidden meaning to a select portion of their public audiences. In their lectures and public sermons the Independent clergy could preach on millenarian themes that were acceptable and even conventional in puritan ears while also conveying, in references to Christ's kingdom, a special meaning to those of their audience who had already entered the gathered church.[12] Independent millenarianism at this time therefore could perform the ambiguous function of both expressing and concealing the fundamental message that Christ's kingdom existed in the gathered churches of visible saints.

This ambiguity leads to the second qualification about Independent millenarianism, that it served less to differentiate the Independent clergy from their puritan brethren than to unite them with the more radical puritan clergy into a clerical war party that triumphantly overthrew the bishops and preached in apocalyptic terms a national regeneration and reformation.[13] Although the Independents formed a recognizable party from the moment of their arrival in London, they were not isolated from the mainstream of puritanism. In November 1641, when the attack upon the bishops was renewed in the House of Commons, the Independent clergy then in London met with the puritan clergy of the City at Edmund Calamy's house to devise a common strategy. The conservative puritan Thomas Edwards described its purpose thus: 'The ministers of both sides, both they and we desirous of reformation in church government and worship, being sensible how much our differences and divisions might distract the Parliament and hinder the taking away of episcopal government and the reformation intended, in a full and great meeting consulted together upon ways to prevent it.' The terms agreed on were that the clergy present would continue to use the least offensive parts of the Book of Common Prayer in an effort to placate moderate Anglicans and isolate the bishops; that some of their number, presumably the Independents present, would undertake to persuade the lay preachers to cease preaching in public and thereby bringing discredit upon the radical puritans; and that a mutual silence would be preserved on disputed issues of church government.[14] Thus these differences were to be subordinated to the larger common cause of extirpating episcopacy, and this cause was conceived in apocalyptic terms by both parties.

In several vivid pages of his biography of William Prynne, Dr William M. Lamont has shown how Prynne, never a friend of Independents, was brought round in 1641 from a moderate episcopacy to a completely anti-episcopal position by puritan clergy who urged upon him the prophetic writings of Thomas Brightman. 'This was Brightman's strength in 1641,' Lamont observes, that 'he could attract separatist and non-separatist, John Goodwin and Thomas Edwards, in the rejection of a totally corrupt, lukewarm episcopacy'; and he did so by a comprehensive exposition of the book of Revelation.[15] Edwards, the implacable enemy of the Independents, scarcely mentions their millenarianism for the very good reason that he was also under Brightman's influence, and it was left for the Scot, Robert Baillie, to expose publicly their attachment to the heresy in his *Dissuasive from the Errours of the Time* in 1645. Yet even Baillie handled the issue gingerly and diplomatically, for as he observed privately in a letter written about the same time, 'most of the chief divines here [in London], not only Independents, but others such as Twisse, Marshall, Palmer and many more, are express chiliasts.'[16] Preachers brought up in the tradition of John Foxe's *Book of Martyrs* and the conception of England as an 'elect nation,'[17] and familiar with Thomas Brightman's more thoroughly anti-episcopal interpretation of Revelation, had at hand a rhetoric in which to discuss the removal of the bishops and the coming of the civil war. This apocalyptic language, in creating an emotional unity in a time of profound crisis, operated at an exalted level of cosmic explanation and served to obscure rather than to define fundamental differences of opinion about church government.

This deeper alliance imposed restraints upon both sides, and this suggests an answer to a complex and difficult problem: namely, why the Independents hesitated so long, until late in 1643, to launch the organization of gathered churches on a large scale. To pose the problem in this way is to presuppose that the Independents were already clear in their own minds in 1641 what their programme was. This assumption has not been made by the leading modern historians of the Independents. Thus Dr G. F. Nuttall finds the first significant event in the mature history of 'the Congregational way' to be the publication at the very end of 1643 of the *Apologeticall Narration* by Thomas Goodwin, Philip Nye, Sidrach Simpson, Jeremiah Burroughes, and William Bridge, all of them exiles in Arnhem and Rotterdam in the late 1630s. This approach avoids not only the question of what these men were doing between their return to England in 1641 and the appearance of the *Apologeticall Narration* but also the larger question of the specific origin of their conceptions.[18] Perry Miller, too, has argued that the English Independents developed their mature position only after their return from exile; he has expressed this classic view in magisterial tones in his remark that 'English Independents like Nye or Goodwin, who in 1640 undertook to spread the New England system in England, were turned aside by the unforeseen course of the wars and forced to preserve their lives in an unholy alliance with the sects upon a platform of toleration.'[19] This view acquires plausibility from the undoubted fact of John Cotton's influence on the apologetical narrators and from their publication of his works with enthusiastic endorsements.[20] But Cotton left England in 1633 as a congregational puritan whose conceptions in England do not appear to have transcended the parochial congregation.[21] The possibility existed in America of one true congregational church in one town, with all of the beautiful simplicity of the New Testament pattern, and Cotton became perhaps the most authoritative master of the theory of this congregational church. But Cotton's horizon in Massachusetts was free of parish churches, and he did not have to face the painful dilemmas involved in creating true congregational churches by 'gathering' the saints out of parish churches and thereby mortally offending puritan friends and allies. Cotton seems never to have understood Jacob's conception of the 'gathered church,' which was devised bearing in mind the problems of living among the parish congregations of England. Thus Cotton's theoretical expositions could be useful to English Independents, who were very cautious about publishing their views themselves, precisely because his conceptions did not embarrass them or commit them in negotiations with other puritans where parochial limits were the central issue in question.

There are indications that by 1641 the Independents were committed to the gathered church in Henry Jacob's sense rather than to a parochial congregationalism. For one thing, there was Henry Jessey's church to serve as a model in every significant detail. Although the Independents seem never to have referred to Jacob in their writings in the revolutionary period, this restraint may have been due to their desire to avoid revealing publicly the degree of their commitment to a non-parochial course of action, just as their use of Cotton's writings may in part have stemmed from the convenience of having a spokesman who was innocent of the separation in which they were engaged.[22] John Bastwick, under no such restraint, certainly knew of Henry Jacob as 'one of the fathers of the congregational way. . .who first baptized their new gathered churches with that compellation of Independent churches.'[23] The Independents sometimes directly echoed Jacob. Thomas Goodwin in 1639 described the covenant of the Arnhem congregation in terms that strikingly resembled the covenant of the Jacob church, 'to walk in all those ways pertaining to this fellowship, so far as they shall be revealed to them in the gospel'; in referring to 'the light that shines, or shall shine,' Goodwin echoed that provision for future light which John Robinson's separatist covenant had in common with Jacob's semi-separatist one.[24] In 1646 Jeremiah Burroughes defined the obligations of semi-separatists in terms similar to the Jacob *Confession* of 1616: 'yet so as not condemning those [parish] churches they join not with as false, but still preserve all Christian communion with the saints as members of the same body of Christ, of the church catholic, and join also with them in all duties of worship that belong to particular churches, so far as they are able.'[25] This was the heart of Jacob's policy of living in a true church in the midst of the parish churches, expressed in words akin to Jacob's.

There is in any case no doubt that by 1641 the leading English Independents were committed to the non-parochial gathered church of the Jacob tradition rather than to a parochial congregationalism. This is evident in Henry Burton's *The Protestation Protested*, published in the middle of the year. The reformation in England, Burton said, would consist in 'the new forming of a church' which was 'properly a congregation of believers, called out from the rest of the world.' He frankly admitted that this was the separatist solution, but it was undertaken not for doctrinaire separatist reasons but because a parochial congregationalism was impractical: 'Nor can we think, at the first especially, that every assembly of people collected in their several parishes is fit to make up a congregation, and so qualified as Christ requireth.' What then were the saints to do, if the parish congregations were unfit places in which to communicate? 'Therefore of necessity there must be liberty granted of setting up churches or congregations where Christ's ordinances are administered in their purity, and so where none are admitted members of the congregation but such as are approved of by the whole assembly for their profession and conversation.' Such churches, although separate from the corruptions of the world, were nevertheless 'not separate from the civil state but are peaceable members thereof, subject and obedient to all the good and just laws thereof.'[26]

The key decision was made in Arnhem, where the most important of the exiled Independents had lived since the late 1630s. As the news arrived of Laud's imprisonment in the Tower and of the root and branch petition for the abolition of episcopacy, many members of the Arnhem congregation decided that the time had come to return to England. A parochial congregationalism must have appeared as impossible to the exiles as it did to Burton, but there may have been anxious weeks of discussion before they made the final commitment to separation and the gathered church in England after Jacob's example. The decision is evident in Thomas Goodwin's sermon on the apocalyptic mission of the gathered church, *A Glimpse of Syons Glory*. We know from the text that the sermon was delivered at the gathering of a church early in 1641.[27] Since this was an unlikely time to organize yet another exiled congregation, the most reasonable explanation is that this was a gathered church formed of those members of the Arnhem congregation (and perhaps others as well) who intended to return to England.

This course of action was typical of Goodwin's subtle mind. By forming the new church in exile and transporting it as a church into England, Goodwin (for he was to be the pastor) could not be reproached by fellow puritans in England for gathering saints out of their parish congregations. Even although they had not secured the magistrate's consent for this congregation, the returned exiles could plausibly argue that their gathered church was nothing more than what they had enjoyed in exile, and that to suppress them was to resume Laud's policy of persecuting saints.[28] To reinforce his position, Goodwin at first refused to admit new members to his gathered church in London 'that it may be said he hath added none to his church,' although this limitation was soon circumvented by the device of accepting probationary members.[29] This gathered church thus served as a carefully calculated compromise which preserved a true congregational church, wherein the returned exiles could worship regularly, without tying the hands of the Independent leaders in their negotiations with the more conservative parochial puritans.* The possibility of a parochial congregationalism was kept open, while the reality of the gathered church was secured.

This interpretation of events is confirmed in petitions addressed to Parliament in 1641 by the religious exiles asking for permission to worship upon their return home in their own gathered churches, on the model of the French and Dutch congregations in England. These gathered churches were not conceived as temporary expedients but as true visible churches, and parochial churches were explicitly repudiated: 'neither are churches to be made by the bounds and limits of parishes. . .but to consist of a company of people called and separated from the world.'[30] Thomas Edwards, who had heard of these petitions, said that messengers were sent over from the exiled congregations to negotiate with Parliament for their transfer to England as separate churches. At their first coming over, he added, some of the Independent clergy had been willing to 'take the charge of parochial churches amongst us upon the reformation hoped for,' but they had since abandoned this policy in favour of gathered churches. Writing late in 1641, Edwards implied that 'the meetings of these separated assemblies'

* For John Bastwick's version of the covenant of an Independent gathered church of about this date, possibly Goodwin's, see Appendix B.

were already well established in London, and he complained that there were 'many falling to that way daily.'[31]

Only two Independent gathered churches, apart from the Jacob church, can be tentatively identified in London at this time, Goodwin's, and Sidrach Simpson's. The latter was probably also imported into London as a pre-existing gathered church, formed by dividing Simpson's original congregation in Rotterdam. The original church continued there under Joseph Symonds' pastoral charge, while Simpson was established in two London lectureships in 1641; if his gathered church dates from this year, as seems probable, it would have taken its origin from the exiled congregation after the model of Goodwin's church.[32]

The decision in favour of the gathered church was probably the most important ever made by the Independents, for it committed them to a protestant pluralism in English society which forever destroyed the principles of universality and uniformity hitherto carefully preserved by the Church of England and accepted by the overwhelming majority of puritans. The profound implications of the Independent decision were obscured for contemporaries by a variety of circumstances. That there was hesitation and uncertainty among the Independents themselves is suggested by Edwards' report that some of the returning Independents were at first prepared to take parochial charges in England, only to abandon this intention after their arrival.[33] One of them, Joseph Symonds, who preached before the House of Commons in May 1641, seems to have found the situation in England so complex that he preferred to return to Rotterdam.[34]

Perhaps most important of all in veiling the full significance of the Independent decision was the idea that the gathered churches in England, like the exiled congregations, were merely a temporary expedient, a kind of puritan way station on the road to the full reformation of the parish churches of the Church of England.[35] Those who joined the gathered churches did not take this view of their action. It was unthinkable that Christians who had shared the dangers and hardships of a separated non-parochial worship in England or in exile should break up their covenanted church, each to return to his territorial parish, upon any kind of reformation whatever within the national church. The Independents also recognized that visible saints were 'thin sown' in this world.[36] Even if the national church were reformed to secure the independence of parish congregations, many of the parishes in England would fail to qualify for recognition as true churches for want of visible saints: 'for how many parishes in England will be found,' Henry Burton asked, 'where scarce one is able to give a reason of the hope that is in him?'[37] Finally, once the voluntary fellowship of the gathered church was experienced, the territorial limitation of the parish church ceased to make any more sense than did the abandoned Laudian ceremonies. The Independents did not reject the Church of England as a false church, and they attached great importance to its reformation. But their deepest aspiration was to gather the visible saints of the nation into a higher church form that transcended the parish churches because it incorporated the voluntary principle into its very essence.

Silent pastors: the reticence of the Independent clergy

The gathering of Independent churches in London began on a large scale in 1643. The earliest report of the new movement appeared in the royalist *Mercurius Aulicus*, which announced from Oxford in April that Henry Burton and Dr Nathaniel Homes, both parish ministers, had set up their 'independent congregations'; and by refusing to administer the Lord's Supper at Easter in their parishes they had in effect unchurched their territorial parishioners.[38] The fall of Bristol in July forced the Llanvaches church under Walter Cradock to move to London together with some members of the Bristol church.[39] The increasing tensions of the civil war induced other Independents to implement their ecclesiastical principles without further delay. Despite Philip Nye's participation in the negotiations in August and September which led to the Solemn League and Covenant with Scotland, the Independents were so alarmed at the implications of the Scottish alliance that along with the 'Brownists' they drew up 'a very high and daring petition to the parliament [which] required that the Scots Covenant might not pass, or at least not be pressed upon them.'[40] The Presbyterian clergy anxiously reassured Nye, who headed off the petition, but it would appear that in the course of this crisis the last constraints felt by Independents who were waiting for the magistrate's consent to gather churches were broken.

The next few months were a period of hectic activity for the Independents. Early in November Nicholas Lockyer was reported to be aspersing the Westminster Assembly and urging the gathering of churches; he was presumably busy at this time gathering his own church.[41] A month later Robert Baillie said that John Goodwin and 'others' were to be admonished 'for their assaying to gather congregations.' Most of the important gathered churches in London in this decade were organized by June 1644, when Baillie wrote that 'the Independents have set up a number of private congregations in the city; they are exceeding busy.'[42] By the time Edwards brought out his *Antapologia* at the end of that month, churches had been organized by two more members of the Assembly, William Carter and William Greenhill.[43] Two years later, when Edwards published *Gangraena*, he could add only two more Independent congregations to this list, those of William Bartlet in Wapping and John Briscoe in Southwark.[44] The shaking loose of the Independent following from the parish churches added to the membership of the Baptist congregations; Baillie remarked that 'sundry of the Independent party are stepped out of the Church' to follow the Seekers.[45]

These momentous events were concealed from the general public by the deliberate reticence of the Independent clergymen, who were also the pastors of the new gathered churches. It had always been their policy to refrain from public statements of their ecclesiastical position. This policy antedated the agreement with the London ministers in 1641 to eschew public controversy about church government.[46] The most important documents relating to the Independents published earlier that year were issued without their consent: the petitions for liberty to gather churches were printed in Amsterdam, perhaps by the separatist John Canne; Thomas Goodwin's *Glimpse of Syons Glory* was printed by Kiffin and Larner (presumably on Goodwin's insistence his initials were removed from the title page to render the pamphlet anonymous); and it was left to Katherine Chidley to answer Thomas Edwards in the name of the Independents.[47] The 1641 agreement therefore involved not so much a change of policy for the Independents as a commitment to persuade others, notably Henry Burton and some of the separatists, to adopt a like restraint in the interests of the anti-episcopal alliance.

The gathering of churches produced a permanent rift with the London ministers, who henceforth consistently opposed any accommodation or compromise with the Independents. On 20 November 1643 they presented a petition to the Westminster Assembly of Divines against the gathering of churches, thus bringing into the open the breakdown of their 1641 agreement with the Independents.[48] This breach with the London ministers led the Independents to prepare their *Apologeticall Narration* for publication six weeks later.

Thomas Edwards complained bitterly, and justly, that the *Apologeticall Narration* was far from being the frank and full statement of the Independents' differences from the Presbyterians that it professed to be.[49] Of the joint authors, Thomas Goodwin and Sidrach Simpson were officers of gathered churches in London, while William Bridge and Philip Nye held office in gathered churches at Yarmouth and Hull, yet the *Apologeticall Narration* does not allude to these institutions in any way. In a famous passage the Independents stated that 'we believe the truth to lie and consist in a *middle way* betwixt that which is falsely charged on us, *Brownism*; and that which is the contention of these times, the *authoritative Presbyterial Government* in all the subordinations and proceedings of it.'[50] In rejecting Brownism the Independents repudiated that doctrinaire separatism which condemned the parish churches as false churches; their own withdrawal from the parishes into their gathered churches was not based on this ground. The substance of the *Apologeticall Narration* dealt with the refutation of the charge that they intended to make the individual congregation 'independent' in the sense that 'every one is left and may take liberty without control to do what is good in their own eyes.'[51] The examples throughout were carefully taken from the exiled congregations where parochial church membership was irrelevant.[52] In this way the issue of whether their congregationalism in England was to be parochial or non-parochial was not only left unresolved but also unmentioned, and the dualism of their position with respect to the parish churches was concealed. One result has been that historians like S. R. Gardiner have read into the 'middle way' professed by the Independents an implicit parochial congregationalism, and the gathered churches have thus acquired the invisibility that it was the intention of the apologetical narrators to secure for them.

The peculiarly dualistic position of the Independent pastors themselves contributed to their reticence. Unlike the Baptist and lay separatist pastors, the Independents were men holding public positions, usually lectureships, within the established church, and also in the case of the most important of them, debating the nature of that church by public appointment in the Westminister Assembly of Divines. They could not have refused this responsibility without placing themselves in the separatist position of denying the Christian validity of the parishes of the established church. They accepted it at the hands of the civil magistrate, and it was their firm grasp of the secular nature of this responsibility that enabled them to attack the *iure divino* presbytery confidently enough to win support from Erastians and laymen not otherwise sympathetic to the gathered churches. Early in 1644, when the Independents were being hard pressed in the Assembly on the theoretical rights of the presbytery in the Scriptures, Philip Nye suddenly turned the tables on the Presbyterians by arguing, in Baillie's words, 'in a crooked unformal way which he could never get in a syllogism the inconsistency of a presbytery with a civil state.' Despite the shocked reaction of the Assembly, Nye persisted in his arguments the following day 'when he saw the Assembly full of the prime nobles and chief members of both houses.'[53] The Independent success in opposing the high Presbyterians depended in part at least on concealing from their secular allies the full degree of their commitment to the gathered church. In any case the gathered church, as a scriptural institution directly under the headship of Christ, was the private business of the saints. Within the Assembly, therefore, it was the fundamental tactic of the Independents to express conscientious or scriptural objections to the Presbyterian programme piecemeal, as it was presented for debate, rather than to challenge that programme with their own. The Presbyterians increasingly realized that the only way to expose this tactic was to force the Independents to produce in public their own positive model of church government. Under pressure from the Assembly the Independents undertook to prepare such a model in the spring and summer of 1645, when Thomas Goodwin was reported to be in the country working on it. The report was postponed from time to time until the victory of the New Model Army at Naseby in June changed the political climate and permitted the Independents eventually to abandon the project.[54] Thomas Goodwin's comprehensive statement on church government, which was remarkably frank in its defence of the gathered church, remained in manuscript until it was published in his collected works by his son at the end of the century.[55]

The position of the gathered church was also concealed by the semi-separatist practices of this generation of Independents. In the conviction that churches made ministers, not ministers churches, the Independent clergymen had rejected their episcopal ordination to derive their pastoral office entirely from the gathered churches, which chose and ordained them.[56] There was thus no difference in principle between their position and that of a lay pastor such as Praise-God Barbone, except that they devoted full time to their religious calling while the lay pastors made their living in a secular occupation. Yet in a very real sense the Independent pastors remained within a traditional clerical caste. When they returned to England they had ready access to important pulpits before Parliament and elsewhere, and they were offered and accepted lectureships.[57] They were offered these positions because they were recognized as clergymen within the Church of England, but they accepted them for the surprising reason that they were private Christians 'exercising their gifts' in an orderly way,[58] or because as pastors of gathered churches they had the evangelical duty of preaching to those outside the church in order to convert the elect.[59] Since the Independents could not announce their reasoning publicly, the general public saw in the pulpits before them only conventional puritan clergymen of the national church. The ambiguity arising from the personal status of the Independent pastors as former clergymen provided a degree of disguise for the gathered churches by rendering them immune against attacks on lay pastors and lay preachers in the accepted sense.

This ambiguity was reinforced by the semi-separatism of the members of the gathered churches, who generally attended the parish churches to hear the sermons of their own church officers; indeed many Independents may have heard more preaching from their pastors in such parish pulpits than they did in the gathered church itself.[60] These semi-separatist practices could be a matter of some anguish to strict separatists who otherwise identified themselves with the Independents. In August 1645, Katherine Chidley of Duppa's separatist Independent church visited Stepney, where William Greenhill and Jeremiah Burroughes were respectively morning and afternoon lecturers, and where members of Greenhill's gathered church, although none of them belonged to the territorial parish, regularly attended the parish church to hear their pastor preach. Mrs Chidley 'with a great deal of violence and bitterness' attacked Greenhill for preaching, and his church members for listening, in a parish church building where idolatrous services had once been performed.[61] On the other hand, more conservative puritans must have been reassured by the regular appearance of the Independents in the parish churches that their repudiation of 'Brownism' was genuine. Furthermore, the Independents also continued the old quasi-separatist practices of the past whereby they held meetings in private houses open to all comers for prayer and conference. These meetings, which were distinct from the meetings of the gathered churches, were a 'pregnant means to steal away men and women from their own pastors,' according to Robert Baillie, but they also formed another link connecting the true Independents with other puritans who remained loyal to their parish churches.[62]

The ambiguity of the Jacob tradition was stretched to its utmost limit by the Independent pastors. As conventional clergymen they debated in the Westminster Assembly of Divines the reformation of the established church and its parishes. As pastors of separate churches they maintained silence, for the fellowship of the saints was solely the business of the saints. Since the Independents did not deny the validity of Christian worship in the parishes nor the legitimacy of parochial reformation, they were convinced in all sincerity that they were not guilty of schism. This dualism was denounced as duplicity by conservative puritan clergymen like Thomas Edwards, for whom the only reformation was parochial; but such controversies for a long time merely confused the general public, who accepted the semi-separatism of the Independents at face value.

Invisible churches: the gathering of the saints

The inner life of the gathered churches was closer in spirit to the sectarian than to the parish congregations. Most of the dozen identifiable gathered churches in London met in private houses, and they offered their members regular worship and all of the Christian sacraments entirely outside the established church.[63] Their semi-separatism did not seem to extend, as it did in the early Jacob church, to the practice of intercommunion with the parish churches, if Edwards' charge against the apologetical narrators on this score is true of the Independents as a whole.[64] Edwards also charged, and the early experience of the Jacob church would tend to confirm, that although the apologetical narrators 'might be such good logicians to make such distinction to salve all' from charges of separatism, some of their followers failed to make these distinctions and regarded themselves quite simply as separatists.[65]

Private members of the gathered churches were permitted to exercise their gifts in an orderly way, a practice defended publicly by Thomas Goodwin and Philip Nye in their preface to John Cotton's *Keyes of the Kingdom of Heaven* in 1644.[66] The Independents showed concern lest their support of such lay preachers should encourage the spread of the rabid anti-clericalism of the separatists into their gathered churches, since it was their intention to reserve the pastoral office for a professional clergy specially educated and devoting full time to their religious calling. Thomas Goodwin carefully spelled out the scriptural arguments for this in his manuscript description of the true church, explicitly distinguishing the Independent conception of the pastoral office as instituted by Christ although the occupant was chosen by the church, from the separatist view of the office as instituted by the church itself.[67] Goodwin also warned against 'the sufficiency of the Spirit's teaching' and defended the professional education of the clergy. In order to support their pastor in a manner 'suited to the dignity and labour of his place and calling,' Goodwin recommended that a competent maintenance should be 'established by mutual covenant and agreement' between the pastor and his church, and that this maintenance be supplemented by the practice of free-will offerings, which 'makes him to have a dependence on the love and affections of the people.'[68] The financial burden of supporting a professional clergyman was eased for most of the gathered churches by the stipends attached to the lectureships and other positions that their pastors were able to occupy within the established church.

The gathered churches recruited their members freely across parish boundaries. At first sight this appeared to be merely a development of the decades-old puritan custom of crossing parish boundaries to hear lectures and sermons from godly ministers or to hold conferences with the godly. Such interparochial movement was by no means limited to the Independents or to those with Independent sympathies. Thomas Goodwin pointed out in 1645 that some Presbyterians, pending the reformation of the established church, were guilty of 'forming up a church in their parishes anew' by 'an addition of members out of divers other parishes in city and country unto the sacrament of the Lord's supper, and to preaching, &c., in a constant way.'[69] It was nevertheless the issue of parish boundaries, rather than the more general issue of church government by classical presbyteries and synods, that proved to be the deepest and most fundamental point of conflict between Independents and the most moderate and accommodating of the English Presbyterians, and that doomed to failure the parliamentary accommodation committee's attempt to find a compromise. The Independent insistence upon gathering visible saints into churches irrespective of territorial parish boundaries involved not merely a congregational but also an essentially sectarian view of church membership which struck at the very heart of the Presbyterian assumption of a uniform national church, organized territorially and universal in its membership. By making church membership at the same time strictly congregational and voluntary the Independents made it portable and transferable out of the territorial parish, thus escaping the godly discipline exercised over elect and reprobate alike which was so dear to the puritan tradition. John Goodwin was outspoken in expressing the scorn that the Independents came to have for anything as superficial and irrelevant to the spiritual life as a mere parish boundary. The Presbyterians, he said, if true to their principles,

> will not. . .admit of any into their church, but only those that are parochialized with them, the formality of that invisible line, which surroundeth so much of the superficies of the earth as times of ignorance and superstition thought meet to appropriate and allow to their respective parishes, the parishes themselves, if not universally, yet more generally, being appropriated unto popish saints; the formality. . .of this invisible line, at first drawn by the hand of blindness, is the only rule and measure of Presbyterian admissions into their churches.[70]

In dismissing parishes as popish devices John Goodwin had travelled a good part of the road to Mrs Chidley's separatist conviction that the parish church buildings had been eternally polluted by the catholic mass.

There was an apparent similarity and even a degree of competition between the exclusiveness of the Independents who restricted church membership to visible saints and the exclusiveness of those Presbyterians who restricted communion in the Lord's Supper to the godly among their parishioners; 'for upon this point,' Baillie observed of the English divines of the Assembly, 'they say, depends their standing, all the godly being resolved to separate from them, if there be not a power, and care, to keep the profane from the sacraments.'[71] It would be wrong to see in this competition merely a difference in strictness and procedures.[72] The exclusiveness was real enough in each case, but it proceeded from opposite premises. The Presbyterians used suspension from the sacrament and ultimately excommunication as instruments of godly discipline upon the masses who were to be kept within the visible church because it was incumbent upon elect and reprobate alike to observe God's worship in a Christian society.[73] The Independents in effect unchurched the reprobate masses in order to restrict the sacraments and the personal associations of church membership as far as humanly possible to the elect. In acting thus exclusively they were not consigning the masses to paganism. Their recognition of the parish churches as imperfect Christian churches was perfectly sincere. Under the supervision of the magistrate, not the Presbyterian hierarchy, the parishes still retained the important function of communicating the Christian gospel to the masses for the gathering of the elect. The parishes were therefore worthy of reformation, and the Independent pastors willingly used parish pulpits for meaningful Christian activity within the larger national society. But for the Independents the parishes remained second-class Christian churches precisely because the Presbyterians refused to accept the Independent principle of voluntary membership, the individual act of joining the church as a visible saint. By insisting that there was a first-class church available to saints in the gathered church, the Independents destroyed the integrity of the parish community and thereby ruined the Presbyterian reformation which was to secure a godly discipline upon fallen mankind in an inclusive church. Between these two views of church membership there could be no accommodation.[74]

The intention of the Independents was to limit church membership to visible saints. Candidates were admitted only after they had given an account of their conversion which satisfied the members of the gathered church that they had experienced the workings of grace in their souls. The admission procedures arising from this requirement gave serious offence to their opponents. Bastwick said that it was the Independent practice that such candidates 'should walk some days, weeks, months, perhaps years' with the gathered church, so that the members 'may have experience of their conversation before they can be admitted,' and he added that any member, man or woman, might block a candidate by challenging the evidence of conversion.[75] Baillie said that to the requirement of evidence of real regeneration the Independents added 'a trial of the sociable and complying disposition' of the candidates and rejected even a saint who lacked this 'suitableness of spirit.'[76] A 'complying disposition' was a relevant qualification for church membership because the Independents took seriously the obligation of 'communion of saints,' that is, the obligation of private members 'to know one another's cases and experiences.'[77] This aspect of church ordinances raised the problem of social differences that might impede the fellowship of the saints. Thomas Goodwin was sensitive to this problem: 'for when will occasion offer for a godly servant to discourse with the master of another family?' 'For some that are rich, and have time to converse much together, may indeed reap the fruits of a blessed fellowship; but others that are poor, or servants, &c., will be abridged.'[78] Goodwin met the difficulty by making the church responsible for mitigating such differences, but their opponents said that the Independents solved it by adding social to spiritual qualifications for church membership. It was charged that the Independents 'scummed the parish congregations of most of their wealthy and zealous members,' that their churches were composed of 'great personages, knights, ladies, and rich merchants,' that the rich were admitted 'speedily' and upon lenient terms, that the poor were put off to 'some other congregation among poor people,' or that the poor were refused admission altogether.[79] These charges, which were not levelled against Brownist or Anabaptist congregations, occur more frequently than the opposite charge, that the Independents exploited the poor by, for instance, collecting five or six shillings yearly from the wages of maid servants for the upkeep of the pastor.[80] It is obvious that the task of identifying visible saints had become considerably more difficult since the time when the Jacob church could rely upon the sheer danger of membership in a separate church to sort the sheep from the goats.

The gathered churches of London

A social difference between the gathered churches and the more overtly sectarian congregations can be inferred but not adequately demonstrated, because of the difficulties of identifying the members of the gathered churches at this period. An initial difficulty is to be confident of the very existence of some of the gathered churches in London when this depends upon the testimony of their enemies. An excellent example is the case of Nicholas Lockyer who, in the modern accounts of Nuttall and Yule, has found no place among the London Independents, yet who was prominent among them in the mid 1640s if we are to credit Thomas Edwards. Lockyer was a divine of more than average importance: born in 1611 and educated at Oxford and Cambridge; a preacher before the House of Commons in 1646 and again in the 1650s; an associate of Oliver Cromwell; a preacher at Windsor Castle, fellow of Eton College, and rector of neighbouring Farnham Royal by 1650, and eventually Provost of Eton; at an unspecified time before the Restoration lecturer at St Pancras Soper Lane and St Benet Sherehog in London.[81] He did not have a London parish, but in the 1640s he was active there as a radical preacher.[82] John Lightfoot recorded in his journal of the Westminster Assembly in November 1643 that Lockyer was attacking the Assembly and urging the gathering of churches. Edwards specifically named Lockyer in June 1644 as having gathered a church, 'a company of weak, ignorant men and women, youths and maids,' and in *Gangraena* in 1646 reported further that the church was troubled with antinomians.[83] This church was also mentioned by John Vicars, and its existence was taken for granted by John Goodwin in 1646 in his reply to Edwards' *Antapologia.*[84] With his appointment at Eton Lockyer moved away from London, his church becomes invisible, and the institutional continuity that distinguishes the mature gathered church from the personal following of a popular preacher cannot be demonstrated. Thus the status of this church remains in doubt.

There is a clue to what may have happened to Lockyer's church in a pamphlet written in 1658. *A Second Narrative of the Late Parliament* denounced the betrayal of the good old cause by prominent members of gathered churches who supported the increasingly conservative Protectorate of Oliver Cromwell. The author was a disgruntled republican sectarian with an intimate knowledge of the gathered churches. His most interesting remark concerned Alderman Robert Tichborn who, he said, 'began to cool, and lose his former zeal and principles, and left off preaching, as his pastor Mr. Lockyer did the church, to his brother George Cokayn.'[85] Tichborn, who appears as one of the uppermost Independents in the Leveller narratives and as 'a peevish sectary' to his enemies in the late 1640s, can thus be identified as a lay preacher and a member of Lockyer's church at that time.[86] This passage also suggests that when Lockyer left London his church chose George Cokayn as pastor in his place. In the next decade Cokayn's gathered church was one of the most important in London, including among its members at least two other aldermen besides Tichborn: John Ireton, brother of Cromwell's son-in-law Henry Ireton, and Rowland Wilson, whose death in March 1650 brought Bulstrode Whitelocke into the church in pursuit of Wilson's widow.[87] Despite the eminence of some of its members, the origins of this church are entirely obscure. Cokayn himself, a younger man than Lockyer, in 1648 secured the living of St Pancras Soper Lane where Lockyer held a lectureship at some point.[88] Members of his gathered church like Tichborn and Wilson did not live in this parish, and there was no necessary connection between a parochial living and the pastoral office of a gathered church.[89] There is nothing incompatible with the known facts in the suggestion that Cokayn's important church of the 1650s may have been originally gathered in the early 1640s under Lockyer's pastoral charge.

Contemporaries were explicit in referring to the wealth and status of the membership of the gathered churches of Sidrach Simpson and Thomas Goodwin which had originated in exile. Edwards described Simpson's church in 1644 as 'a rich and numerous church, consisting of so many gentlemen and gentlewomen, rich citizens, rich virgins, &c.' Another contemporary spoke in 1643 of the ease with which Thomas Goodwin could raise £200 among his congregation for political purposes.[90] There were 'gentlemen and merchants of figure' in the exiled congregations at Rotterdam and Arnhem, but the continuity of membership between the exiled and the London churches is conjectural.[91] One of the most interesting possibilities is that of Thomas Andrewes, who became a London alderman and sheriff in 1642 and the first Lord Mayor under the Commonwealth in 1649. Andrewes was a linendraper in the parish of St Margaret New Fish Street, where Sidrach Simpson was curate and lecturer until he fled to Rotterdam in 1638. Andrewes followed Simpson into exile, according to the eighteenth-century historian of the puritans, Daniel Neal, and this seems to be confirmed by Andrewes' absence from his customary shop premises in the period between 1639 and 1641. Upon his return Andrewes became a key man among radical London puritans, and early in 1642 his eldest son and namesake married the daughter of the late puritan MP for the City, Matthew Cradock. Andrewes was probably a member of Simpson's gathered church in London from the beginning, although there is no direct evidence for this. Two of his sons died prematurely in the 1650s, and both left legacies to Sidrach Simpson, indicating that they too belonged to this church.[92] The case of other exiles is even more conjectural than this. Thus among the founding members of Sidrach Simpson's church in Rotterdam was a merchant named White. In the late 1640s one of the most active lay leaders of the religious Independents in London was a lieutenant-colonel of the London militia named John White, but there is no certain way of identifying him with the Rotterdam exile.[93] Still more obscure is the case of John Aske, a silent member of the group of lawyers who formulated the charge and conducted the prosecution against King Charles in 1649. Neal lists a lawyer named Aske among the exiles of the Laudian period, and there is a possibility that this was another member of Simpson's London church.[94] Simpson himself returned to his lectureship in Andrewes' parish church of St Margaret in 1641, but his pastoral office no longer had any connection with the parish.[95]

The Arnhem congregation of Thomas Goodwin and Philip Nye was socially more eminent than Simpson's Rotterdam church. Sir William Constable and Sir Matthew Boynton returned to England about the same time as Goodwin and continued as members either in Goodwin's gathered church in London or in Philip Nye's in the neighbourhood of Hull. Constable brought to the Independents the lustre of an old Yorkshire family rather than wealth. He was elected to the Long Parliament for Knaresborough. His military career in the first civil war was interrupted by the Self-Denying Ordnance and resumed on the eve of the second civil war. Sir Matthew Boynton, who distinguished himself by discovering and forestalling the attempt of Sir John Hotham to surrender Hull to the royalists in 1643, took an active part in helping Sir Thomas Fairfax to organize puritan and parliamentary strength in Yorkshire at the beginning of the civil war, and he too entered the House of Commons, as a recruiter for Scarborough. Boynton was a wealthy man whose eldest son had married a daughter of Lord Saye and Sele.[96] A Huntingdon gentleman, Henry Lawrence, for several years remained behind in Arnhem where he served as a ruling elder and lay preacher, but he was back in England by 1645 when he was elected as a recruiter for the county of Westmorland. His Baptist views, which were widely shared among the exiled groups at Rotterdam and Arnhem in the 1640s, would have been no bar to his membership in Goodwin's London congregation.[97] Radical Yorkshire gentry, however, could hardly form the core of constant membership in a London congregation, even if they did belong to it.[98] The identification of the London members of Thomas Goodwin's church must remain a matter of conjecture. One probable member was Dr William Parker, a well known 'doctor of physic' who was one of the most prominent of the lay members of the gathered churches in London.[99] Finally, an undoubted member of this church was the radical London business man Samuel Moyer, who was perhaps one of the early probationary members mentioned by Edwards.[100]

Thomas Goodwin was very cautious about taking official responsibilities within the established church. He was an active member of the Westminster Assembly, but he did not accept a regular parochial lectureship until 1646, when he was appointed to a fortnightly Sunday lecture at St Michael Crooked Lane. By mid 1648, as the climate within the established church changed, Goodwin sought permission from the rector and vestry of St Michael Crooked Lane to administer the sacrament of the Lord's Supper to his gathered church in the parish church. It was clear that Goodwin had support in the parish vestry, but this was unavailing against the opposition of the senior churchwarden supported by the Fourth London Classis.[101] In 1650 Goodwin was appointed President of Magdalen College, Oxford, and he resigned his pastoral office in the London congregation to gather a new church in Oxford. The London church continued under the successive pastorates of Thomas Harrison, Thomas Mallory, and John Collins, but nothing in its later history serves to illuminate its condition in the 1640s.[102]

Philip Nye was associated with Thomas Goodwin in the pastorate of the Arnhem congregation, but in England his career followed a different course. Goodwin was the intellectual and spiritual leader of the Independents in England, with a deep commitment to the gathered church and an almost separatist degree of detachment from the institutions of the national church. Nye was the politician among the Independents. His commitments were much more deeply divided than Goodwin's, for he was thoroughly dualistic in according full recognition both to the gathered church and to the national church.[103]

Upon his return from Arnhem Nye seems to have gathered a church in Hull or its neighbourhood; it was perhaps this Yorkshire congregation that Constable and Boynton joined.[104] But he was also vicar of Kimbolton in Huntingdon, and in 1643 was appointed to the rectory at Acton, just beyond Westminster, in place of Dr Daniel Featley. In addition, Nye was the son-in-law of Stephen Marshall, his opposite number as an ecclesiastical politician among the English Presbyterian clergy; the personal relations of the two men are unknown, but they had in common a suspicion of the Scots which permitted collaboration.[105] Thomas Edwards remarked in 1644 that Nye 'lived a great part of his time since his return into England in noblemen's houses.'[106] No nobleman is known to have joined a gathered church, but parish discipline sat lightly upon peers who with their domestic chaplains had something resembling a gathered church in their own households.[107] Such men as Lord Brooke, Lord Saye and Sele, and the Earl of Warwick were not unsympathetic to the Independents, and Nye's contact with this circle dating back to the Saybrook project in 1635 was undoubtedly one of the sources of his influence.[108] Nye was selected by Parliament to join Stephen Marshall in accompanying the English commissioners to Scotland to negotiate the Solemn League and Covenant in 1643, and the English Presbyterian clergy seem to have turned naturally to him when they wanted to conduct behind-the-scenes negotiations with the Independents.[109]

Such a man in such a position was necessarily the soul of caution, and it is impossible to uncover the traces of Nye's personal career in the 1640s. Nothing is known of his relations with his parishioners at Kimbolton. The parishioners of Acton seem to have found themselves virtually unchurched, so far as receiving the sacrament was concerned.[110] Nye gathered a church in London, but it remained invisible until it surfaced in bizarre circumstances in 1655. In that year John Loder, the pastor of the gathered church of which Nye was the teacher, was intruded with dubious legality into the parish of St Bartholomew Exchange by the Protector. The presentation was usurped from the parishioners themselves, thus precluding the exercise of a parochial congregationalism by the members of the parish in choosing their own minister. Instead, Loder brought an existing gathered church with him into the parish church. The resulting conflict, between the parishioners and the gathered church and between the parishioners and their rector, continued to the Restoration.[111]

Jeremiah Burroughes, the teacher of William Bridge's church at Rotterdam and one of the apologetical narrators, did not have a gathered church of his own in London. Presumably he belonged to one of the early congregations, but his would seem to be a case of a private member of a church exercising his gifts in an orderly way in public. Because he had not himself 'gathered' a church and was not vulnerable to criticism on this score, he spoke on questions of church order and national politics with less restraint than other Independents.[112] He had ample opportunities to exercise his gifts, for until his death in an accident in 1646 he was the Sunday morning lecturer at Stepney, and he held lectureships at St Mildred Bread Street, St Michael Cornhill, and St Giles Cripplegate.[113] He may also have influenced William Greenhill, with whom he had been associated in the Stepney lectures since 1641, in the radical step of gathering a church there in 1644, none of whose early members in fact lived in Stepney. Members of the Stepney gathered church attended the preaching of both Independents in the parish church, but until Greenhill became vicar of the parish in 1654 the private meetings of the gathered church may have taken place in Greenhill's home.[114]

In the case of other gathered churches, their very obscurity suggests that their membership was small and lacking in social prominence, but this is no more than an inference. The most we can attempt is to establish their existence. Edwards is quite specific about the churches of William Carter, William Bartlet, and John Briscoe, yet they have left no further trace behind them. Carter had left the rectory of St John Zachary as long ago as 1630, and he never accepted another parochial appointment. He was a member of the Westminster Assembly of Divines, where he cooperated closely with the other Independents; and he was known in the Jessey church, being one of the Independents consulted at the time of the baptism crisis early in 1645.[115] His church was already in existence when Edwards published his *Antapologia* in June 1644, and its radicalism was illustrated by a story in *Gangraena* in 1646:

There is an Independent of Master Carter's church, who speaking against our public assemblies, often quotes that Scripture in Revel. 17.5. 'Babylon the great, the mother of harlots,' interpreting it thus, 'Rome is the mother church, and all the parish congregations of England are the daughters, which are harlots'; and this having been objected against this interpretation, that the Apologists acknowledge many of our congregations to be true churches, he and divers other Independents say, they are not of the Apologists' minds.

The only other reference to this 'great congregation' is Henry Jessey's assertion that it met on Sundays in the forenoon in the same premises in which Jessey's church met in the afternoon.[116] The churches of Bartlet and Briscoe are referred to only in passing in *Gangraena* in 1646, yet in each case there are reasons for accepting Edwards' assertion of their existence. William Bartlet described himself as a minister of the gospel at Wapping when in 1647, ignoring the self-imposed restraint of other Independents, he published a full defence of the Congregational way. He left London, however, when he was reappointed to his original parochial living at Bideford in Devon in 1651.[117] The continuity of the Wapping congregation remains uncertain. There was an otherwise unidentified separatist church meeting in Wapping in 1656 under the pastoral charge of George Huntley, who may be identical with an elderly nonconformist clergyman of that name who had suffered under Archbishops Abbot and Laud, who had been the occasion of a celebrated legal case challenging the jurisdiction of the Court of High Commission, and who gave evidence against Laud at his trial in 1644.[118] These coincidences are suggestive rather than conclusive. Geographical continuity was not of course necessary for gathered churches, but it perhaps provides a clue in Briscoe's case as well. Briscoe was appointed chaplain to St Thomas Hospital in Southwark in 1643, and although he left London in the next decade for Abingdon he returned just before the Restoration to share Henry Jessey's lectureship at St George's, Southwark.[119] These Southwark connections suggest that his gathered church might have continued under the pastoral charge of Ralph Venning, the lecturer at St Olave's, Southwark, who was the pastor of a gathered church in 1654.[120]

There is no doubt of the existence of Walter Cradock's church, the remnant of the Llanvaches church now in London. According to Edwards, Cradock administered the Lord's Supper 'in a house at evening,' and the church seems to have attracted London members.[121] Cradock became lecturer at Allhallows the Great in Thames Street, a crowded and poor parish with a large parish church where members of his church were accustomed to hear him preach. Although the gathered church had no official connection with the parish of Allhallows the Great, it became familiarly known among radicals as the church at Allhallows. After Cradock's departure from London in 1647 to become an itinerant preacher in Wales, the church eventually chose John Simpson as pastor.[122] Simpson and Cradock were well known as antinomians, and perhaps both placed more importance on their role as public preachers of the spiritual message of Christianity than on their office as pastor, with the result that the church remained small. Simpson became a Baptist early in the next decade, but like Henry Jessey he made believer's baptism a personal rather than a church matter, and his congregation continued as an Independent church. It also continued its association with Allhallows, where lectureships were freely handed round among radical preachers to make this church one of the centres of radical millenarian preaching under the Commonwealth. Although he too preached at Allhallows, Simpson held an official lectureship not in this parish but at St Botolph Aldgate.[123] The continuity of this church is reasonably well established on the testimony of the radical saint, Anna Trapnel, who in 1654 spoke of her membership for the past four years with 'the church meeting at Allhallows (whereof Mr. John Simpson is a member),' and in the funeral sermon of John Simpson in 1663, which reminded the church at Allhallows of 'those many exhortations you had from that blessed man Mr. Cradock.'[124]

These churches do not exhaust the list of Independent gathered churches in London in the 1640s. The remaining churches, however, pose an additional difficulty: although they were Independent gathered churches like all of the others, and true separate churches, in each case the man holding pastoral office also held a parochial living in his legal possession at the same time. The two earliest such cases, those of Henry Burton and Dr Nathaniel Homes, can be merely glimpsed. Homes was the rector of St Mary Staining and lecturer at St Michael Bassishaw.

Both Thomas Edwards and John Vicars were explicit in assigning a gathered church to him, and Vicars gave a graphic account of its relationship to his parish church in *The Schismatick Sifted* in 1646. Homes, he said,

> gathered an Independent congregation, excluding all his foresaid loving parishioners from Christian communion in their own parish church, except they would enter into a covenant with him, to walk according to his rule, which they not willing to yield unto he having got the keys of the church from their clerk, keeps all the parishioners out, and will not administer the Lord's Supper to any of them, not baptize any of their children, nor do any act of a minister or pastor to his people, save what he would do to a very Turk or pagan, unless they will dance after his Independent pipe. And thus now the parishioners wander as sheep without a shepherd, glad to run into others' pastures.[125]

In this case the gathered church seems to have been intruded into the parish church building, while the pastor served his territorial parishioners as a Christian evangelist among an unchristian people who, as unconverted, were undeserving of the Christian sacraments.

Burton's case seems to have been a similar one. After his triumphant return to London in 1641 he was restored to his lectureship at St Matthew Friday Street, but a parliamentary order restoring him to the rectory was blocked by the presence of a legal incumbent in the parish. Upon the latter's desertion to the royalists the way was clear for Burton to resume the parochial ministry, although it is not certain that he did so in any legal sense. Burton also had a Tuesday lecture at St Mary Aldermanbury, from which he was physically locked out by parish officials in 1645 after the rector of the parish, Edmund Calamy, accused him of stealing a parishioner away to his gathered church.[126] One member of Burton's church was perhaps the lawyer John Cook, a prominent Independent layman who was to achieve fame as the chief prosecutor of King Charles.[127] According to *Gangraena*, there were internal problems in Burton's church, including a quarrel that erupted during a church meeting between Burton and a butcher, and differences 'about singing of psalms, baptizing of children, prophecying, and somewhat else.' Against his better judgement Burton suspended the singing of psalms in his church and agreed 'to forbear baptizing some of his people's children,' presumably because they had developed scruples about infant baptism.[128] Burton appears to have differed from Homes in holding the meetings of his gathered church in his house rather than in his parish church. Nevertheless his anomalous position in the parish gave serious offence to the strict separatists. In June 1645 a delegation from Duppa's strict separatist church, including Duppa himself, David Brown, and Samuel Chidley, met at Burton's house with the elders of Burton's church to ask why, 'both their professions and covenants seeming to be alike,' the practice of the two churches differed so much in the matter of 'both your [Burton's] preaching, and all your members hearing in those parish assemblies.' Burton said that he had renounced his ordination in the Church of England, and that there was no holiness in the parish churches, but he and his elders insisted that the 'exercise of gifts' and 'hearing' could occur in parish church buildings without offence. The separatists could not reconcile themselves to Burton's continued presence, however qualified, in 'those shops of Antichrist.'[129] Burton died at the beginning of 1640, and the succession of his church is unknown.

The gathered church and the parish: the case of John Goodwin

The gathered church under the pastoral charge of John Goodwin differed from those of Homes and Burton in that it appears to represent a deliberate attempt to build a gathered church on the foundation of a parochial congregationalism. This attempt is so complex as to require special consideration; fortunately it can be traced in some detail. John Goodwin had succeeded John Davenport as vicar of St Stephen Coleman Street upon the latter's departure for the New World in 1633. The parsonage was impropriate in the hands of the parishioners, who chose their own vicar. This parish congregation was one of those which had been regarded by radical puritans as an implicit congregational church with an implicit congregational ministry.[130] The puritans of the parish were highly organized and forthright in controlling the spiritual affairs of the parish through the vestry; in this respect this parish contrasts strongly with those London parishes that supinely accommodated 'wandering ministers or such as are not settled by lawful authority.'[131] Of all London parishes, St Stephen Coleman Street was the best qualified to undertake the experiment of an explicit parochial congregationalism. The critical step was taken late in 1643 when every form of superior ecclesiastical jurisdiction had lapsed into the hands of Parliament while the Assembly debated the principles upon which it was to be based.

The actual 'gathering' of the church is the most obscure part of its history.[132] Some of the saints of the parish seem to have joined together with some outsiders in a regular church order, and then this new body chose Goodwin as its pastor. It is clear that from the beginning this church included outsiders and that it was not merely an exclusive body of the parishioners of St Stephen's. Indeed one of the principal motives in gathering the church may have been to bring saints from outside the parish into a regular church relationship with the saints inside the parish. At the same time Goodwin ceased to administer the sacrament of the Lord's Supper in his parish church, although he continued to offer it in the gathered church, probably in his own house. Goodwin pointed out that, in refraining from offering the sacrament in the parish until the principles and procedures of admission in a reformed church order were established, he was only acting like 'very many godly ministers' in London, including members of the Assembly.[133] He continued to preach regularly in the parish church, where his gathered church heard him along with his parishioners; he claimed in 1644 that he never preached to his gathered church apart from his parishioners, although he confessed that he had prayed apart with them, 'and now and then debated a question in mine own house.'[134] Goodwin also gave permission to his parishioners 'to choose what minister they pleased, either to preach or to deliver the sacrament unto them,' and he offered to contribute financially towards such an appointment.[135] But he did not resign his parish living back into the hands of the parishioners. Thomas Edwards described the situation as one in which 'the known godly in the parish church of Coleman Street (which amongst parish churches is one of your [the Independents'] true churches in England) cannot be admitted to the sacrament of the Lord's Supper by virtue of their relation of membership they hold in the parish church.'[136]

These arrangements were the subject of prolonged negotiation in the parish vestry. Apart from Goodwin himself, there were three parties to these negotiations: the 'visible saints' of the parish who had joined the gathered church, the 'known godly' of the parish who had not joined the gathered church although eligible for membership, and those who in Goodwin's opinion were eligible neither for membership in the gathered church nor for admission to the sacrament in the parish church at the hands of any conscientious minister. At the time of gathering his church Goodwin secured the formal agreement of the parishioners in a public vestry meeting for the admission of people from other parishes into the church. This agreement was a key stage in the development of the gathered church; 'drawn in writing in a parish vestry,' it was the closest thing to a church covenant that the new church possessed. When a group of his parishioners complained to the parliamentary committee for plundered ministers because Goodwin had ceased to offer the sacrament in the parish church, Goodwin countered this move with a petition from forty-five parishioners in his support and with the written agreement with his vestry.[137]

This was where the issue stood when Goodwin published his *Inno-*

cencies Triumph in 1664. He had survived the first challenge to his position, but the controversy continued within the parish. In the end the balance turned against him and he was ejected from the parish by the committee for plundered ministers in mid 1645. Although the parliamentary committee made the decision, Goodwin's survival in 1644 and his ejection in 1645 reflected the will of his influential parishioners. What happened can be reconstructed from Goodwin's *Anapologesiates Antapologias*, published a year after his ejection from his parish. His agreement with the vestry governing admissions to the gathered church caused increasing uneasiness to the 'known godly' in the parish who had not joined the gathered church, and Goodwin said that they 'multiplied rules and conditions, to order, umpire and limit him. . .in his proceedings and ways.' The controversy boiled down to one issue, that the godly of the parish 'would acknowledge the persons who had joined themselves unto him as a pastor fellow members of the same particular church with themselves.' Otherwise, Goodwin said, he would find himself in the impossible situation of being pastor to two churches at once, the visible saints in the gathered church, the known godly in the parish church.[138]

The heart of the problem was the outsiders. The known godly of the parish who in the end refused to join the gathered church had probably initially accepted the apparently innocuous idea of admitting people from other parishes into *their* parochial church of saints. But when they failed to join in the actual gathering of the church, for whatever reason, these godly members of the parish found themselves unchurched as effectively as the reprobate of the parish; for Goodwin ceased to offer the sacrament outside the gathered church. The godly were henceforth in the position of having to ask for admission to the gathered church in order to enjoy the sacrament, and they found that the decision upon their admission to church and sacrament was in effect transferred from the parish vestry to the gathered church. Furthermore, since the gathered church included a number, perhaps even a majority, of outsiders, the godly of the parish found their church membership and their enjoyment of the sacrament in their own parish church to depend upon strangers from outside the parish, and this was more than they could stomach. When such eminent godly puritans as the former Lord Mayor, Isaac Penington, threw their influence against Goodwin, his fate in the parish living was a foregone conclusion.

From Goodwin's point of view, these godly members of the parish were guilty of separatism because they failed to take up the church membership in the gathered church for which they were qualified, and their separatism deprived them of the sacrament. For, said Goodwin,

'I know no rule whereby a pastor stands bound to admit such to the sacrament, who separate themselves both from him, and from such of their [parish] fellow-members who cleave unto him, and are willing to walk with him in the way of the Gospel, and of God.'[139] The two points of view had become irreconcilable. One regarded the essence of the individual congregation as parochial, the other as 'gathered,' and Goodwin was ejected from the parish living by the influential proponents of the first view. Both were in a sense 'Independent,' and we have from this point two individual congregations to consider: the gathered church of John Goodwin, now reduced to the position of the Jacob church as extraneous to the parish system, and the parish church of St Stephen Coleman Street where the vestry exercised such remarkable control over its spiritual affairs.

Goodwin's gathered church met at his house in Coleman Street from 1645 to about 1648, when the vestry of the parish of St Mary Abchurch agreed to allow them the use of the parish church of St Mary.[140] What the parish gained from this arrangement was the services of John Goodwin as preacher, for he undoubtedly resumed his former custom of preaching openly in the parish church and meeting his gathered church privately only for the sacrament and for business meetings. In November 1649 Goodwin made the same agreement with the vestry of his former parish at St Stephen's, which secured Goodwin's preaching services once again, without further cost to themselves than permitting the gathered church to use the parish church for its private affairs and dividing equally the offerings for the poor collected on fast and thanksgiving days. This new arrangement seems to have contented both sides.[141]

The agreement between the gathered church and the vestry of St Stephen's in 1649 preserved the property rights in the pews for the parishioners and left the members of the gathered church without pews of their own. This has been interpreted as signifying a social difference between the wealthy parishioners of St Stephen's and the members of the gathered church, who could not afford pews; the true interpretation is that as outsiders in the parish the members of the gathered church were not entitled to usurp this particular right of the territorial parishioners.[142] Some members of the gathered church were men of established wealth at the beginning of the civil war. Robert Smith, a grocer, and Mark Hildesley, a vintner, invested three hundred and one hundred pounds respectively in the Irish Adventurers in 1642. During the civil war Hildesley was a leader among London radicals, and his activism was recognized with his appointment to the radical London militia committtee of September 1647.[143] Other members exploited the opportunities of the revolutionary situation. William Walwyn the Leveller, who knew many members of this church well, provides a vignette of one such member in his description of Henry Brandriff:

how, and by what means he got good store of monies, in the midst of the wars, by rising early in mornings, and searching in inns what goods were brought to town (indeed most commendably and industriously), how he many times ventured to buy goods he had little skill in, nor knew not when he had bought them where he was like to vent them; yet how well he sped with abundance of things I will not repeat.[144]

A number of members were merchants. William Allen, a merchant of Tower Street, and Thomas Lambe, a linen draper in Cornhill, were smaller fry in the circle of aggressive and thrusting merchants and financiers around the rising figures of Maurice Thompson and Samuel Moyer. Lambe, with his fellow member Captain Nathaniel Lacy, had investments in the Excise farm, and he was a partner in the French trade with Captain Nathaniel Manton, one of the important radical figures in the next decade.[145]

Other members are known in a political context. Thomas Davenish leased Winchester House in Southwark and acted as keeper of royalist prisoners there in the civil war; later he was John Lilburne's landlord. Davenish was a key figure in a complicated intrigue in 1643 between the royalists at Oxford and the Independents in London.[146] Richard Price the scrivener and his uncle Richard Price the mercer, who was also Hildesley's son-in-law, were active in the parish politics of St James Garlick Hill in Vintry ward in 1643, when they cooperated with William Walwyn in an important radical remonstrance to the London Common Council.[147] Daniel Taylor, Richard Arnold, and Bartholomew Lavender were all active among the London radicals in the late 1640s.[148] Henry Overton, the stationer of Pope's Head Alley who published many of the Independents' books and pamphlets in the 1640s, had acted as Henry Jessey's London posting address from the early 1630s.[149] Finally, there was John Price 'an Exchange man,' an active lay preacher and pamphleteer who was Goodwin's principal assistant within the gathered church.[150] Many of these men were to occupy positions in both the City and the national administrations in the next decade.

Goodwin's congregation is the clearest, and perhaps the only, example of the evolution of a gathered church out of a parochial congregation. Goodwin began not with a covenanted congregation but with his parish vestry, and his intention was to implement a congregationalism on this foundation that could admit saints to membership from beyond the parish boundaries. The experiment failed. Once the outsiders were admitted, the non-parochial gathered church replaced the parochial vestry as the source of authority, and the territorial parishioners were unchurched with respect to the sacraments, although not with respect to regular services and sermons from their vicar. When the vestry reasserted its control of the parish by securing the removal of Goodwin as vicar, Goodwin's gathered church became as completely a separate church as the original Jacob church. In the revolutionary upheaval of the next few years, it was to be the most important separate church in London.

'Presbyterians Independent' or parochial Independents?

In John Goodwin's place as vicar and lecturer, the parish congregation of St Stephen Coleman Street appointed William Taylor, a clergyman who as a Presbyterian was guaranteed not to gather a church. In January 1646 the vestry established a board of thirteen laymen to determine with the vicar who should be admitted to the Lord's Supper, thus acting as a parish presbytery.[151] From this point onwards St Stephen's can be regarded as a Presbyterian parish, but, in Bastwick's famous phrase, 'Presbyterian Independent' rather than 'Presbyterian Dependent.'[152] The godly puritans of St Stephen's resisted the latter as a Scottish tyranny, and among London Presbyterians they retained a distinctly radical or 'Independent' cast.

At this point we encounter serious problems of terminology. The leader of the godly puritans in the parish of St Stephen's was Isaac Penington, the Lord Mayor of London in 1642 and 1643, a leader of the war party and of the 'political Independents' in London. As the leader of the godly puritans in the parish, Penington was influential in removing Goodwin, appointing Taylor, establishing the board for determining admission to the sacrament, and in arranging for the return of Goodwin and his gathered church in 1649. Penington decisively rejected the gathered church in favour of a congregational presbytery within the traditional parish congregation, and on this point he can be described as Presbyterian. But the Presbyterians were themselves divided on a number of important issues: the autonomy of the parochial presbytery and the authority of classes and synods, the issue of free or restricted admission to the sacrament, the rights of clergymen to control admission to the sacrament, and the question of tolerating the existence of the gathered churches. On these points Penington took an 'Independent' rather than a Scottish line, whereas his opponents the 'political Presbyterians' tended to take some or all of these points of church order in a Scottish sense. The religious issues which divided the Presbyterians were very real ones; confusion arose because on the autonomy of the particular congregation, the exclusiveness of the sacrament, and lay participation in control of admission to the sacrament, the Independent clergymen were the most articulate spokesmen for positions held by radical lay puritans like Penington. Thus Penington might be termed a 'Presbyterian Independent' or a 'parochial Independent.' Both terms have drawbacks and need qualification, but the latter conveys more emphatically that there were important religious issues that gave some significance to Penington's activity as a political Independent. The most important of these issues was to be that of tolerating the existence of the gathered churches alongside the parish congregations. On this point Penington was perhaps influenced by the presence of his son and namesake, the future Quaker leader, in a gathered church.[153]

In their role as spokesmen for radical parochial puritans the Independent clergy were able to win support far beyond the limits of their small gathered churches, and this was an important element in their success as radical minority leaders. Their appeal to 'parochial Independents' went beyond laymen to include clergymen who had not ventured as far as the gathered church. Towards the end of 1643, Robert Baillie in analysing the strength of the Independents in the Westminster Assembly included among their number Joseph Caryl, John Phillip, and Peter Sterry.[154] These men were neither members of nor advocates for gathered churches in the 1640s. Phillip, a brother-in-law of William Ames, associated himself with one of the Independent 'dissents' in the Assembly, but none of them signed the *Apologeticall Narration* or the published dissents of the Independents. Caryl and Phillip had regular parochial livings, and both were appointed by name to the Presbyterian classical system in 1645.[155] Such clergymen, if they were Independents at all at this period, were 'Presbyterian Independents' or 'parochial Independents.' Even after 1649, when both Caryl and Phillip became overt Independents, they remained closely linked with their parishes in implementing a parochial congregationalism of sorts.[156]

The long controversies over church government and the failure of Parliament to implement an effective reform at the parochial level had a demoralizing and disruptive effect on parochial life in London which fed the 'Presbyterian' reaction of 1646. When in turn this reaction was broken by the Army's revolution in 1647, parochial disarray in London reached really serious proportions. By 1648 a third of the parish congregations in the projected Presbyterian province of London were without ministers.[157] It is against this bleak background that the appearance of Independent clergymen in parish livings must be judged.

Sidrach Simpson and George Cokayn secured parish appointments at St Mary Abchurch and St Pancras Soper Lane. Another Independent lecturer, Thomas Brooks, secured the parish living at St Margaret New Fish Street, where Sidrach Simpson had so long been lecturer. Brooks set an interesting set of conditions for his acceptance of the parochial living: the parish elders had to resign, the parish vestry had to divest itself of all spiritual responsibilities, and the 'godly party' were to 'gather themselves together and. . .own one another's grace, in a way of conference.' 'Strangers,' that is, believers from other parishes, were to be admitted 'so you find them fit.' This new church was to choose officers and receive the sacraments.[158] Since church membership was no longer parochial, the parishioners of St Margaret New Fish Street were simply unchurched unless they met the criteria established by the Independents in the gathered church. Although it never won wide acceptance outside East Anglia, the gathered church in a parochial shell proved to be the fulfilment of the dream of a parochial congregationalism which satisfied many 'parochial Independents' like Caryl and Phillip.[159]

It may be doubted if the ordinary parishioner in London noticed that he was 'unchurched.' Sunday services continued in the parish church, and the standard of preaching may have improved with an Independent incumbent.[160] The test of church membership was admission to the sacrament of the Lord's Supper, and here the situation had been so confused for so long that the peculiar regulations of the gathered church went unnoticed by the average parishioner. By the late 1640s, many people no longer automatically sought admission to the sacrament in their own parish; in a similarly confused period of change after the Restoration it was observed that 'in many great parishes, in which there are perhaps 20,000 or more communicants after the old way of reckoning, from 16 years old upward; and now, it may be, about 10, 20, or 40 present themselves' at the sacrament.[161] Some Presbyterian clergymen had ceased to offer the sacrament in their parishes, others competed with the Independents in restricting it to the godly few, still others admitted godly puritans from other parishes, and yet others secured their parishes only on the undertaking of free admission.[162] A gathered church therefore was scarcely noticeable when intruded into a parish where there had not been a strongly organized group of parishioners who were prepared to direct the spiritual affairs of the parish through the vestry. Only those people with strong convictions were concerned about these matters, and they were perhaps scarcely more numerous than the members of the gathered churches. John Goodwin remarked in 1646 that not half 'of persons truly conscientious in the kingdom' were Presbyterians.[163] The key is in the words 'truly conscientious.' The godly puritans were a minority, and that minority was divided.

The parochial Independents lie beyond the scope of a book dealing with separate churches except as illustrating another source of the wide influence of the Independent clergymen, for this cannot be explained in terms of the small circle of the gathered churches. As champions of the parochial Independents in the Westminster Assembly and in the political pulpits of London, the Independent clergymen found ample scope for challenging the high Presbyterians in a parochial context; and the sheer complexity of their controversy with the Presbyterians served to obscure the real nature of the gathered churches as truly separate churches. Their success in this role made the Independents credible as 'puritans,' and this made it correspondingly difficult for their clerical rivals to brand them as schismatics or 'sectaries.'

By the end of the first civil war in 1646, the Independents were entrenched in at least a dozen gathered churches in London. The programme of reformation on the basis of ecclesiastical uniformity was irrevocably broken not by wayward Baptists and Brownists but by respectable puritans. John Goodwin's church had illustrated the incompatibility of the gathered church of visible saints with the parochial framework; the experience of the Interregnum, when the Independents possessed political power, was to confirm this incompatibility. The lesson had already been learned by 1646. The Independents were willing to work with other puritans for a national reformation, but their minimum price was the acceptance of the separate church alongside the parish. The real name for this policy was toleration, that is, toleration of pluralism on the original semi-separatist principles. It was typical of the confusions and ambiguities of this revolutionary period that this policy should be obscured with the euphemism of 'accommodation.'

6

ACCOMMODATION OR TOLERATION?

Unity in pluralism

The ephemeral manoeuvres of the religious factions of the civil war period gave rise to a false dichotomy between Independents and 'sects' that has been enshrined in the historical literature in terms of the 'alliance,' even the 'unholy alliance,' with the 'sects' which the Independents were forced into by a common dread of Scottish Presbyterianism enforced by Scottish arms.[1] There was no division among the separate churches that would require an 'alliance,' and those who postulated this division did so because they could not understand the pluralism at the very heart of the congregationalism of the Independents. Their semi-separatism led the early Independents to recognize the Christian validity of parochial congregations alongside the separate churches. This dualism had quickly given place to a true pluralism when, since congregational theory required each separate church to constitute itself as a congregation, differences in details of church order inevitably appeared. This diversity of separate churches did not endanger the fundamental unity of Christian churches any more than the diversity of national reformed churches endangered the larger unity of Christendom.

The Independent gathered churches themselves contained 'sectaries'. Their congregations included without friction strict separatists and Anabaptists as well as semi-separatist Independents. Thomas Goodwin announced at the second parliamentary accommodation committee in 1646 that 'he cannot refuse to be members, nor censure when members, any for Anabaptism,' and Henry Lawrence, the elder of the Arnhem congregation who became convinced of believer's baptism, probably joined Goodwin's congregation when he returned to London in 1645.[2] Independent pastors refrained from baptizing the children of church members who had decided against infant baptism, but if such members themselves wanted to undergo believer's baptism they could not secure it from their Independent pastors. In this case the Particular Baptists cooperated by baptizing believers as individuals rather than as church members, thus supplying the deficiency without requiring that those rebaptized repudiate their membership in their gathered churches.[3] Robert Baillie reported with disgust and alarm in his *Dissuasive* that the Independents accounted Anabaptism 'a very tolerable error' and admitted both Brownists and Anabaptists to communion in the gathered church.[4] Thus the Independent notion of a 'tolerable error' related in the first place to the internal order of their gathered churches. This Independent perception that visible sainthood was not impaired by holding 'tolerable errors' in good conscience formed the real foundation of the Independent policy of toleration.

This latitudinarianism was also extended to differing church orders. Thomas Goodwin's unpublished statement on church government included a passage that appears to reflect the experience of the Independents at the time of Kiffin's withdrawal from Jessey's church. In the case of members who are convinced in their consciences on mistaken grounds, the Independents should 'not only permit them to go from them, but assist them in gathering a new church, according to the principles of their own consciences, whilst they therein set up the substance of God's worship, and profess to hold all communion in other ordinances with them as far as possible they can.' Goodwin's reasoning was that the obligation 'to all sorts of believers to be in church fellowship wherein to enjoy all ordinances' was a greater obligation of conscience than the variable requirements of particular individual churches. 'If there were churches extant of their judgement anywhere in the world, why might they not be permitted to remove to them?' And if so, why not admit their right to Christian ordinances despite their errors?[5] Such tolerance was to be extended to all who in the words of another Independent were 'the children of truth in the main, though scabby or itchy children through some odd differences.'[6] In this way the legitimate diversity of Christian worship within Christendom might be reproduced within the nation, and protestant pluralism would replace ecclesiastical uniformity without endangering the underlying principle of a Christian commonwealth.

Their pluralism did not destroy the spiritual unity of the separate churches. In the period before organized and distinct denominations appeared, this unity was embodied in what appears to have been a formal association of representatives of all of the separate churches in London except the General Baptists. Although there were frequent meetings to consider common problems, the precise nature of the association remains indistinct because of the secrecy practised by the Independents.

TABLE 3 *Separate churches in London circa 1646* (listed by pastor with date of formation. For a fuller listing, see the Index of Separate Churches on page 245

Independent gathered churches

Henry Jessey (1616)
Thomas Goodwin (1641)
Sidrach Simpson (1641)
Walter Cradock (1639, 1643)
Nicholas Lockyer (1643)
Henry Burton (1643)
Nathaniel Homes (1643)
William Carter (1644)
John Goodwin (1644)
William Greenhill (1644)
William Bartlet (1645)
John Briscoe (1645)
John Loder (164?)

General Baptist churches

Thomas Lambe (1612 or 1640)
Edward Barber (1612 or 1640)
John Clayton (1624)
John Griffith (1646)
Samuel Loveday (164?)

Separate churches with lay pastors

Stephen More (1621)
John Duppa (1630)
Green and Spencer (1639)
?Richard Rogers (163?)
Praise-God Barbone (1640)
Edmund Rosier (1641)
John Bolton (1641?)
Samuel Highland (1642?)
John Fenton (164?)

Particular Baptist churches

Spilsbury–Richardson (163?)
Kilcop–Cox (1642)
Munden–Tipping (1642)
Kiffin–Patience (1644)
Hobson–Goare (1644)
Gunne–Mabbitt (1644)
Knollys–Holms (1645)

Thomas Edwards had discovered such meetings by early 1644 when he remarked that the *Apologeticall Narration* was the product of a conference among the Independents.[7] The records of the Jacob church provide evidence for the working of this association. The meeting in May 1644 at Shambrook's house to advise the Jessey church on Kiffin's Baptist defection from the church was attended by Praise-God Barbone, Edmund Rosier, and Sabine Staresmore of Duppa's church, by Thomas Goodwin, Philip Nye, Sidrach Simpson, and Jeremiah Burroughes, by William Erbury, a clergyman earlier associated with Walter Cradock and already launched on his career as an itinerant preacher, by Dr Parker, possibly of Thomas Goodwin's church, and by John Cook, possibly of Henry Burton's church. A year later further conferences were necessary to consider Jessey's own conversion to Baptist principles. The records mention 'many conferences' and list those present as Nye, Thomas Goodwin, Burroughes, Greenhill, Cradock, and Carter, and Mr Jackson and Mr Bolton, and others.[8] Another such meeting was held in 1645 or 1646 at the request of the Duppa church to consider the objections of this church to the attendance of Christians in the 'high places' (the parish church buildings) and on this issue the separatists were unanimously voted down. Those present at the conference included Burroughes, Burton, Homes, the Particular Baptist Hanserd Knollys, the radical clergyman John Saltmarsh, 'and divers others.'[9] A conference of 'some brethren' was held to consider the differences about singing of psalms and the baptizing of children in Henry Burton's church, and Burton was apparently persuaded to moderate his stand on these questions.[10] Finally, Edwards reported that late in 1645 there were 'some meetings' at which 'some persons of the several sects, some Seekers, some Anabaptists, some Antinomians, some Brownists, some Independents' met with some Presbyterians to discuss the issue of toleration.[11] These meetings were exceptionally large, but they seem to have grown out of the conferences which had become a regular feature of the life of the non-parochial churches of London. The effects of such conferences can perhaps be traced in other episodes, when the Independents were able to persuade the lay separatists to cease preaching in public pulpits at the end of 1641, or when Nye was able to head off the petition of the Independents and the Brownists against the Solemn League and Covenant in 1643.

These conferences had in part the character of a ministerial association, for radical clergymen like Erbury and Saltmarsh did not have London congregations; Hugh Peters was undoubtedly another such participant. These men provided links with radicals beyond London, and especially with those in the Army. It is not known whether the conferences were held regularly to discuss common problems, like the regular meetings of the London clergy at Sion College, or whether they were summoned on an *ad hoc* basis to deal with problems as they arose. What is certain is their essentially interdenominational character, including Independents, separatists, and Baptists, and their willingness to consider problems of the internal order of individual congregations, which implied a spiritual unity rather than a political alliance.

There were among the non-parochial churches important cross-currents of hostility and division as well. The General Baptists were not drawn into the conferences with other separate churches, although they were defended by parliamentary Independents when attempts were made to molest their meetings. John Goodwin's Arminianism made him a doctrinal black sheep among Independents. Nathaniel Homes accused him of Socinianism in 1643, and John Simpson held two famous disputations with him at Allhallows the Great on free grace and free will early in 1650.[12] Homes and Burton were opposed to tolerating Baptist views within their churches, although Burton reluctantly gave in on this point at the urging of other Independents.[13] Members of the Duppa church engaged in what were clearly acrimonious disputes with Greenhill, Burton, and John Goodwin over the Independents' presence in the 'high places.' Separatist and Baptist churches were exclusive in their membership, rejecting the principle of internal tolerance that seems to have been generally accepted in the Independent churches. These strains on the spiritual unity of the separate churches strengthened the tendency towards an organized denominationalism in the next decade, although the practice of interdenominational meetings persisted.[14] In the mid 1640s, however, as the crisis deepened over religious toleration, unity was strengthened by the consciousness of common dangers, to the point, eventually, of organizing direct political action.

Accommodation

Considering that they were schismatics, the separate churches enjoyed a surprising degree of freedom from molestation during the first civil war. This was in part due to the collapse of the Court of High Commission and to the urgent necessity for unity in the civil war. But it was also the result of very substantial confusions in the project of reformation undertaken by the Westminster Assembly of Divines at the behest of Parliament. Nothing illustrates these confusions better than the accommodation policy pursued by the Assembly on Parliament's order. The majority of those advocating accommodation did so on the premise that the gathered churches of the Independents could in some manner be accommodated within the parochial framework, thus isolating the 'sects' and permitting their suppression without disrupting 'puritan' unity. The premise being false the accommodation policy failed, but not before it had given the separate churches the opportunity to consolidate their position in London.

From the meeting of the Long Parliament the offence of separation from the parish churches ceased to be punished in London. In his campaign to stamp out puritan 'conventicles' Archbishop Laud had failed to distinguish between interparochial puritan meetings and true separate churches. A puritan regime fighting a civil war simply reversed this policy and by affording full scope to quasi-separatist puritan meetings also permitted the existence of separate churches. Indeed it seems unlikely that the puritan clergy even perceived a serious threat coming from schismatic churches under lay pastors; what they saw instead were ephemeral groups of wayward laymen and misguided individuals. Accordingly, when the Westminster Assembly of Divines met in 1643, the conservative puritan clergy launched an unsuccessful witch hunt on heterodox clergymen and heretical books.[15] The Independents, for their part, denied that their gathered churches were schismatic, and they succeeded in raising such a cloud of uncertainties over the definition of schism that separation was no longer identified as the chief offence of the sectaries.

The gathering of the Independent churches in 1643 soon induced the London clergy, as they found their parochial congregations losing their 'fattest sheep,' to take a more realistic view of schism. In November they petitioned the Westminster Assembly for action against the gathering of churches.[16] The Assembly responded instead on 23 December 1643 with an official declaration, *Certaine Considerations to Dis-swade Men from Further Gathering of Churches*, which established the accommodation policy.

Certaine Considerations is a remarkable document. It was written by Stephen Marshall and signed by twenty-one divines of the Assembly, including the five apologetical narrators as well as leading English Presbyterians. It was accepted by the Assembly, although only after a sharp debate, and published with their authority. By arguing that the gathering of churches out of the parishes was merely 'unseasonable,' the declaration implied that there were circumstances in which *de facto* separation from the parishes might be lawful. By promising that Parliament and Assembly would 'concur to preserve whatever shall appear to be the rights of particular congregations. . .and to bear with such whose consciences cannot in all things conform to the public rule, so far as the word of God would have them borne withall,' it provided the idea and in part the terminology of the accommodation order passed by the Commons the following September.[17] The leading Independents were able to sign the paper because it did not refer to existing gathered churches and did not challenge the separated congregations in principle; 'one of their own profession,' wrote Alexander Forbes in a pamphlet published in June 1644, 'who ought to know it, told me they might well dehort others, when themselves had already gathered their own churches.'[18] The acceptance of *Certaine Considerations* by a reluctant Assembly marked a defeat for the conservative London ministers who had called for action against the gathered churches, and an important victory for the Independents, albeit they felt it to be a precarious and limited victory and continued with their plans to bring out the *Apologeticall Narration* a few days later.[19] More fundamentally, the Assembly threw away the one ground, separation from the parish churches, which would have permitted a decisive and simple definition of the sectarian offence against the national church, and it never recovered the initiative sufficiently to base the case against the sects upon the principle of uniformity. The policy of accommodation established by Marshall and later confirmed by Parliament proved a will-of-the-wisp that enabled the Independents to manoeuvre for endless delays and permitted the issue of non-parochial congregations to flounder in a sea of ambiguities.

The accommodation policy was endorsed unanimously by the House of Commons on 13 September 1644, when they voted to establish a committee to resolve the differences of the divines on church government or, failing that, to establish how far 'tender consciences' might be permitted to deviate from the 'common rule' to be established in the Church of England.[20] Robert Baillie thought at first that it was an Independent trick to secure toleration for themselves, but a month later he had seen more deeply into the move and named Stephen Marshall as one of the chief contrivers.[21] The intention of the accommodation order, which had secured its unanimous acceptance in the Commons, was to permit effective steps to be taken against the sects by isolating them from the Independents. The assumption implicit in this policy was that the moderate English Presbyterians and the Independent clergy had more in common than the latter had with the sects, and that the Independents could be detached from the sects by reasonable concessions. It soon appeared in the accommodation committee that the Independent price was too high. Their minimum requirement was freedom to cross parish boundaries and to gather in separate churches that could define for themselves the terms of schism and heresy. These terms were sufficiently alarming that the conservative puritans, aided by the victory of the Scottish army at Newcastle, were able to persuade the Commons to dissolve the accommodation committee on 1 November.[22]

The problem of the 'huge increase and insolencies intolerable'[23] of the sectarians remained. After long negotiations, Parliament and Assembly in October agreed to establish a temporary procedure for ordaining clergymen to supply the London parishes, and this suggested another approach to the problem of isolating the sects from the Independents. On 15 November the House of Commons resolved that 'no person be permitted to preach who is not an ordained minister, either in this or some other reformed church, except such as, intending the ministry, shall be allowed for the trial of their gifts by those who shall be appointed thereunto by both Houses of Parliament.' The resolution did not result in a parliamentary ordinance until 26 April 1645, and even then its passage was finally precipitated not by the activity of sectarian pastors but by the disorders caused by a preaching colonel at the organization of the New Model Army at Abingdon. Offences against the ordinances were to be regulated by referring the violators back to Parliament itself.[24]

The intention of the ordinance against lay preaching was to attack the sectarians by discriminating between their lay pastors and the ordained clergymen who were the pastors of the Independent gathered churches. It proved to be totally ineffective for this purpose. The Lord Mayor of London promptly made a test case of Thomas Lambe, who was easily the most visible of the sectarian pastors in London, and one of his associates. Lambe denied that he had transgressed against the ordinance on the ground that he was a properly ordained preacher in a reformed church, so the Lord Mayor referred the case to a parliamentary committee. According to Edwards, the Baptists

> were committed for a while, and then let out by the means of some friends they have, and have preached since more openly and frequently than before; so that the late Mayor when he saw that the committees of Parliament suffered their own ordinances to be thus condemned, committed no more of them, neither doth this present Lord Mayor, seeing it is in vain.[25]

Another famous test case occurred in the Army when Sir Samuel Luke, the governor of Newport Pagnell, arrested Captain Paul Hobson and Captain Beaumont for lay preaching and sent them to Fairfax's headquarters for disciplining. The lay preachers were immediately released and returned to Newport Pagnell, where the exasperated governor arrested them once again and sent them up to a parliamentary committee. 'I know not how it came about,' wrote Edwards, 'instead of some exemplary punishment, this Hobson was presently at liberty and preached the very next Lord's day in Moorfields or thereabouts. . .and preaches ever since on week days and Lord's days.'[26]

Equally unsuccessful was an attempt by the Presbyterian clergy in the Assembly to expose the Independents as being themselves schismatic sectaries and to alienate from them their influential supporters in Parliament and the nation. 'We were glad to have them declare this much under their hands,' said Baillie of the Independent propositions in the accommodation committee, confident that they had given themselves away in their true sectarian colours.[27] In this same spirit the Westminster Assembly debated some of these propositions for over a month in the spring of 1645 in an inconclusive effort to prove the Independents guilty of schism. Early in April the Assembly constituted the dissenting brethren a committee to bring in 'the whole frame of their judgements concerning church government,' and clarified its purpose some months later by adding that in this order 'was and is included the business of gathering of churches.'[28] The Independents delayed and finally abandoned the project, but the Assembly's move was effective in securing the withdrawal of the leading Independents from the Assembly while the Presbyterian majority proceeded with the drafting of a Presbyterian church government.

The disillusionment that the Presbyterian clergy confidently expected would follow promptly upon the 'exposure' of the Independents as schismatics was a long time coming. Puritan laymen, including Presbyterian laymen, did not see their way through the ambiguities surrounding the Independents with the clearsightedness shown by some of the puritan clergy. An illustration, albeit a special case, is John Bellamie, a Presbyterian bookseller in the 1640s and a consistent supporter of a hard line against the sects and the Independents. His bookshop at the Three Golden Lions in Cornhill was one of the best known meeting places in London for zealous Presbyterians.[29] He was the publisher of Edwards' *Reasons* in 1641 and of his *Antapologia* in 1644. For Edwards the issue was crystal clear: the gathered churches of the Independents were schismatic and no better than the outright sectarian congregations. Yet when Bellamie was accused by John Price of John Goodwin's congregation of having himself been a member of 'a separate congregation' many years before in the Jacob church, and despite his own acknowledgement that he had withdrawn from the parish churches as a member of this church, Bellamie vehemently denied that this was 'a separate congregation' and quoted the semi-separatist principles of the 1616 *Confession* to prove it.[30] The same uncertainty was evident in the popular response to a citizens' petition circulating through the parishes in September 1645 which urged the speedy settlement of church government in order to bring the sects under control. The petition was opposed by the more liberal newspapers and by the Independent lecturers; in the end it was not presented, one Independent minister, according to Edwards, publicly giving thanks to God 'for breaking the neck of that wretched petition of the citizens.'[31]

A final effort at accommodation occurred with the re-establishment of the parliamentary accommodation committee in November 1645. In the committee meetings the Independents abandoned all pretence that they were working for accommodation within the parochial system of the national church and bluntly demanded toleration for the 'sects.'[32] More important than the accommodation committee itself, and certainly more obscure, were the informal meetings arranged behind the scenes by the Independents to bring together with moderate Presbyterians the sectarian leaders whom they wished to include within the scope of toleration. There were 'some meetings lately in the City,' said Thomas Edwards,

> wherein some persons of the several sects, some Seekers, some Anabaptists, some Antinomians, some Brownists, some Independents met; some Presby-

terians also met with them, upon their desire the better to understand what they would have; the intent of which meeting was, to consider how all these might have the liberty of their way and practice in this Kingdom, and to persuade the Presbyterians to be willing to it, and to help to effect it for them: now the result of these meetings was, that all these several sects were agreed and held together for pretended liberty of conscience, the Independents as well as the others holding together with the rest of the sects, as buckle and thong; some professing at one of the meetings, it was the sin of this Kingdom that the Jews were not allowed the open profession and exercise of their religion amongst us; only the Presbyterians dissented and opposed it.[33]

Apart from Clement Wrighter, William Walwyn, and John Price of John Goodwin's congregation, the identity of the participants on the sectarian side can only be inferred from the inter-sectarian meetings with the Independents which are already familiar. On the Presbyterian side, the attendance of Stephen Marshall could be expected as the chief advocate of the accommodation policy, and Baillie perhaps had these meetings in mind when he later remarked that Marshall was one of the 'faithful divines who have had more dealing with the Anabaptists than any other on this side of the sea.'[34]

Stephen Marshall had no more sympathy than Robert Baillie or Thomas Edwards with Seekers, antinomians, Anabaptists, or Brownists. His accommodation policy was premised upon the assumption that the clerical Independents could be detached from the lay sectarians, and to achieve this end he was prepared in the second accommodation committee to go to the length of granting toleration to the separate gathered churches of the Independents while attempting to deny it to the sects.[35] Marshall's clerical prejudices were so deeply embedded that while he grasped that the Independent gathered churches with their ordained ministry were recognizably churches, he saw in the sectarian churches only an inchoate mass of wayward laymen who were to be disciplined individually for their errors and disorderly practices. The meetings between sectarians and Presbyterians ended in failure, although only an isolated anecdote from Edwards survives to indicate their rancorous tone.[36] The failure is also evident in Marshall's massive *Defence of Infant Baptism*, which appeared in April 1646, where he gave it as his considered judgement that believer's baptism was the gateway to all other heresies and that the Particular Baptists in England were Anabaptists in the full sense. This identification was no longer very credible in England, but Marshall was the prisoner of his own policy. In the battle for public opinion, his *Defence of Infant Baptism* was ineffective, and the work of rallying conservative opinion for action against the sects was performed by tougher men.

The confusion of the accommodation policy was the chief advantage derived from the silence of the Independents about their church order. By emphasizing their rejection of strict separatism, the Independents sought to preserve a place for themselves in the overlapping coalitions of the anti-episcopal alliance and the parliamentary war party fighting the civil war. They succeeded, and by diverting attention away from schism disarmed the conservative clergy and secured a practical freedom for all of the separate churches. The conservative puritan strategy of detaching the Independents from the 'sects' was bound to fail, but as long as this hope lasted all of the separate churches benefited. The failure of the accommodation policy brought the separate churches face to face with more determined enemies.

Confrontation: Gangraena *and the new Presbyterians*

Both the substance and the arena of the new conservative attack are important. The substance was to attack the Independents themselves as schismatic sectaries, and the arena was London. The resulting political polarization in London gave control of the City to determined Presbyterians, but it also brought into existence a corresponding Independent faction, centred around separate churches fighting for their existence, whose minority position in London was to a degree offset by their influence with the sectaries of the New Model Army and with the political Independents in Parliament. The initiative in this polarization rested with the conservatives, but the important result was to mobilize the radical minority for a revolutionary advance entirely unforeseen in 1641.

The failure of the citizens' petition in September 1645 caused the conservatives to move more deliberately in following months. The London Common Council, after overcoming opposition, joined with the London clergy in petitions to Parliament at the revival of the parliamentary accommodation committee in November; the Commons regarded these petitions as evidence of a conspiracy of the Presbyterian faction and referred them to the committee of examinations.[37] A citizens' petition was again abroad in the City parishes in December, this time with the limited objective of stirring up the Common Council to petition Parliament against toleration, but carefully timed to secure the election in the wards of conservative Common Councilmen.[38] The failure of the secret meetings of the Presbyterians with the sectarians encouraged the City clergy to attack the Independents directly in a petition on 1 January 1646 against toleration. This impassioned document made it clear that the central issue at stake in the toleration controversy was not the existence of Anabaptists and separatists but the schismatic practices of the Independents themselves; indeed this famous letter against toleration did not even refer to sects or to heretics except to remark in passing that they also would secure toleration if the schism of the Independents were allowed.[39] The City government followed in mid January with a petition to Parliament asking for the suppression of all private and separate congregations; this, remarked Bulstrode Whitelocke, 'was looked upon as tending to persecution.'[40]

The petition of mid January marked the opening of the great City campaign that determined the future course of the toleration controversy and gave the City its reputation as a citadel of Presbyterian orthodoxy. After years of debate the Presbyterian church government was approaching completion, and the most efficacious manner of controlling the sects now appeared to be the prompt institution of an authoritative Presbyterian church government without exemptions, accommodation, or toleration. The new conservatism was therefore thoroughly 'Presbyterian,' but it was so less from dogmatic considerations than from determination to secure a solution to the sectarian disorders of the church. The social rather than the dogmatic character of the new Presbyterianism was manifest in the rapid growth of citizen participation in the conservative campaign. This was evident in an episode at the Guildhall on 17 March 1646. On that day a committee of the Lords and Commons came to communicate to the Common Council the displeasure of Parliament at their petition of the previous November in favour of Presbyterian church government. The Independents found this an opportune moment to organize a demonstration of their supporters 'from all parts of the City and suburbs.' They were met at the Guildhall by 'many godly orthodox Christians,' and from four until nine in the evening the two sides talked and argued 'in several companies and knots in the Hall' over the issue of toleration.[41] This direct confrontation of the citizens symbolized the polarization of London puritanism into two political camps in the City which were henceforth fundamentally opposed to each other over the right of the non-parochial protestant congregations to continue in existence.

The growing popular participation in the toleration controversy took the issue of the separate churches out of the realm of clerical manoeuvres in the Assembly and into the larger realm of public opinion. In the task of mobilizing opinion and polarizing London politics no single event matched in importance the appearance of 'Gangreen after Gangreen' in 1646. Edwards' *Gangraena* is an underestimated minor classic of the English revolution, a new form of popular journalism of great power, deliberately conceived and executed to influence public opinion beyond the range of the formal sermons, the learned treatises of the divines, and the conventional pamphlet literature of the day.[42]

Two motives impelled Thomas Edwards to bring out *Gangraena*, the first his undying hatred of sectarianism in all its forms, the second his very considerable alarm at the failure of the citizens' petition in London in September 1645. The overriding passion of his later life was the exposure of the voluntary principle of the Independents and its fundamental conflict with the traditional parochial life of a Christian society. He had published his first plea against the toleration of Independent congregations in England in 1641 only to find himself muzzled by the agreement of the London ministers later that year to avoid public controversy. The appearance of the *Apologeticall Narration* gave him his opportunity, and his *Antapologia*, a book of over three hundred pages, was out by the end of June 1644, a closely reasoned and exhaustive line-by-line analysis of the thirty-one page long *Apologeticall Narration.* Edwards must have been confident that he had finally exposed the Independents; his book was well received by the London ministers who set up a weekly lecture at Christ Church to enable him to continue his public exposure of the radicals.[43] Few laymen read it, however, regarding it as part of the interminable squabble among the clergy which was delaying the work of the Assembly. Edwards learned his lesson from this experience, and in *Gangraena* skilfully made a direct appeal to lay public opinion. He abandoned reasoned argument and any attempt to refute the principles of sectarians and Independents in favour of direct reporting of their opinions and practices, intending by a massive disclosure of the facts to bring home to his readers what was to him the self-evident enormity of the results of toleration. 'I aim,' he said in his preface, 'to yield fruit every month,' and the reader must remember that 'all the following errors, blasphemies, practices, letters, be of persons in this time, and in this kingdom, yea of such who live and dwell among us.'[44]

Edwards' object in *Gangraena* was to provide the conservative case against the sectarians with a new foundation. The first part of *Gangraena* appeared in February 1646, at the height of the controversies over the *ius divinum* of Presbyterian church government and the power of excommunication which bedevilled relations between Assembly and Parliament, which filled Baillie's letters, and which occupied the City government from time to time.[45] These controversies divided the Presbyterian clergy from conservative (in the sense of anti-sectarian) laymen, causing among the latter as much confusion as the ambiguities of the parliamentary accommodation policy had done. The absence of these controversies from *Gangraena* is striking. Edwards was seeking not to defend the Presbyterian system as such but to open up the perspective of the problem of church government and to present the sects as something much more than a temporary phenomenon that could safely be left to the remedy of the long-awaited establishment of a reformed church discipline. Such controversies were in Edwards' view in danger of becoming academic and irrelevant in the face of a practical degree of toleration which undermined their basic premise, church uniformity in the parochial system of the Church of England.

Gangraena substituted for a dogmatic a social conservatism. Edwards sought to show how the principle of toleration spread disruption and disorder from the parish churches to the institutions of society, delaying the reform of the church in both Parliament and Assembly, frustrating attempts to maintain discipline through parliamentary committees, infesting the Army, and finally spreading anarchy in the very fabric of society itself, in the family and in the relationships of masters and servants:

> In September last, *Die* 25, being at a merchant's house in London, there came in one Mr. Y. who related that in his family there were but four persons, himself, his wife, a man and a maid servant, and saith he, we are of several churches and ways; I am of the Church of England, my wife was of one Mr. Jessey's church; but she is fallen off from that church (as many others have) and is now of none, doubting whether there be any church or no upon the earth; my maid-servant is of Paul Hobson's; my man belongs to a company of which there are some twenty or more young men, who meet together to exercise, but sing no psalms, abominate the hearing of our ministers, keep none of our days of fasting nor thanksgiving.[46]

Or again, one of Edwards' correspondents writes of William Kiffin, who 'hath by his enticing words seduced and gathered a schismatical rabble of deluded children, servants and people without either parents' or masters' consent.'[47] From its author's perspective, *Gangraena* presented a vivid picture of society faced with imminent dissolution into anarchy and moral confusion.

Edwards' books were not, of course, the only works directed against the sectaries. Among others those former heroes of the London separatist community, William Prynne and John Bastwick, were active in this field, and Robert Baillie's *Dissuasive From the Errours of the Time* preceded the first part of *Gangraena* by three months, although Baillie drew heavily upon Edwards' *Antapologia* for his material. But *Gangraena* was the only book that systematically compiled the errors and practices of the sectarians and treated them as evidence of the dangers of toleration rather than as matters to be controverted. There can be little doubt about the impact of his approach. With his racy, gossipy style and his obsessive concern for the homely detail, such as the fact that the tablecloth was not removed for the administration of the Lord's Supper in Edward Barber's church,[48] Edwards produced an ephemeral best seller. The London printers were kept busy through 1646 publishing recriminations and denials from every section of the radical spectrum. On the other side, Edwards was able to publish or summarize in the third part of *Gangraena* in December a flood of sympathetic letters from every part of the country. *Gangraena* must have carried conviction because it dealt with phenomena within the personal experience of so many of its conservative readers.

The reaction first took shape in London, where conservatives had rallied to defeat an attempt to secure the election of Independents 'and Independentish persons' to the Common Council at the end of 1645.[49] The decision of the City government to support a Scottish solution to the problems of church government was evident in their petition to Parliament in January 1646, mentioned earlier, in which they asked for the suppression of non-parochial congregations. The City's decision placed it squarely in the middle of the conflict between Parliament and Assembly over the power of excommunication, and for a time the City government wavered in its support of a strict Presbyterian settlement.[50] The House of Commons, for its part, although intransigently opposed to a divine right Presbyterian system, was beginning to show signs of uneasiness in the face of the demands from the City and the Scottish commissioners for action against the sectarians, and the problem was brought home to them in the early months of 1646 by their own inability to find any satisfactory method of dealing with the Socinian Paul Best. On the monthly fast day of 29 April 1646, therefore, the House met in the evening to order the preparation of an ordinance for the 'punishment of heresies and such as divulge them.' But this project, first moved in the previous June, did not either then or now lead to action of any kind.[51]

The City government renewed its attack upon the sectarians with a *Humble Remonstrance and Petition* to both Houses of Parliament on 26 May. Reminding Parliament that 'it hath been long since declared to be far from any purpose or desire to let loose the golden reins of discipline and government in the church, or to leave private persons or particular congregations to take up what form of divine service they please,' the City demanded first of all the suppression of all 'private and separate congregations,' and secondly that 'all Anabaptists, Brownists, schismatics, heretics, blasphemers, and all such sectaries as conform not to the public discipline established, or to be established, by Parliament, may be fully declared against; and some effectual course settled for proceeding against such persons.' A third request specifically asked for the maintenance of uniformity in church government, and the fourth, 'That no person disaffected to the Presbyterial Government set forth or to be set forth by Parliament may be employed in any place of public trust.'[52] The City *Remonstrance* caused divisions in both Houses: the Lords declared themselves, after a division, to be 'well satisfied' with the religious clauses of the *Remonstrance* and, after another division, ordered its publication together with their answer; the Commons, after a division, announced curtly that the *Remonstrance* would be taken into consideration 'when time shall be convenient.'[53]

Whitelocke remarked that many members of the House of Commons expressed great offence 'that the City should now prescribe to the parliament what to do,' but the sectarians could take little comfort from this.[54] The day following its summary treatment of the City petition, the Commons voted a second time to revive the committee to prepare an ordinance against heresies, and this time the conservative pressure was sufficient to ensure that a draft bill was prepared. Introduced in September and debated with some regularity in the autumn of 1646, this bill was finally to issue in May 1648 as the notorious blasphemy ordinance whose draconic penalties upon the divulging of errors clearly reflected the desperation of conservatives who had lost all initiative against the sects on grounds of schism, which was the real sectarian offence against society. The debates on the proposed ordinance in 1646 were inconclusive, and the attention of the House was finally diverted from this measure by the London conservatives themselves.[55]

The conservative citizens of London exhibited an unprecedented vigour in the summer of 1646 in countering every move made by the Independents in the City. The Independents had attempted to forestall the *Remonstrance* by petitioning the City government on 22 May, and to counter its effect by petitioning Parliament on 2 June.[56] By 5 June a conservative petition, which George Thomason and several other booksellers had a hand in composing and promoting, was being circulated in the wards and was presented to the City government on 23 June in support of the *Remonstrance*.[57] Anonymous Independent pamphlets attacking the *Remonstrance* or the citizens' petition were promptly answered by Presbyterian pamphlets written by citizens; Thomason identified the author of one of these replies as Captain Jones, a well known conservative who was appointed to the conservative London militia committee in the spring of 1647, and the bookseller John Bellamie had the last word in his more substantial controversy with the

Independent John Price.[58] The vigour of this lay conservatism reflected the impact of *Gangraena*; social rather than doctrinal in its nature, the attack was directed against the separatism of the Independents rather than in favour of a divine right Presbyterian system of church government.

It was perhaps more than a coincidence that Parliament's successful negotiations in the City to raise two hundred thousand pounds to pay off the Scottish Army in England were immediately followed by a citizens' petition for the suppression of the sects. Baillie had heard of the new petition by 1 December, Whitelocke by 5 December, and it was presented to the City government on 10 December.[59] Nine days later the City government forwarded the petition to Parliament with its own covering petition. In its religious clauses, the 'Covenant-engaged citizens of the city of London' asked for the suppression of lay preaching and 'separate congregations, the very nurseries of all damnable heresies'; for the passage of an ordinance 'for some exemplary punishment to be inflicted upon heretics and schismatics'; and for the removal from office of all who refused to take the Covenant. The short petition of the City government endorsing the citizens' petition went considerably farther. To the citizens' request for the disbanding of the Army on the ground of expense, the City government added the observation that the Army was the stronghold of the sectaries and 'we humbly submit it to this Honourable House to consider what security or settlement can be expected while they are masters of such a power.' The same motive, although not in this case thus openly acknowledged, lay behind their request that control of the London militia should be transferred back into the hands of the City.[60] The suppression of the sects, the disbanding of the Army, and the restoration of the London militia to the control of the City: these were to be the basic policies of a resurgent conservatism in the House of Commons in the early months of 1647.

For more than a year the London conservatives had based their fundamental attack on the sects upon social rather than dogmatic grounds by attacking schism rather than heresy, and *Gangraena* had provided them with an arsenal of arguments. The London petitions of December were the climax of this campaign. It is ironic that the citizens' petition inadvertently spoiled the aim of the House of Commons by complaining of lay preachers, and typical of the conservative leadership in the House that they seized upon that ineffective and already discredited measure for disciplining the sects. For weeks both Houses of Parliament busily discussed measures against lay preachers as if the ordinance against lay preaching had never been passed, while the ordinance against heresy was quietly dropped.[61] S. R. Gardiner saw in the 'long and stormy debate' in the House of Commons on 31 December, in which the ordinance against lay preaching was confirmed by a vote of 105 to 57, the decisive moment in the 'shifting of parties' which marked the resurgence of the political Presbyterians in the House of Commons, but in its context this vote was virtually meaningless. Had the Independents carried their amendment which limited the prohibition to public pulpits, the House of Commons would have implicitly afforded an unprecedented degree of recognition to sectarian practices; that it was defeated without a division is hardly surprising. The size of the conservative majority on the main vote, which was not matched on more substantial issues in following weeks, was due to the simple fact that the vote did nothing beyond confirming a position the House had already taken two years before.[62]

Such a hollow victory could hardly mislead even the most naive conservative, and for the following six weeks the House devoted all day each Friday to sitting as a Committee of the Whole to debate, sometimes hysterically, a schedule of punishments that would give the ordinance against lay preaching some teeth.[63] On 25 January the 'Covenant-engaged citizens' of London urged the City government to attend the Houses daily until effective measures were taken, but this increased City pressure could not overcome the inability of the Commons to organize a programme of religious persecution. The Commons responded by appointing a national fast day for the rooting out of heresies and blasphemies on 10 March; by the time this day arrived the attempt to find a legislative solution to the sectarian problem had completely collapsed.[64] To placate the City, however, the conservatives in the Commons had steeled themselves for administrative action against the sects in an exemplary way. The line of approach was already determined by the debates on lay preaching, the instrument chosen was the parliamentary committee of examinations chaired by Colonel Leigh, and the principal victims were the Particular Baptists.

Mrs Hutchinson, whose husband came to London about this time, spoke of a 'violent persecution, upon the account of conscience.'[65] William Walwyn said that 'Mr. Leigh's committee extremely perplexed honest people about their private meetings and doctrines,' and also, 'That committee was of a most persecuting disposition, and dealt most frowardly with divers conscientious people; with whom, and in whose behalf, I continually appeared; as for Mr. Kiffin, Mr. Patience, and many others, I cannot now remember.'[66] Yet it is difficult to find evidence that this persecution amounted to very much, apart from the prominence of its victims among the sectarians. In the first week of February William Kiffin, Thomas Patience, and Hanserd Knollys were brought before the committee along with Samuel Gorton of New England on charges of lay preaching; for this purpose Knollys's formal renunciation of his ordination in the Church of England was accepted at face value. The Baptists' defence was that they were duly ordained in true reformed churches, and they found support from the Independent members of the committee. The outcome of this episode is not known, but an opponent reported anxious heart-searching at a meeting of Anabaptists near Old Street in March, at which it was 'resolved to persist on, and adhere to the rules of their own reformed churches,' even if they had to 'take their leave of this their native soil.'[67]

The religious and political polarization of Presbyterians and Independents in 1646 was much sharper in London than in Parliament, where the religious confrontation was blunted by an awareness of the Independent influence in the New Model Army and by a determination to circumscribe both Scottish and clerical influence in a Presbyterian church settlement. Such considerations had less force within the local framework of London politics. Here the Presbyterians had seized and maintained the initiative against the Independents as sectaries throughout 1646. The result was to disrupt old political alliances among 'puritans' and to force the separate churches of London into direct popular agitation in their own defence.

Sectaries and London politics

For their survival in politics the Independents had depended on coalitions as assiduously as in religion they relied on the ambiguities of their position. There was at first no political party composed of religious Independents. Membership in separate churches was risky enough to be undertaken only by determined people, and the churches themselves were secretive groups in which the members could be assumed to be both personally loyal to one another and in regular communication. These were admirable qualifications for secret political cells that could take concerted and disciplined action with a political impact entirely out of proportion to their tiny numbers. At times of acute danger to their own existence the separate churches could be briefly mobilized in this fashion, but normally these churches were too individualistic and, being congregational in principle, too suspicious of any form of supra-congregational leadership to permit the existence of anything like a centralized political directorate. The interdenominational association of Independent, separatist, and Baptist congregations, even if it had more than an episodic and *ad hoc* character, seems to have been limited to spiritual or ecclesiastical purposes, although these could sometimes overlap with political objectives, as when Nye was able to stop the petition against the Covenant in 1643. Quite apart from the inherent difficulties in mobilizing the churches for political purposes, the political activists among their members were alert to the potential political isolation of such a policy. From the beginning of the Long Parliament the religious Independents were active members in larger political coalitions, in the anti-episcopal alliance and, after the outbreak of civil war, in the puritan war party.

On the other hand, the massive 'root and branch' organization of 1640 and 1641 and the puritan war party in the City in 1642 and early 1643 contributed significantly to the gathering of Independent churches in the latter half of 1643. Friendships and personal loyalties developed across parish boundaries in the course of political collaboration in an undifferentiated 'puritan' cause to create a climate in which certain political attitudes became an implicit, unarticulated ingredient in the definition of 'visible sainthood' which was the common bond of the gathered church. This can be illustrated only in the case of John Goodwin's church, which seems almost as if it had been organized expressly for such political activists, and it was perhaps less true of some of the other gathered churches. William Walwyn, the future Leveller leader and a principal source of information about the inner workings of the puritan war party at the popular level, describes this climate in his vignette of Richard Price the scrivener, a radical member of the London Common Council and promoter of an important anti-episcopal petition of the citizens in December 1641:

My first aquaintance with this Mr. Richard Price was by occasion of our parish business, in his trade, and that about our ward; and after that, about a Remonstrance presented to the Common Council [March 1643],[68] in all which I found him ingenuous, and so grew to intimacy with him: this was when alderman Penington was Lord Mayor, and before Mr. John Goodwin had gathered his church, or at least, before this Mr. Price was a member of it; and I took so much content in his company, that I brought such as I loved most entirely, acquainted with him.

I, through God's goodness, had long before been established in that part of doctrine (called then Antinomian) of free justification by Christ alone. . .upon which point, I was frequent in discourse with him, and he would frequently come home to my house, and took much delight in that company he found there; insomuch as we fell to practice arms in my garden, and whither he brought his friends; and Lord's days, and Fast days he spent usually with us: As for Fasts then, some circumstances of the times and proceedings considered, neither he nor we were satisfied therein, nor hardly any of those that we called Sectaries (or Antinomians, which was then the beam in the eye) about the Town.[69]

Price soon joined Goodwin's church. Before the end of 1643 he and another member, Thomas Davenish, were deeply involved in the tortuous negotiations of Ogle's plot, in which the royalists sought to detach the religious Independents led by Thomas Goodwin and Philip Nye from the war party by offering to tolerate separate churches. The attempt was an interesting one, for it indicates that the gathering of churches was recognized as giving the religious Independents a distinct political objective within the larger puritan war party. The Independents saw the danger; from the beginning they revealed these negotiations in the parliamentary committee of safety, and outsiders like Walwyn were taken into their confidence.[70]

The political context in which the Independents operated is as obscure as the membership of the gathered churches. For instance, nothing is known about the activity of a merchant-tailor named William Hawkins, yet he was regarded with great aversion in 1645 by both Prynne and Bastwick and described by the latter as 'the sagamore of the Independents'; he was personally known to John Lilburne at this time, and he was named to an important commission in the officers' version of the Agreement of the People in 1649, a pretty sure indication of his membership in a gathered church. A heavy investor in the Irish Adventurers in 1642, he was appointed secretary of the committee of both Houses for Irish affairs in 1645.[71] Dr Valerie Pearl, in her important book on the early years of the puritan revolution in London, has identified some of the other leaders of the 'active and godly citizens' in the popular war party as Sir David Watkins, Richard Shute, and Maurice Thompson.[72] In 1645 these men were named in the parliamentary ordinance appointing triers to regulate the selection of elders in the Presbyterian classes of London. At first sight it would appear that they had become religious Presbyterians, but nothing more can be inferred from their appearance in this ordinance than that they were parish Christians who were willing to accept a watching brief by parliamentary appointment in the establishment of London Presbyterianism, a function not at all incompatible with political Independency.[73] They remained loyal to their alliance and friendship with the religious Independents of the gathered churches, and their political Independency therefore had a religious implication. Watkins, a merchant and another very heavy investor in the Irish Adventurers in 1642, got into trouble with the House of Commons in December 1646 for remarking loudly in the Exchange that the Army should be sent for to deal with the London citizens when they delivered their petition against the separate churches to Parliament.[74] Richard Shute had become a member of a gathered church by 1651, when he signed an important *Declaration* along with other Independents and Particular Baptists.[75] Maurice Thompson remained, like Penington, a parochial Independent, but his daughter became a member of Greenhill's gathered church, and in 1649 he contributed a commending epistle to a pamphlet published by the Particular Baptist merchant Samuel Richardson.[76] The politically influential members of the gathered churches, men like Thompson's business associates Thomas Andrewes of Sidrach Simpson's church and Samuel Moyer of Thomas Goodwin's, were fully aware of the importance to their own survival of the political coalition that historians have come to designate as the 'political Independents.'[77]

The gathering of the churches had nevertheless weakened the old godly party. The London clergy had broken with the Independents as soon as they realized that the gathering of churches was occurring on a large scale. Lay puritans were slower to react. John Bellamie was an active leader of the radicals from his election to the Common Council in 1641, and he was an associate of Walwyn's on an important City committee in 1642; in September 1643 the royalist *Mercurius Aulicus* denounced his bookshop as a 'Brownists' nest.' By mid 1644 Bellamie published Thomas Edwards' *Antapologia*, and henceforth his shop earned its reputation as a centre for the religious Presbyterians. Bellamie's position was made particularly difficult because his religious conservatism, which led him to give wholehearted support to the City *Remonstrance* of May 1646, came into conflict with his political radicalism and his equally wholehearted championing of the rights of Common Council against the oligarchic tendencies of the bench of aldermen.[78] The oldest level of the anti-episcopal alliance in London had fractured in 1645 when Prynne, fresh from his prosecution of Archbishop Laud, and Bastwick, recently released from a royalist prison, both turned on the sects. Penington's leadership of the radical war party weakened not so much because of his surrender of the lieutenancy of the Tower under the terms of the self-denying ordinance as because of the inner tensions of his party, especially as they were brought home to him in his own parish of St Stephen Coleman Street. Penington and other political radicals in the parish like Owen Rowe and James Russell must have given at least their tacit approval to the effort to eject John Goodwin from the vicarage, and they may have been active participants in this notable manoeuvre.

This faltering of the radical organization permitted the formation of a new conservative coalition in London politics which had control of the Common Council by the end of 1645. The conservatives were able to use the machinery of City government to petition Parliament and to endorse the petitions of citizens and clergy on behalf of Presbyterianism.

But they could not become masters in their own house as long as there was a strong Independent representation on the London militia committee and in the militia itself. The City militia committee, a relic of the heyday of the godly party, was based on parliamentary ordinance, and until the spring of 1647 members of Parliament were too cautious to return the control of the London militia to the reckless conservatism of the City.

The separate churches of London, as the City conservatives focussed their attack on them, became increasingly inclined to undertake that unilateral political agitation their leaders had always avoided. This is a subject of great obscurity, but it is possible to glimpse a kaleidoscopic series of meetings in 1645 and 1646 in which the religious radicals met to discuss their common problems, to plan petitions to 'counterwork' the conservative City petitions or to protest against the intolerance of Prynne and Bastwick, to discuss the election of Lilburne and Walwyn as members of Parliament for Southwark or to influence the Common Council elections of 1645 and 1646, to meet with the Presbyterians at the time of the second accommodation committee or to petition on behalf of the imprisoned Lilburne and Overton.[79] This intense activity comes into clearer view as the Leveller agitators became more influential in this circle, for the Levellers used the techniques of self-dramatization to advance their cause. But the appearance of the Levellers also indicates that the mobilization of the separate churches for political agitation provided the conditions for a new and more radical political movement in London.

One of the important characteristics of the sectarian response to the toleration controversy is that it was, in a sense, leaderless. The natural leaders of the sectaries, the important Independent clergy and the politically influential members of the gathered churches, the 'uppermost Independents' as the Levellers later called them, as they lost ground in London concentrated their attention on the national institutions of Assembly, Army, and Parliament. Until the time of the second accommodation committee the leading Independent clergymen worked in the Assembly to provide breathing space in England for 'tender consciences.' The New Model Army was widely believed to be under the control of the Independents and the sectaries. Most important of all to the London Independents was the survival of the coalition of the 'political Independents' in Parliament to the end of 1646, for this sheltered them from the full force of the conservative reaction in the City. The uppermost Independents were too tied by these manoeuvres to be free at the same time to lead a movement of popular agitation in London. Many of the most influential pastors of the sectarian congregations were inhibited from a role of political leadership by the fear that political action would confirm their enemies in the conviction that they were Anabaptists subversive of all political order. Yet the relentless pressure of the conservatives through 1646 was felt by many members of separate churches to require direct countermeasures in London. The Leveller leaders found here a ready-made audience, and were able to give direction and purpose to a popular movement that was in search of such leadership.

7

'THE GENERALITY OF CONGREGATIONS'* AND THE LEVELLERS

Salters' Hall and the Windmill Tavern

The Levellers were the most important political gainers on the radical side in the wake of the polarization of London politics over toleration. With astonishing boldness, and with equally astonishing success, they were able to seize the initiative in organizing what Walwyn called 'the generality of congregations' to respond to the conservative threat in London. At its most successful moments, in the spring of 1647 and the autumn of 1648, this movement was able to deflect the course of the revolution in England. But the Levellers were not mere lobbyists for the separate churches. The Leveller organization had a deep sectarian taproot that shaped their aspirations and their polemic in a distinct way. They were free of the dualism of the Independents and the resulting ambiguity towards the established church. They shared with Baptists and separatists the principle of the complete separation of church and state, and they were prepared to disestablish the national church and its tithes. They went beyond the sectaries in accepting the secular state as a legitimate sphere of moral action in its own right, and they attempted to find principles of natural equity appropriate for political action in a secular state. This incipient liberalism was unacceptable to the politically powerful classes of the nation, but it failed also to command the unqualified support of the sectarians, who could not free themselves from lingering aspirations for a Christian magistrate and for 'righteousness' in a Christian society.

In the earliest phase of the Leveller movement William Walwyn, John Lilburne, and Richard Overton made brilliant use of the unlicensed press to provide an articulate defence of religious toleration and an increasingly reckless attack upon the conservatives which by mid 1646 landed both Lilburne and Overton in prison. This phase was essentially one of pamphleteering and propaganda, but each man had

* *Leveller Tracts*, p. 355.

a distinct range of contacts among the London radicals and was able to make an organizational contribution to the inner core of the Leveller party. It is at this organizational level that much about the history and ultimate fate of the Leveller movement in London becomes clearer.[1]

William Walwyn came from the mainstream of the political Independents in London. He was involved, he tells us, 'in all the proceedings of Salters' Hall.'[2] Penington's term as Lord Mayor in 1643 had afforded the war party radicals their greatest opportunity to establish an autonomous political base in London. By offering to raise volunteer regiments they secured the establishment of a militia sub-committee at Salters' Hall which was firmly under their control, but their subsequent attempt to free the sub-committee from its subordination to the London militia committee failed.[3] Salters' Hall remained the main meeting place for the political Independents in London, and the committee there appears to have taken on the function of a political directorate over the broad Independent interest in the City. Its activities can be glimpsed in 1644 and again in 1645, but it was increasingly limited to the direction of popular agitation.[4] Walwyn, Clement Wrighter, and John Price, the most prominent lay preacher in John Goodwin's church, attended the joint meetings of Independents, sectarians, and Presbyterians at the time of the second accommodation committee in December 1645.[5] Walwyn and Wrighter could not have attended as representatives of sectarian or Independent congregations, whose continued existence was the main subject of discussion in the meetings; they must have attended as the secular representatives of the political Independents in the context of the Salters' Hall organization or of something very like it.

'I am not in fellowship with those good people you call sectaries,' Walwyn told Edwards in 1646, 'yet I join heart and hand with them in anything that I judge to be right, and tending to the public good.'[6] He was sceptical of religious dogmatism and deeply anti-clerical, but there is no evidence that he was concerned with parochial congregationalism and no reason to describe him as a parochial Independent in religion. He was a vehement opponent of the high Presbyterians on the issue of the toleration of the sects, and it was this that gave a religious content to his career as a political Independent in London. In 1643 he joined Samuel Eames, one of the founders of the Particular Baptists and soon a Seeker, to provide a bond for Laurence Saunders, the author of the notorious pamphlet, *The Fulness of Gods Love*. In 1644 he defended the Baptists in his *Compassionate Samaritane* in terms which directly anticipated the Particular Baptist confession of that year. He was familiar with members of strict separatist churches; indeed the primary purpose of his *Samaritane* was to defend the separatists who had been 'left in the lurch' by the Independents in the *Apologeticall Narration*, although this suggests that he was unaware of the inter-denominational meetings of this period.[7] His sympathy towards the sects led him in 1645 to give his support promptly to John Lilburne, who represented a distinctively sectarian interest in the broader Independent spectrum in London.

To mid 1646 the radical organization in the City appears to have remained under the control of the uppermost Independents and their political allies. Thomas Edwards reported that in the last week of February 1646 there were meetings of 'sectaries' in the City to prepare a petition to Parliament 'to counterwork the Common Council' and its petition of 15 January. It was proposed to get forty or fifty thousand hands to the petition, including 'the hands of all those that keep separated meetings, to send the petition to their several meetings to be subscribed.'[8] This petition was not presented, but early in June another with twenty thousand hands, to counterwork the City *Remonstrance* of 26 May, was presented to the House of Commons and received by the House with thanks. According to Edwards, Hugh Peters had a part in the preparation of this 'anti-petition,' which was 'carried up and down the City by his man, to get hands to it.' Another enemy of the Independents identified Robert Tichborn as one of those who had presented this petition 'from the sectaries of London' to the House of Commons.[9]

In his brief narrative of the year 1646, written in 1649, Walwyn related the fate of two 'lamentable' petitions, 'a large petition' and one 'not so large,' which failed despite the support of the 'Anabaptists and Brownists congregations' and 'all sorts of conscientious people,' because 'Master Goodwin's people, and some other of the Independent churches' were 'against the season.'[10] The chronology of these petitions is vague, but if, as was likely, the imprisonment of Larner, Lilburne, and Overton in March, June, and August respectively were the 'sad stories' and persecutions of Walwyn's 'lamentable' petitions, then these may be placed in the second half of 1646.[11] The most interesting implication is that the petitions were discussed in the main circle of the political Independents in the old Salters' Hall connection. This is evident in Walwyn's involvement, in the scope of the meetings, including Independents, Brownists, and Anabaptists, in the prominence of members of John Goodwin's congregation, and in the fact that 'the Independents' were able to frustrate the petitions on the grounds that they were untimely. On the other hand, the 'lamentable' petitions obviously went beyond what was politically expedient and were premised on a psychology of confrontation and protest that was more characteristic of John Lilburne and his following than of the political Independents of Salters' Hall. The contents of the petitions, the emphasis on persecution, the support of the sectarians, and the fact that one of the key meetings is known to have taken place at the Windmill Tavern,[12] all point to the active participation of the group that had gathered around Lilburne in the previous year, which met customarily at the Windmill in Lothbury. In this context, the failure of the petitions is considerably less significant than the nature of the body that debated them, representing the union of Salters' Hall with the Windmill Tavern, of the more radical political Independents with the sectarians around Lilburne. The initial failure of the future Levellers was negligible compared to the immense widening of the prospect for mass agitation that opened before them in this union.

If Walwyn was a political Independent with a special concern for the sects, John Lilburne stood at the very heart of the sectarian interest in London. Between the publication of his letter to Prynne on 15 January 1645, after his return from the Army, and the debate over the 'lamentable' petitions in late 1646, it was Lilburne's achievement to gather around himself the support of the London sectarians, to give them an initiative of their own among the London radicals, and in the course of his personal encounters with authority to give this movement a distinctive political programme. The centre of the movement in 1645 and 1646 was the Windmill Tavern.[13] Lilburne's activity produced a tendency towards polarization between Independents and sectarians. This was the result of his personal connections with the oldest and best established level of the separatist community. He was a member of Edmund Rosier's separatist church, and among his closest friends and associates were such people as the Chidleys, mother and son, David Brown and Sabine Staresmore of Duppa's church, Samuel Highland, the pastor of the most important separatist church in Southwark, Josiah Primate of Praise-God Barbone's church, William Kiffin, Paul Hobson, and William Larner, the separatist printer. Lilburne was well known personally in the Particular Baptist congregations whose members had been recruited from the separatist churches; on 10 August 1645 Hanserd Knollys, the most popular of the sectarian preachers in London, prayed at his church next to St Helen's in 'these words, or to this effect, Lord, bring thy servant Lilburne out of prison, and honour him, Lord, for he hath honoured thee.'[14] The separatist context of Lilburne's movement is evident in the profound sense of the betrayal of the common cause of 1637 by William Prynne and John Bastwick which haunted the movement in 1645 and 1646. Some of Lilburne's own sharpest encounters were with Prynne and Bastwick in 1645, and his followers proposed to petition the House of Commons 'to have Mr. Prynne's and Dr. Bastwick's books called in,' annexing to the petition 'a large schedule. . .of offensive passages.'[15] In the autumn of the next year, when Elizabeth Lilburne led a delegation of women to Parliament to petition against the renewed imprisonment of her husband, they met John Bastwick and, according to one of Bastwick's friends, 'upbraided you to your face before all the people that you had once been one of them, and called you an apostate, and persecutor of the saints.'[16] This intense personal antagonism suggests the degree to which the separatist community in London had a sense of its own identity and its own perspective on the revolutionary cause.

The separatist circle immediately around Lilburne was to provide the hard core of the future Leveller organization, but it was too small a group to explain the shift of the whole revolution to the left. Edwards spoke of meetings of four or five hundred people at the time of Lilburne's imprisonment, and the petition to the Commons on Lilburne's behalf on 26 August 1645 was supported by two or three thousand citizens, according to Lilburne himself.[17] This was a long way from the reputed twenty thousand supporters the Independents could muster in mid 1646; it was this larger popular base that was to give the Leveller movement its significance. Also, Lilburne's movement did not have the unqualified support of the sectarians themselves, and it cannot be regarded simply as a kind of sectarian pressure group. Speaking of the time of his encounters with Prynne in 1645, Lilburne said that the 'leaders in the churches of God. . .durst then do nothing manlike for themselves, but sat in silence like a company of sneaks without souls or hearts.'[18] In the case of the Particular Baptist leaders, the source of the restraint was their concern to avoid overt political activities that would justify their condemnation as 'Anabaptists'; but also, the important separatist pastors Barbone, Rosier, and Stephen More cannot be traced in open support of Lilburne's movement or of the subsequent Leveller movement. Too much should not be made of this. Lilburne's early support undoubtedly came from the rank and file of these congregations; here his pamphlets found their most eager audience, and here the petitions proposed by the Windmill Tavern meetings, like the later Leveller petitions, were undoubtedly read and discussed in the effort to secure mass support. The distinction to be made is between the sectarian congregations acting jointly as congregations, the saints acting as a pressure group, and the support that members of the sectarian congregations could give as individuals and citizens to Lilburne's movement as a political phenomenon.

Lilburne's empirical and intensely personal approach to a secular political programme had deep roots in the common sectarian tradition. As well as his stand against the 'black-coats' with their tithes and their religious persecution, Lilburne's attack on the privilege and authority of the King and the Lords, the oligarchy of the City, and the economic privileges of the Merchant Adventurers, which grew into the Leveller programme of political and social reform, amounted to an expression of the aspirations of the sectarian community at large. Insofar as republicanism had a popular base in England in the next decade, it was to be found among the sectaries who identified a monarchical constitution and a privileged social order as the bulwark of religious persecution. It was the sectarian congregations that most violently opposed the offer of the crown to Cromwell; Praise-God Barbone, no Leveller agitator, was one of the most intransigent republicans just before the Restoration, and William Kiffin fell heir in the next decade to Lilburne's role as leader of the attack upon the privileged position of the Merchant Adventurers.[19] Despite a common programme of desirable reforms, the sectarian leaders differed from the Levellers in their view of the role of the political radical and a secular political party; they in the end decided that the common cause was best left in the hands of the saints. But these developments lay in the future. In the summer of 1646, Lilburne was easily the most prominent spokesman, and martyr, for the sectarian interest in London.

The union of the Independents, or at least their more radical wing as represented in the Salters' Hall meetings, with the movement supporting Lilburne and meeting at the Windmill appears to have occurred in the aftermath of the great City *Remonstrance* of 26 May, and it involved several levels of activity. At the organizational level, the Independents joined the meetings at the Windmill to debate Walwyn's 'lamentable' petitions. In the area of tactics, John Goodwin's congregation adopted John Lilburne's cause as their own sometime after his imprisonment in June and were, more than all other congregations, responsible for 'large kindnesses manifested unto me in this my present imprisonment in supplying my necessities.'[20] At the ideological level, John Price's pamphlets against the City *Remonstrance* moved far in the direction of accepting the House of Commons, the representatives of the people, as the supreme authority in the constitution; Thomas Edwards commented upon the change: 'Certainly these books of Master Price were not written in the year 1645, but in the year 1646 that they agree with Lilburne, Overton, &c.'[21] There is little evidence about the financing of Leveller propaganda, which reached its mature form with the publication of *A Remonstrance of Many Thousand Citizens* on 7 July 1646, but the Independents certainly provided a greatly enlarged audience for the Leveller pamphlets and may have had a hand in distributing them widely outside London.[22]

Mass agitation in London was inhibited by the deadlock that ensued over the 'lamentable' petitions. The history of this episode is overshadowed in Walwyn's account by an attack on his religious scepticism at this time led by John Price. Price was 'an Exchange man,' according to Thomas Edwards, and John Goodwin's 'beloved disciple, and one of his prophets, who among others preach for him when he hath any book to answer, or some Libertine tractate to set forth.' Price and Walwyn had advanced together towards a more prominent role at Salters' Hall. They were both prolific pamphleteers, but while Walwyn was writing persuasive defences of toleration during the civil war, Price had specialized in devotional handbooks for the parliamentary armies. By the summer of 1646 Price was fully engaged in the political crisis in London and was one of the leaders of the Independent radicals; at the end of the year Edwards had heard reports that he had preached at Bury St Edmunds, and he may have contributed to the spread of radical agitation outside London.[23] That Walwyn's opponents should choose his supposed religious scepticism as the ground of their attack arose from his personal involvement with members of John Goodwin's church extending back over many years. A typical example was his brief friendship with Thomas Lambe, a linen draper in Cornhill, whom he met in the course of his business. Lambe was scarcely able to overcome his suspicion of Walwyn because he had not joined a gathered church, and the brief friendship ended when Walwyn criticized some of Goodwin's books. Such suspicions were dangerous to Walwyn's role as a political leader because they were not limited to Goodwin's church or to the Independents. It was Richard Wollaston, a member of Hanserd Knollys' Baptist congregation, who aspersed Walwyn as an anti-scripturist at a meeting in Cromwell's house, one of the nerve centres of the London radicals; this, according to Walwyn, 'served their turn at that meeting to blast all the reason I spake, and to destroy that petition' at a critical meeting at the Windmill.[24] Price, with his tendency to limit the role of the political activist to the saints, secured the appointment of a committee in Goodwin's congregation to examine the charges against Walwyn's faith, but the matter was blocked by Walwyn's supporters within the congregation, and then temporarily forgotten when the renewal of persecution early in 1647 reunited the London radicals. But there were deep antagonisms here that were to follow the Leveller movement to its end.

The March petition of the Levellers

The adherence of the General Baptist congregations to the radical organization appears to have broken the deadlock of late 1646, shifting the initiative to the Leveller side and making possible Walwyn's victory in establishing the terms of the March petition the following spring. The General Baptists were drawn into the Leveller movement through Richard Overton, of whom men like Price, Kiffin, and Rosier could say in 1649 that 'we know him not but by his pen,' adding, 'the complexion whereof hath quit our desires of any further acquaintance with him.'[25] Overton's early pamphlets against religious persecution were the product of his individual genius, and although they were thoroughly consistent with General Baptist principles he was not acting as an official spokesman on behalf of the sect. Nevertheless his outlook was profoundly shaped by the intellectual tradition he shared with the General Baptists. In a rare personal apologia published in 1649, Overton gave a clear expression to his radical view of the separation between church and state which permitted the formulation of a secular notion of citizenship upon the basis of reason, justice, and equity:

> I confess, for my part, I am a man full of sin and personal infirmities, and in that relation I will not take upon me to clear or justify myself; but as for my integrity and uprightness to the commonwealth, to whatsoever my understanding tells me is for the good of mankind, for the safety, freedom and tranquillity of my country, happiness and prosperity of my neighbours, to do to my neighbour as I would be done by, and for the freedom and protection of religious people: I say as to those things, (according to the weak measure of my understanding and judgement) I know my integrity to be such, that I shall freely (in the might of God) sacrifice my life to give witness thereunto.[26]

By focussing on the right of the individual to an autonomous spiritual life rather than on the right of the gathered church to exist, the General Baptist tradition freed itself from confusion as to the respective roles of citizenship and sainthood or church membership. Overton's own career was explicitly that of Leveller, not that of a General Baptist in politics.

Richard Overton and Nicholas Tew of Lambe's congregation controlled a secret press in Coleman Street before the end of 1644. This brought them into contact with Lilburne and with the separatist printer and bookseller William Larner, and led to Tew's arrest for unlicensed printing early in 1645.[27] Overton relied on members of his sect to distribute his pamphlets, which could not be safely handled by regular booksellers. The General Baptist Samuel Fulcher was brought before a justice of the peace for selling copies of *The Last Warning to all the Inhabitants of the City of London*, a pamphlet that in Edwards' judgement was 'against all kingly government.' Two days after the pamphlet appeared on 20 March 1646, Edward Barber announced that a book had appeared that 'had cut the legs off the Presbyterian government.'[28] Later in the summer, perhaps after the appearance of the *Remonstrance of Many Thousand Citizens* in which Overton had a large hand, 'Crab of Southwark side,' who shared Overton's views on the mortality of the soul, was brought before the Lord Mayor and bound over to the sessions for saying that 'it was better to have a golden calf or an ass set up. . .than to have a king over them.'[29] By July 1646, when he worked with Walwyn and Henry Marten to bring out the *Remonstrance*, Overton was fully engaged in the concerted Leveller propaganda effort, and he was soon to follow Lilburne to prison. There is no further trace of General Baptist activity through the rest of this year, but in the agitation over the March petition in 1647 members of this sect occupied a central position in the Leveller organization.

The context of the March petition was established by the conservative citizens' petition and the accompanying City government petition of 19 December 1646, and by the House's revived attempt in January and February of 1647 to regulate the sects. John Price suggested that the March petition was initially intended as a demonstration of the whole of the 'honest party' in London.[30] Walwyn confirms this. The revival of religious persecution, and Walwyn's efforts on behalf of the persecuted Particular Baptists and others, healed over the breach of the previous year between himself and members of Goodwin's congregation; 'the generality of congregations, and others, resolved to bear testimony' against the persecution.[31] The debate over the content of the petition was sharp. Walwyn and his supporters wanted to adopt a programme of fundamental reform which was to become the Leveller party platform, and to present it without regard for political expediency. Price and the Independents were at a disadvantage in this debate, in that they appear to have envisaged the petition in terms of political manoeuvre at a time when the Independents had lost room for manoeuvre in Parliament. Price said that Walwyn's programme contained 'such things, which though in themselves desirable and (were they attained) hopeful and promising to the well-being of honest men, and the interest of the nation,' were unseasonable, an argument that scarcely concealed the Independents' lack of an alternative initiative. The manner in which Walwyn won his victory in determining the content of the petition is not known, but his hand must have been strengthened by the accession to the movement of the General Baptist congregations with their foothold in London's lower classes. Price's account suggests that the Independents were swamped by the popular element, by

> men of low and mean birth, breeding and quality, proud, heady, high-minded, vain-glorious, giving out themselves to be always the well-affected party, by whom, chiefly and mainly, if not only the Parliament have been chosen, maintained, preserved, as if the whole burden of the charges and service of the wars was undergone by them and by none else.[32]

The petition was circulated to the congregations for signatures in the week following 10 March, the national day of humiliation for heresies and blasphemies. It was detected by an informer at the regular Sunday meeting of Thomas Lambe's General Baptist congregation on 14 March where, after a young man had 'endeavoured to prove free will' and Thomas Lambe had preached a sermon, yet another person at the front of the congregation read out the petition while Lambe corrected him. The petition was then subscribed by members of the church.[33] The matter, described by Whitelocke as 'a counter-petition to the London petition' of the previous December, was referred by the House of Commons on 15 March to Colonel Leigh's committee of examinations which had shortly before harassed the Baptist preachers. On the 18th, Lambe appeared before the committee accompanied by 'abundance of conscientious people,' two of whom, Nicholas Tew, 'one very active in this business' and Overton's associate two years earlier, and Major Tulidah, a friend of Lilburne's, were imprisoned.[34] On the 20th, a second petition was presented by 'divers citizens' in support of the first and asserting the right of the citizens to petition. The petition 'termed Independent' was the subject of comment in a newsletter to the Army on the 30th in which it was reported that 'the petitioners or a great company of them will attend the House daily to have their petition restored.'[35] A large group of citizens waited upon the House on 3 April and again on 4 May for an answer; on the second occasion the House told the petitioners they did not approve of the petition or the manner of its presentation. On 20 May the Levellers presented a third petition to Parliament in prosecution of their former petitions, and this time the House replied, by a vote of 94 to 86, with an order for the burning of the petitions, duly executed on the 22nd.[36]

During this period, 'most of the uppermost Independents stood aloof and looked on, whilst Mr. Stasmore [Staresmore], Mr. Highland, Mr. Davis, Mr. Cooper, Mr. Thomas Lambe of the Spital, and very many more, for many weeks continually plied the House.'[37] The agitation was sustained, that is, by leading separatists and General Baptists, while the Independents stood aloof and the Particular Baptist pastors refrained from overt support of the movement. Yet the position of the Independents was becoming increasingly desperate as the conservatives proceeded with the rest of their programme. On 15 April Parliament transferred control over the London militia to the City government, and on 27 April the Common Council purged from the militia committee leading political Independents such as alderman Penington, as well as religious Independents like Colonel Robert Tichborn, one of Lilburne's 'gentlemen Independents' and a member of Lockyer's gathered church. The House of Commons confirmed the new militia commissioners in office on 4 May, and the purge of Independent officers of the militia began immediately and continued for some weeks as the City conservatives recklessly contemplated an armed conflict with the New Model; the victims of the purge were not obscure sectarians but prominent men like Lieutenant-Colonel William Shambrook of Jessey's church, who lost his command because 'he was of a particular congregation.'[38] Overshadowing everything else was the conservative drive to disband the New Model Army. On 30 March the House of Commons had reprimanded the senior officers of the Army and condemned their petition expressing the grievances of the Army, and a month later they summoned before them the representatives of the newly elected agitators who carried an open letter to the general officers in London. The Army's revolt began with its refusal to disband as ordered by Parliament on 1 June, and by the morning of the 3rd Cornet Joyce had seized control of the King from the Parliament's Commissioners at Holmby. The three crises, over the London petition, the London militia, and the disbanding of the Army were thus contemporaneous.

Seen in its wider context, the completeness with which the Levellers established control over the radical initiative in London during the period of crisis is astonishing. The Leveller petition, 'termed Independent,' and the agitation on its behalf became the representative cause of the whole of London radicalism, and this was implicitly acknowledged by the political Independents in the House of Commons in the close vote on the burning of the petition. As the crisis deepened, even John Price faced the realities of the situation. 'The eyes of the people in all places,' Walwyn said, were opened by 'this bustling unkind dealing with petitioners for many weeks together, and the burning of a petition so just and necessary.' Price and the Independents who had originally opposed the terms of the petition 'began to approve of our motions, and they and I began to come a little nearer together, and had joint meetings and debates.'[39]

The threads of the several crises crossed in Cromwell's house in Drury Lane at the end of May. On the evening of the 31st Cornet Joyce had his interview with Cromwell in the garden before setting out on his expedition to secure the King. 'Mr. Price may, and cannot but remember an evening's journey he and I made into Drury Lane to the Lieutenant General,' Walwyn said, 'and what satisfaction we received.' The result of this joint visit was that 'we all, both his friends and mine, joined in a petition, the last and most sharp of any,' and the decision to petition was probably made in Cromwell's house about the 29th or 30th. The petition, delivered to the Commons on 2 June, had representative rather than mass support, with one thousand hands, according to Whitelocke. Since it linked the grievances of the Leveller petition, the London militia, and the Army, the object of this 'sharp' petition was hardly to persuade the House of Commons, although a major effort was made to turn out votes by the parliamentary Independents.[40] In part the petition may be related to efforts to persuade Cromwell to act. It demonstrated the unity of the London radicals as well as the intransigence of the conservative majority in the House of Commons. When Cromwell rode away from the City to join the Army on 3 June, he knew that the London radicals were united, that they had made their demonstration in Parliament, and that they had lost by the slim margin of 128 votes to 112.

Sectaries and the New Model Army

The men 'that did all the hurt,' wrote Richard Baxter, chaplain of Whalley's regiment of horse in 1645, in explaining the religious radicalism of the Parliamentary armies, were men 'that had been in London, hatched up among the old separatists.'[41] There is solid evidence to support the charge. In his own regiment the most prominent and outspoken of the junior officers was Lieutenant Edmund Chillenden, a member of Samuel How's congregation in 1637 and the author of a defence of lay preaching published in 1647; he became a General Baptist at some undetermined time before 1651. Lieutenant John Webb of Hewson's regiment, an active lay preacher (in competition with his colonel) who in 1646 figured prominently in the third part of *Gangraena,*[42] was also a former member of How's church who had appeared as a separatist along with Chillenden before the House of Lords in 1641; he had become a Particular Baptist and signed the first edition of the London *Confession* for one of the seven churches. Robert Barrow, a lieutenant in Colonel Birch's regiment, was a former member of Samuel Eaton's church and the author of one of the earliest

Particular Baptist replies to Praise-God Barbone; he had been rewarded by the House of Commons for his prominent part in the capture of Hereford in 1645.[43] Paul Hobson, formerly of Green and Spencer's church and the founder of one of the seven Particular Baptist congregations, was a captain in Fairfax's regiment of foot and perhaps the most renowned lay preacher in the Army. One of his closest associates in the regiment was a former London apothecary, Captain Richard Beaumont, whose troop was responsible for the baptism of a horse in a parish church in 1644.

Many London sectarians remained private soldiers through the civil war. William Allen, a Southwark feltmaker and a Particular Baptist, served first in Colonel Holles's regiment, later in Skippon's; he had been captured once and wounded twice.[44] Thomas Shepard, a strict separatist in Eaton's church in 1633 and an organizer of one of the seven Particular Baptist congregations, had originally joined the Earl of Bedford's cuirassiers and later served in Ireton's regiment in the New Model.[45] A more tentative case is that of Robert Lockyer, the trooper in Whalley's regiment who was executed at the age of twenty-three for his part in a revolt in 1649. A Robert Locker rebaptized by Richard Blunt in January 1642 was perhaps the son of the 'Mary Lock' who was also rebaptized on that occasion, and who was listed as a householder in her own right as 'Mary Locker' in the parish of St Botolph without Bishopsgate in 1638.[46] If this is the same Robert Lockyer, his youthfulness might have been unusual in a sectarian congregation in 1642, but it was certainly not impossible; Kiffin was preaching to his fellow apprentices at the age of sixteen, and Lockyer himself had joined the Army in 1642 at the same age.

Other radical Londoners advanced to high rank at the formation of the New Model Army. Lieutenant-Colonels John Hewson and Thomas Pride and Colonel John Okey had all been London tradesmen before the war. Pride was a member of Duppa's strict separatist church,[47] Hewson a radical Independent and a famous lay preacher,[48] Okey a member of Jessey's congregation and perhaps himself a Baptist.[49] Hewson became colonel of his regiment in 1645. His major in 1647, and later the lieutenant-colonel, was Daniel Axtell, a member of William Kiffin's congregation in London, and according to Richard Overton, originally a pedlar in Herefordshire.[50] One of Hewson's captains, the Particular Baptist Alexander Brayfield, had formerly been Beaumont's lieutenant in Fairfax's regiment. Pride did not secure control of his regiment until the withdrawal of the Presbyterian officers in 1647. Among his captains were the General Baptists John Mason, a former apprentice to a coach harness maker in London,[51] and John

Pym; although these men later moved to the regiment of Charles Fairfax, General Baptists remained entrenched in the lower levels of Pride's regiment, where Samuel Oates served as chaplain in the next decade. Among the captains of Okey's regiment of dragoons was another active General Baptist, John Garland.

Scarcely less important than the Londoners in shaping the radicalism of the Army was Oliver Cromwell's regiment of Ironsides.[52] Cromwell's practice of recruiting godly men without regard to their sectarian affiliations was well known. His principle in this matter was stated in 1644 in a letter to Major General Crawford on behalf of Crawford's own lieutenant-colonel, a Baptist named Warner of whom little is known: 'Sir, the State, in choosing men to serve them, takes no notice of their opinions, if they be willing faithfully to serve them, that satisfies.' About the same time Cromwell had to intervene on behalf of one of his own lieutenants, William Packer, a Baptist whom Crawford had arrested, probably for the offence of lay preaching.[53] Packer was to be one of the most successful of the Baptist officers in the New Model Army. He was a man of humble origins and of no determinable geographical roots; in a moment of anger his friend John Lilburne railed at him that his Army career under Cromwell had raised him from a 'dung-hill.'[54] He originally enlisted as a trooper in Cromwell's own troop of the Ironsides; as the regiment expanded he was transferred to Walton's troop as lieutenant, and he became captain of the troop at Walton's death at Marston Moor. Other men who were Baptists or were shortly to become so were rising through the ranks. John Gladman became captain-lieutenant of Cromwell's own troop in 1644; one of the corporals, Peter Wallis, became a cornet by 1647, and eventually the colonel of a regiment in Ireland. In Captain Berry's troop in 1644, the lieutenant was William Disher and the cornet, William Malyn; both eventually rose to the rank of captain. Another Baptist, Thomas Empson, was a lieutenant by 1647; he was said to be a better preacher than a fighter, a remark that prompted Cromwell to write, 'Truly I think he that prays and preaches best will fight best.'[55]

When the double regiment of the Ironsides was divided at the formation of the New Model Army, these men, all Particular Baptists, remained with that section of the regiment that became Fairfax's. This regiment remained a stronghold of the Particular Baptists through the rest of the revolutionary period; Packer eventually became major and the effective commander, and a man of wide influence. The second half of the regiment was placed under the command of Colonel Whalley. Here the Particular Baptists were negligible, but General Baptist opinions were widespread among the lower ranks; it was probably while he was serving in this regiment that Chillenden was converted to the General Baptists. Baxter said that the men of Major Bethel's troop were particularly radical, and that they 'took the direct Jesuitical way' in favour of free will, an indication of the presence of General Baptists.[56] One of the troopers elected as an agitator for this regiment in 1647 was the General Baptist William Russell, and about the time of the second civil war, the General Baptist Jeremiah Ives succeeded Hanserd Knollys to serve in Baxter's old position as chaplain of the regiment.

A number of Baptists left the Army at the end of the first civil war, but this trend was suddenly and perhaps significantly reversed late in 1646 when Baptists and separatists began to join or to rejoin the Army. William Allen rejoined the Army about the middle of the year as a trooper in Cromwell's own regiment of horse.[57] Paul Hobson, after preaching a farewell sermon to the Army in the spring of 1646, was back within a year and soon promoted to the rank of major in Robert Lilburne's regiment. The Baptist clergyman Edward Harrison joined Thomas Harrison's regiment as chaplain in 1647.[58] Another former clergyman, the General Baptist Henry Denne, joined Colonel Scroope's regiment as a cornet. John Turner, who would soon become a Baptist, appeared in 1647 as a lieutenant in Lilburne's regiment. The separatist John Spencer, another Londoner soon to become a Baptist, also appeared in the Army as a cornet in July 1647.[59] All these men were important leaders in the sectarian movement. Their actions suggest that, faced with the ominous approach of an intolerant Presbyterian settlement, they anticipated the exercise of some form of political influence on their behalf by the Army in securing a final religious settlement in the nation.

The departure of the Presbyterian Officers from the regiments of the New Model Army when the Army refused to disband in 1647 afforded substantial opportunities of advancement to religious radicals in several regiments. The radical Independent Robert Overton became colonel of Herbert's regiment of foot. At least three of Overton's five new captains, William Knowles, William Gough, and Robert Reade, were Particular Baptists, and two more Baptists, John Gardiner and Benjamin Groome, were appointed to the rank of captain within the next year or so.[60] Much the same thing happened in Robert Lilburne's regiment; Lilburne, the brother of John Lilburne, was a friend and patron of Baptists.[61] Paul Hobson was appointed major, Richard Deane, soon to be appointed one of the treasurers of the Army, joined the Particular Baptist Abraham Holmes among the captains,[62] and John Turner and the Devonshire Particular Baptist Nathaniel Strange served as lieutenants. By 1649 Hobson had become lieutenant-colonel and effective commander of the regiment. Yet another Particular Baptist, Richard Lawrence, served as marshal-general of horse in the New Model in 1647.

Some measure of the influence of the religious radicals over the lower ranks of the Army can be gathered from the number of Baptists among the representatives elected by each regiment to serve on the General Council of the Army in 1647. Among the officers elected to represent the regiments of horse were Lieutenant Empson and Cornet Peter Wallis of Fairfax's regiment, the General Baptist Captain Henry Pretty of Ireton's regiment, Lieutenant Chillenden of Whalley's regiment, and Captain Richard Creed of Thornhaugh's regiment. Among the troopers elected were William Allen of Cromwell's regiment and Thomas Shepard of Ireton's. Captain Holmes and Captain Deane represented the officers of Lilburne's regiment of foot, Captain Brayfield was elected in Hewson's regiment, and the General Baptist Captain John Mason in Pride's; among the soldiers were the General Baptist John Miller of Lambert's regiment and the Particular Baptist Robert Mason of Sir Hardress Waller's regiment. There were also at least two General Baptists, Robert Everard of Cromwell's regiment and William Russell of Whalley's, among the more radical agents who were elected to represent five regiments of horse in the autumn of 1647.[68] The Baptists are the most easily identifiable because they were branded as 'Anabaptists,' but there were probably members of other sectarian churches as well among the soldiers' representatives.

The Baptists were in any case important in their own right, not merely as being typical of religious radicalism as a whole. With a decade or more of illegal religious activity behind them, they had a wide range of sectarian connections throughout the Army and in London. They had a more urgent concern than the Independents over the prospects of a Presbyterian settlement, and sufficient experience to form their own political judgements on the course of events. When the parliamentary Presbyterians set about the delicate task of disbanding the New Model Army without first securing the rights of the disbanded soldiers or establishing satisfactory conditions of service in Ireland, grievances were shared by the whole Army. Baptists played a leading role in the spontaneous organization that sprang up to give expression to the grievances of officers and men. There is nothing to suggest that the revolt was deliberately planned by the Baptists and separatists who entered or rejoined the Army in the months immediately preceding the crisis, but the implications of their political instincts are clear. Their experience and their aspirations ensured that leadership was available to exploit to the full the discontent created in the Army by the policy of the parliamentary Presbyterians.

Two men, Lieutenant Chillenden and Trooper William Allen, were especially active in the initial stages of the organization of the soldiers in the spring of 1647. Chillenden was deep in the counsels of both the officers and the soldiers who organized in March and April to prepare petitions setting forth their grievances. He was one of the seven officers who delivered the *Petition and Vindication* of the officers to the House of Commons on 27 April. Three weeks later he was in London to secure political intelligence for the agitators who had been elected by the soldiers. He reported a rumour that Parliament would seek to divide the soldiers from their officers, and he urged the agitators to persuade the soldiers to stand by the officers. He also took the opportunity to send to the Army copies of the Leveller petition addressed to the House of Commons in March. On 25 May, the day Parliament published its orders for the disbanding of the first regiments, Chillenden was again sent to London post-haste to collect political intelligence for the agitators, and during the critical days that followed he served as one of the principal channels of communication between London and the agitators.[64] William Allen was a leading spirit in the organization of eight regiments of horse in April. Elected as the agitator for Cromwell's own regiment, he remained the most prominent spokesman of the agitators for several months. Allen was sent, with Thomas Shepard and Edward Sexby, to deliver the initial letter of the eight regiments to the Generals in London, and he acted as the main spokesman when the three men were questioned at the bar of the House of Commons on 30 April.[65]

In the end, neither Allen nor Chillenden were Levellers, but it is a difficult task to trace the stages by which the sectarian and Leveller interests in the Army were disengaged, to leave the initiative as spokesmen for the Army radicals with the Levellers. The key is probably to be found in the channels of communication between the radicals in the Army and in London, and here the story is obscure. Men like Chillenden, Allen, and Shepard had a natural entry into the circles of London radicalism and especially into the sectarian circle around Lilburne. But as the soldiers arrived in London in the period between March and June, they would find that their circle was already organized for political action under the leadership of the Levellers, who were occupying the common ground among the several varieties of religious radicalism and giving a political leadership independent of the sectarian pastors. Here Edward Sexby, the agitator for Fairfax's regiment and a future Leveller leader in the Army but not, as far as we know, a sectarian, could feel as much at home as Chillenden and Shepard, the one associated with Lilburne in 1637, the other a member of Eaton's separatist church as long ago as 1633.

'Well, very good friends we were all,' wrote Walwyn of the period from the June 'sharp' petition to the entry of the Army into London in August, 'and I was by very eminent persons of the Army sent for to Reading, to be advised withall touching the good of the people, a study my conscience had much addicted me to.'[66] On 16 July the General Council of the Army met at Reading to debate the proposal of the soldiers' representatives for an immediate march on London in response to the purge of the Independents from the London militia.[67] Chillenden gave the opening statement of the case for marching on London, but the principal spokesman was Trooper William Allen, whose arguments with the grandees dominated the meeting.[68] On the following day, 17 July, the General Council moved on to consider the wider issue of the settlement of the kingdom and the procedures to be used in preparing the Army's plan for settlement. The *Clarke Papers* unfortunately contain only a fragmentary report of the first few minutes of the debate, but the single radical speech reported is once again Allen's, and what he had to say is extremely interesting: although 'we are most of us but young statesmen,' the business of settling the kingdom is 'truly the work we all expect to have a share in, and desire that others may also.'[69] Allen was claiming a role for the agitators, the representatives of the common soldiers, in the settlement of the kingdom; in claiming a place for 'others' in preparing the Army's proposals for settlement he was making the initial move that culminated in the important participation of the civilian Levellers in the Putney debates three months later. This brief speech strengthens the clear impression left by the previous day's session: Chillenden and Allen still controlled the radical initiative in the Army, they were engaged in establishing firm communications with the London Levellers, and they had as yet no inkling that the sectarian and the Leveller interests were distinct.

It was the issue of the militia that brought on the crisis in London at the end of July. On 23 July Parliament responded to Army pressure by restoring the old militia committee with its strong Independent representation. The City conservatives, who had met the Army's challenge to Parliament at the beginning of June with 'one unanimous consent' in the Common Council 'that they would have no more war,'[70] reacted much more vigorously to the loss of their control over the militia. On 26 July, under threat of mob violence directed by the City conservatives, Parliament was forced to reverse itself again and to restore the new conservative militia committee, an act which by itself appeared to make use of the London militia against the Army virtually inevitable. The House voted an adjournment to the 30th, by which time the two Speakers and a significant portion of the members of both Houses had taken refuge with the Army, which had already begun its march on London in earnest. On 4 August the Southwark militia, always a weak link in the conservative hold on London, opened the gates for Colonel Rainsborough. On 6 August Fairfax marched into the City. The Houses of Parliament were restored, and Fairfax was immediately appointed Lieutenant of the Tower of London.[71] Thomas Edwards fled into exile to Amsterdam.[72] However, as Cromwell had warned at Reading, the effects of an act of force on the part of the Army, even if taken in response to the force upon Parliament on 26 July, were incalculable, and so it soon proved.

From Reading to Ware via London

Much of the uncertainty and confusion that overtook the English political scene and the Army itself in the late summer and autumn of 1647 arose from the rivalry between uppermost Independents and Levellers for control of the radical initiative. On 17 July, the same day that the deeply religious William Allen was initiating at Reading the steps which led to the appearance of the civilian Levellers at Putney, Richard Overton warned the agitators in his *Appeal from the degenerate Representative Body* to 'trust no man, whether officer or soldier, how religious soever appearing, further than he acts apparently for the good of the Army and Kingdom; mark them which would and do bring you into delays and demurs, let their pretences be what they will, their counsels are destructive.'[73] This warning was prophetic, for in the aftermath of the Army's march on London deep divisions appeared among the radicals. The Levellers complained in their later narratives of three episodes which may serve as a guide into the confusion that beset the radicals at this period. In the first place, the imprisoned Levellers were not freed during the Army's 'glorious march through London' on 7 August.[74] This was the kind of affront Lilburne could not swallow, and he immediately turned on Cromwell. When William Allen conveyed to him from the Army a suggestion that he ask the House of Lords for his freedom, he denounced Allen as Cromwell's 'officious and extraordinary creature' who was corrupting the agitators. To Allen, this experience may have come as a shock, creating for the first time a conflict of loyalties which was to trouble the Army radicals for months to come.[75]

The second episode also followed directly in the aftermath of the

Army's march on London, when the Independents faced the problem of securing the military control of the City. In the second half of August Walwyn attended the Army headquarters at Kingston with a delegation of civilian Levellers, 'friends of London, Southwark, and the places adjacent,' to urge Fairfax to secure 'the Tower, City and Borough' under the control of the 'well-affected inhabitants,' envisaging apparently a popular citizens' militia controlled by Levellers and Independents. This visionary scheme was rejected by the Council of War, 'the proposers themselves being dismissed with reproaches,' in favour of raising a new Tower regiment, to be placed on the regular Army establishment and commanded by Colonel Tichborn, Fairfax's deputy in the Tower, Lieutenant-Colonel Shambrook, and other City Independents. The Levellers were sharply displeased both with this decision and with the manner in which it was made by the 'grand officers' in the Council of War, with 'the agitators thrust out.'[76] The breach between the Levellers and the Army grandees widened, and the Levellers broke with the City Independents.

The episode of the Tower regiment plays a key role in Walwyn's personal narrative: 'and then afresh, we were atheists, non-scripturists, Jesuits and anything to render us odious.'[77] But it is reasonably clear that the Levellers simply ignored those prudential considerations that weighed heavily with the City Independents at this juncture. The Army's march on London had produced a modification but not a revolution in the political balance in the City. The Independents secured a much larger voice in the settlement of the militia committee, with new committees in Westminster, Southwark, and the Tower Hamlets, but this division of authority in itself encouraged new antagonisms in the City. Parliament imposed the 'schismatical' John Warner on the City as Lord Mayor at the end of September, but this was far from securing Independent control of the City government, which remained stubbornly, if more circumspectly, conservative.[78] That 'peevish sectary' Tichborn, Lieutenant of the Tower and colonel of the Tower regiment, whose martial valour was little regarded in the City, occupied an insecure position. Cromwell regarded Tichborn's lieutenancy as negotiable, if he could reach agreement with more conservative elements in the City, and Tichborn lost his position at the outbreak of the second civil war when the Tower was restored to the control of the City and to the command of Colonel Francis West, whom Fairfax had displaced. In the wider context of London politics, the Tower and its regiment were under the control of what Clement Walker termed the 'pure Independents' as distinct from the 'mixed Independents'; in the eyes of conservative citizens the Tower regiment was controlled by 'sectaries' whose political position was exposed and precarious.[79] Viewed in this light, it is scarcely surprising that the City Independents reacted violently to the Leveller attack on the Tower regiment, which was an attack on their rear just as they had with the Army's help won a precarious victory against their common opponents in the City. The Levellers, however, had no patience with men who were 'mere politicians. . .governed altogether by occasion.'[80]

The third source of division among the radicals was the persistence with which Cromwell and Ireton pursued their policy of securing a general settlement of the kingdom by negotiating directly with the King, to the point where they virtually forfeited the confidence of the Army.[81] The Particular Baptist leaders in London and in the Army, in their capacity as sectarian leaders, took a direct political initiative in these negotiations. The details come from the letter-book of a Royalist, Sir Lewis Dyve, a fellow prisoner with Lilburne in the Tower at this period. The initial approach was made by Paul Hobson soon after the King was brought to the Army in early June; it was arranged through Sir Lewis Dyve, who gave Hobson a letter of introduction to the King.[82] Hobson and Dyve in turn must have been brought together by John Lilburne when Hobson visited him in the Tower, which in itself suggests how close the Particular Baptists were to Lilburne. That this initiative was taken in Lilburne's circle through his contact with Dyve is confirmed in a pamphlet published in 1651 by Cornet Joyce, now a lieutenant-colonel, in which he linked Major Tulidah, Lilburne's friend and a Leveller, with Hobson, and said that they spoke with the King 'and immediately were lifted up, and nothing would serve them but a personal treaty with the King.'[83] The most important Baptist contact with the King was made at Hampton Court in September by William Kiffin, acting on behalf of the Particular Baptist leaders in London; Dyve's letter to the King on 5 October speaks of the 'satisfaction. . . which Mr. William Kiffin, an anabaptist teacher in London, lately received from you when you were graciously pleased to speak with him.'[84] The result of this 'satisfaction' was the preparation of a petition for a personal treaty with the King in an effort to give popular support to the policy of Cromwell and Ireton.

The initiative in this petition appears to have been largely Particular Baptist. Joyce said that it came from the soldiers, 'and immediately upon their resolution, some progress was made in the petition at London and other places, by them and others'; the suggestion finds some confirmation in Dyve's correspondence, where Hobson remained a key figure into October. The Levellers, in the *Second Part of Englands New-Chaines* in 1649, said that immediately after Cromwell and Ireton had defeated Henry Marten's motion in the Commons of no further addresses to the King on 23 September, they took pains 'to work every man at the headquarters, upon which petitions were attempted in the Army in favour of a treaty, and some conscientious but weak people were drawn to second their design with a petition for a personal treaty, which they had ready at the House door.' Another remark of Lilburne's in 1649 serves to identify the 'conscientious but weak people': he describes Samuel Richardson as 'a preacher amongst those unnatural, un-English-like men. . .the first promoters in England (as Cromwell's beagles to do his pleasure) of the first petition for a personal treaty almost two years ago, and [who] commonly style themselves the preachers to the 7 churches of Anabaptists.'[85] According to Joyce, when this petition was dropped by the 'Independents,' who repented, it was immediately taken up by the 'Sion College men,' the Presbyterian clergy of London.[86] A settlement arrived at by Army and King on the basis of toleration was admirably suited to remove from the Baptists the taint of being rebels, and as such was especially attractive to men like Kiffin. Such considerations, however, did not carry the same weight with the rank and file of the Particular Baptist sect; William Allen was to be a fully committed participant a few months later at the famous prayer meeting of the Army leaders at Windsor in which it was decided to bring 'that man of blood' to justice, and Daniel Axtell of Kiffin's church was to become notorious for his brutality as the commander of the guard at the King's trial.

By the time of the King's flight from Hampton Court on 11 November, the hopes of the Army grandees and Particular Baptist leaders alike had collapsed, and 'hereupon the whole frame of the design alters.'[87] The Levellers were working to recover the radical initiative in the City and had captured the leadership of the lower ranks in the Army, while strong forces were pushing the sectarians into the Leveller campaign for the Agreement of the People. No sectarian could entirely trust Ireton's circumscribed view of religious toleration or afford to give blind obedience to the leadership of the Army grandees;[88] the Particular Baptist leaders had supported the grandees longer than other radical groups only for peculiar reasons of their own. Still less could the sectarians regard with satisfaction the progress of events in Parliament, where 'one of the first fruits' of the restored House of Commons in August 'was the passing of an ordinance for tithes upon treble damages,' where 'clamorous women' petitioning for Lilburne's release were ordered cleared by the guard from the passages around the Commons 'in respect of the danger of infection,' and where Biddle's Socinian pamphlet was ordered burned by the common hangman and

Biddle himself imprisoned.[89] The response of such a House to the Agreement of the People in November was a foregone conclusion: on the 9th it was voted destructive of the privileges of Parliament and of the fundamental government of the kingdom, although an attempt was made to soften the blow by finally allowing Lilburne out of the Tower without his keeper.[90]

The Agreement of the People was a purely Leveller document, and it was promoted in the Army by what was now a Leveller organization. The Levellers accomplished this advance by taking over the communications between the lower ranks of the Army and the London radicals, displacing men like Allen and Chillenden. By 29 September Sir Lewis Dyve learned from Lilburne that several regiments of horse 'cashiered their old agitators as unfaithful to the trust reposed in them by the soldiers, and have chosen new men in their places, who had a solemn meeting yesterday in this town with divers other well-affected brethren of the city.' Lilburne, Dyve said, 'set this business first on foot,' and a week later he reported that the new agents were meeting regularly.[91] The result was *The Case of the Army Truly Stated*, signed by the new agents of the five regiments on 9 October at Guildford and published on 15 October. Its collaborative authorship may have included Sexby, the old agitator, and the civilian John Wildman. The Agreement of the People came from this same combination of Army radicals and civilian Levellers and was written, perhaps by Walwyn himself, expressly for presentation to the General Council of the Army as a statement of the soldiers' demands.[92] Ireton was angry about these meetings because they were 'a divided party or distinct council from the General Council of the Army.' Bulstrode Whitelocke, cryptically reporting in his diary the events leading up to the Ware mutiny on 15 November, referred to the Army radicals' support of the Agreement as 'the late proceedings in London, tending to divide the Army,' and as 'the late endeavours of the London agents to raise a mutiny in the Army.'[93] In essence, the 'London agents,' as they were generally called, had taken over the role of spokesmen for the radical party in the Army.

The representatives of the soldiers at the famous debates at Putney were three of the old agitators, Allen, Nicholas Lockyer, and Sexby; two of the new agents, one of them Robert Everard, a General Baptist from Cromwell's regiment; and two civilians, John Wildman and Maximilian Petty. Chillenden was among the junior officers present, but he and Allen found themselves displaced as spokesmen for the soldiers by Sexby, Everard, and the civilian Levellers. Allen and Chillenden had been excluded from the Leveller meetings that produced the Agreement. Allen questioned whether the new agents and their civilian allies 'have a power to debate, and if they have not, that they may have recourse to them that sent them, to see what [powers] they will give'; while Chillenden was suspicious of these new representatives: 'I hope that these gentlemen of the five regiments their ends are good, and hope their hearts do tend to peace.'[94] Neither man took any part in the great controversy on 29 October over the nature and extent of the franchise proposed in the Agreement, but Allen made two brief speeches early in the debate at the General Council on 1 November. Searching his heart for a 'cure for a dying kingdom,' he found a basis for unity in the earlier declarations of the Army; in the second speech, he remarked that the Army was engaged to 'set up the King as far as may be consistent with, and not prejudicial to the liberties of the kingdom.' Cromwell himself reprimanded Allen for this speech, suggesting that the agitator 'did not mean all' that the setting up of the King might import; no party in the Army was any longer engaged in 'setting up' the King.[95]

Allen gave the impression at Putney of an uneasy man unwilling to face the issues which were dividing the Army, and his conflicting loyalties were soon to meet a serious test. To assert discipline, the Council of War appointed three separate rendezvous in place of the proposed general rendezvous of the Army set for the middle of November. At the first of these near Ware on 15 November, several officers and men were arrested for distributing the Agreement in the ranks; among them was William Allen, whose own regiment was not present and who was acting therefore in clear defiance of the General's orders.[96] Yet Allen was not fully committed to the Leveller cause, and he was personally suspect to the Leveller party; his decision to defy the Army grandees must have been motivated by a sense of obligation to the common soldiers. The main weight of the sectarian interest at Ware was thrown decisively against the Leveller demonstration and in favour of the Army grandees. The commanders were well aware of this, and to bring the point home to the London sectarians they chose Lieutenant Chillenden to escort to London one of the mutineers arrested along with Allen, Major Thomas Scott, a member of Parliament and a man suspected of secret royalist sympathies; the selection of a man as well connected in London as Chillenden to escort a mutineer whose motives were distrusted even by the Levellers was too apt a choice to be a casual coincidence.[97] The divergence between Leveller soldiers and sectarian officers was particularly evident in the case of Colonel Robert Lilburne's regiment, which drove away its officers and appeared at Ware led by the Leveller Captain Bray. The officers, including the large Particular Baptist group led by Major Paul Hobson, published a

Remonstrance at the end of the month in which they asserted their loyalty to Fairfax and blamed the trouble in the regiment on 'malcontented spirits' outside the regiment who divided the Army 'for such things as are in themselves very disputable, whether just or unjust, and which is more than probable may be more destructive to the commonwealth if granted, than the refusal of them will be.'[98]

The restoration of discipline at Ware was conclusive and marked the end of the concerted Leveller organization in the Army. The Ware mutineers, including Allen, were forgiven and restored to their regiments on 23 December, and Allen was afterwards offered a commission.[99] The Levellers retained some influence over the soldiers, but this influence was never again to be mobilized in an Army-wide organization that was capable of bringing pressure to bear on the Army grandees from within the Army. There were to be isolated outbreaks of Leveller activity in the Army, sometimes quite serious, but they were controlled with the full support of the sectarian officers, especially the influential Particular Baptists. When a group of soldiers attempted to revive the Leveller agitation in a meeting at St Albans on 24 April 1648, the meeting was broken up by a group of officers acting on their own initiative and led by the Particular Baptist captains, William Packer and John Gladman.[100] The future significance of the Levellers was to be found in the influence of their ideas on the Army, and no longer in their capacity to organize the lower ranks behind their programme.

The collapse of the Leveller organization in the Army can be explained by two things, apart from those general pressures that worked in favour of the maintenance of military discipline. In the first place, the political organization of the lower ranks of the Army in the spring of 1647 had been essentially a sectarian rather than a Leveller achievement. The intrusion of the Levellers or the 'London agents' into this organization, although intended to supplement the sectarian initiative, had by the time of the Putney debates ended by replacing it. At Ware, when these interests appeared as rival rather than complementary forces, the sectarian influence was thrown decisively on the side of discipline and the effect was to destroy the radical representative machinery initially constructed by the sectarians themselves in the spring. Thus the Levellers lost the benefit of the existing representative machinery, and insofar as they had alienated the sectarians they were left without the capacity to create a new one among the soldiers.

The second thing that undercut the Leveller organization in the Army was the steady advance of sectarians, especially the Particular Baptists, in the officer corps, at the formation of the New Model, at the withdrawal of the Presbyterian officers in the spring of 1647, and again in the second civil war. These men were closely connected with the radical initiative in 1647, and the very success of that initiative and their own advance in rank rendered the representative machinery that had helped to launch them less necessary to them. They attended the General Council of the Army in increasing numbers as representatives of the officers, and they were thereby the less inclined to follow the Levellers into exalting the representation of the soldiers as a fundamental principle of the revolution. The Baptist officers still represented a sectarian interest in the Army, they could differ sharply with the grandees about religious toleration, and the stability they were able to give the Army would be eroded by differences of principle over the next decade. But in the course of the year 1647 their advance in the officer corps increased the stability of the Army, and minimized the gap between the officers and the soldiers and between the lower ranks and the grandees. The new reality in the Army was implicitly recognized in the disappearance of the General Council with its soldiers' representatives; thereafter decisions were made by the council of officers, in which the sectarian voice was assured.

Levellers or saints?

By the autumn of 1647 the uppermost Independents and the respectable pastors had taken the measure of the Leveller leaders as reckless men whose determination to have their own way even to the point of dividing the saints was revealed in the mutiny at Ware. The Leveller leaders, however useful they were in organizing public agitation at moments of crisis, could not be allowed to control the tactics and the objectives of the saints. For their part, the Leveller leaders, although unconscious of the full extent of the reservations towards them felt by important sectarian pastors, hoped to break free of 'the generality of congregations' to establish a secular political party. This growing divergence between Levellers and saints was concealed for the time being, especially for the Levellers, by the continuing threat of a conservative reaction that would sweep sectaries and Levellers alike into oblivion.

In London, while the City Independents were once again limited in their manoeuvres by the requirements of the parliamentary situation, the Levellers recognized no such limitation. On 26 September and again on 5 October 'divers Londoners' presented petitions asking for the purge of members who sat 'during the force upon parliament' in the summer; the only name that can be linked with these petitions is that of Samuel Highland, indicating that the radical initiative was back in the hands of the Levellers.[101] On 9 November the House of Commons condemned the Agreement of the People, to which the Levellers responded on 23 November with a petition in defence of the Agreement. The Commons imprisoned five of the petitioners 'for seditious and contemptuous avowing and prosecuting' of the Agreement: Thomas Prince, Samuel Chidley, Jeremiah Ives, William Larner, and Captain Thomas Taylor. A month later the House of Lords received a complaint that Samuel Oates 'by himself or agents' was scattering the Agreement through Rutland.[102] This group of names indicates that the Levellers still relied heavily upon the General Baptist and separatist congregations for leadership. Highland, Chidley, and Larner represented the separatist community, Ives and Oates were two of the most prominent evangelists connected with Thomas Lambe's General Baptist congregation. Taylor was perhaps the Captain Taylor of Wapping who had been purged from the London militia in the spring, and he too may have been a General Baptist.[103] Thomas Prince, who now appeared in a leading role in the Leveller organization, was a parochial Independent; Walwyn remarked in 1649 that 'Mr. Prince hath not a congregation to cry up his parts.'[104]

The 'generality of congregations,' however, would not support the Levellers and the Agreement in defiance of Parliament. The day before the Leveller petition was presented to Parliament, George Thomason picked up from the bookstalls a pamphlet with the title *A Declaration by Congregational societies in and about the City of London, as well of those commonly called Anabaptists, as others*; the pamphlet also appeared with an alternate title page omitting the reference to the Anabaptists. In the name of 'the generality of people fearing God,' the pamphlet solemnly repudiated polygamy and community of property, and it defined liberty exclusively in terms of religious liberty. The *Declaration* expressed the long range policy of the saints in stating their preference for governors who 'fear the Lord' because they are bound in conscience to faithfully discharge their trust and because they 'will be more ready to protect godly men. . .and to propagate the Gospel in their territories.' Because men are unequal in their capacities and understandings, the authors said, 'it cannot but be very prejudicial to human society, and the promotion of the good of the Commonwealth, cities, armies or families, to admit of a parity, or all to be equal in power.'[105] The *Declaration* had an impact on the Levellers, if on no one else. Walwyn said it was a way of rendering the Levellers odious 'by vindicating yourself in those things whereof no man suspected you, that others may be thought guilty,' and the Levellers found it necessary for the first time to introduce a disclaimer in the 23 November petition against the slander that they sought 'to level all men's estates and subvert all government.'[106]

The *Declaration* was published anonymously, and the Levellers were ignorant of the authors. Walwyn, writing in 1649, attributed it to his enemies in John Goodwin's congregation and sardonically reported his wife's reaction to the *Declaration*: 'Says she, They against magistracy? Who can suspect them, that hunt and seek for offices as they do?'[107] But John Goodwin's congregation had no part in the document. The same group published another declaration 'of divers elders and brethren of Congregational societies in and about the city of London' in 1651, acknowledging the 1647 *Declaration* as theirs, and this time appending their names. The leading names were those of William Greenhill, the pastor of the gathered church at Stepney, and Richard Shute, one of the most prominent radicals in London from the beginning of the revolution. John Simpson and Christopher Feake, who with John Rogers were soon to form the triumvirate of the Fifth Monarchy movement, appeared along with Thomas Brooks, who preached the funeral sermon for (and was perhaps the pastor of) Colonel Rainsborough, the most articulate and influential of the senior Army officers who endorsed the Leveller programme.[108] Fully half of the sixteen names were Particular Baptist, led by Henry Jessey and two, possibly three, members of his congregation. Three other Particular Baptist pastors signed, William Kiffin, Hanserd Knollys, and William Conset, and of the two remaining Baptist laymen one was that Richard Wollaston of Knollys's church who had spread rumours about Walwyn in 1646.[109] The extent of Baptist participation in the 1647 *Declaration* would have come as a shock to the Levellers had it been known. Men like Kiffin and Knollys stood in the circle around Lilburne, and Walwyn could write in 1649 that 'as for Mr. Kiffin, I never had an unfriendly word or countenance from him, nor from Mr. Rosier, but kind respects wherever I met them.'[110] The later Leveller narratives display a surprise and anger at the Particular Baptist betrayal of their movement in 1649 that would scarcely be intelligible had they been aware of this earlier attempt to organize the Particular Baptist congregations against the Leveller movement.

The suppression of the Ware mutiny and the publication of the *Declaration* warned the Levellers that the saints were not fully behind the Agreement of the People; they therefore determined to break free of the 'generality of congregations' to organize their movement on an entirely secular basis. The intention was one of the most remarkable conceptions of the Levellers, but the achievement is considerably more difficult to assess. An informer reported to the House of Commons in January the grandiose scheme of 'method and order' by which the Levellers were planning to mobilize mass support for their programme, with 'commissioners' (although 'the honest blades of Southwark did not like the word Commissioners') and agents to distribute petitions, with treasurers and collectors to gather weekly subscriptions towards the costs of printing and distributing their literature, and with regular correspondence with like organizations throughout the country. Prince and Chidley were appointed treasurers, and collections were in fact made to print some of the Leveller literature of this period.[111] Nevertheless, in the business of mass petitioning the conservative elements in society commanded the greater resources, as the reputed one hundred thousand signatures to the conservative Engagement in July indicated.[112] A 'plain man' at a Leveller meeting in Wapping made the point: 'we know that the generality of the people are wicked,' and if they had power 'we may suppose and fear' that they would cut the throats of all the 'honest, godly, faithful men in the land.'[113] Although Lilburne swept this objection aside, it haunted the Leveller movement to its end. The Levellers were to remain vulnerable to appeals for unity among the saints as the only sure road to survival in the midst of a hostile society.

The successes of the Levellers in 1647 came from their capacity to articulate the established emotional loyalties of the 'generality of congregations' and of the 'honest, godly, faithful men,' especially in times of deep crisis when the more cautious leadership of the uppermost Independents failed to mobilize a mass movement. In their campaign for the Agreement of the People, the Levellers could hold the loyalty of a section of the sectarian community, but it was not yet clear whether these Leveller sectaries, if they were forced to choose, would place their fundamental trust in the Levellers or the saints. It was still less clear whether the Levellers could succeed in freeing themselves from dependence on the sectaries when these sectaries stood at the very centre of the organization which constituted the Leveller movement.

8

THE TRIUMPH OF THE SAINTS

The second Agreement of the People

The year 1648 was dangerous for sectaries and Levellers. They could both expect violent suppression at the hands of a threatening threefold combination of Royalists, English Presbyterians, and Scots. This combination did not occur, in part because the religious Independents worked desperately to preserve any parliamentary coalition that would prevent this particularly dangerous conjunction. The Independents could hardly forestall the alliance of Royalists and Scots which gave rise to the second civil war and the Scottish invasion, but in the New Model Army they possessed an effective defence against this danger. They were more vulnerable to an alliance of Royalists and Presbyterians, which their parliamentary coalition could not withstand. By the autumn of 1648 this alliance, whose religious policy was already evident in the projected Blasphemy Ordinance of May, was pushing the saints towards that unilateral political action they had always sought to avoid. Until the execution of the King in January 1649 it remained uncertain whether the saints would act on the political premises of the Levellers or on distinct political grounds of their own.

The inner history of the radicals in the months following the crisis over the first Agreement of the People in November 1647 is obscure. The Army grandees moved appreciably closer to the Leveller position in throwing their influence behind the successful vote of no addresses to the King on 3 January.[1] The City Independents, however, could derive scant comfort from a supposedly Independent Parliament. On 17 December 1647 the House of Commons voted to disenfranchise supporters of the Agreement of the People in City politics. Ostensibly aimed at the Levellers, in fact this move struck at the popular base of the Independents in London.[2] There are signs of an attempt at reconciliation among the radicals in the unsuccessful Leveller petition of January 1648, from which the abolition of tithes was omitted,

Wildman said, in order not to 'disengage any considerable party.' But Wildman and Lilburne were sent to prison for their efforts on behalf of this petition, and the Derby House Committee, the tool of the political Independents, according to Clement Walker, ordered the militia to break up Leveller meetings.[3] The failure of Cromwell's approach to the City conservatives was followed, Edmund Ludlow said, by his approach to the 'Commonwealths-men,' in Ludlow's language an amalgam of Levellers and republican members of the Commons. The outcome was inconclusive, the Commonwealth men maintaining that 'monarchy was neither good in itself, nor for us,' while Cromwell replied that he 'was convinced of the desirableness of what was proposed, but not of the feasibleness of it'; in any case Cromwell continued 'his usual practice to gratify enemies even with the oppression of those who were by principle his friends,' and Lilburne remained in the Tower.[4] The reconciliation, when it finally came, occurred in the Army in the remarkable three day prayer meeting of the Council of War at Windsor at the end of April. William Allen many years later described the meeting in which the officers unanimously decided to call the King, 'that man of blood, to an account for that blood he had shed and mischief he had done to his utmost against the Lord's cause and people in these poor nations.'[5]

The coming of the second civil war and the tortuous manoeuvres of City and Parliament created what must have been irresistible pressures to force the minority party of the radicals back into some semblance of unity. The pressures are clear to see, the results on the radicals unfortunately not. On 2 May 1648 Parliament passed the intemperate Blasphemy Ordinance that had been stalled since early in 1647; among its penalties was indefinite imprisonment for those who denied infant baptism. In mid May the Tower and the militia were restored to the City, and the Tower regiment marched off to Kent at the end of the month to put down the royalist insurrection.[6] During the following months the City government kept up its pressure on Parliament to restore the centralized control of the London militia committee and to bring the militia of neighbouring counties under unified command in an obvious effort to create a military counterbalance to the Army. The City also protested the commission granted by Parliament to Major-General Skippon to raise a force of horse in the City free of the control of the militia committee, and at the beginning of August the Common Council threatened to enlist its own horse without Parliamentary sanction. The House of Commons for the most part resisted these pressures, but it gave in to even stronger demands to revive the personal treaty with the King, this time in the conservative interest on the basis of a

Presbyterian settlement. Petitions from the counties for a personal treaty began to reach Parliament early in May, and were followed by a citizens' petition in London in June, endorsed by the City government. On the 30th, Lords and Commons agreed to set aside the vote of no addresses, on 28 July they voted to open negotiations with the King for a personal treaty, on 24 August they formally repealed the vote of no addresses and by mid September the parliamentary commissioners were on their way to the Newport negotiations. To secure their religious position in these negotiations, Parliament passed the ordinance for a Presbyterian settlement on 29 August; neither in the ordinance itself nor in the Newport negotiations was any attention paid to provision for tender consciences.[7]

These events forced the elements of London radicalism together as the conservative campaign in the early months of 1647 had done. There are glimpses of their response. On 18 July and again on 21 August there were counter petitions on the militia, the first with ten thousand supporters against the centralization of the county militias, the second with 'thousands' against the centralization of the suburban militia. The main effort of the radicals, however, was the establishment of their own military force under Skippon, which created an army of 'sectaries' and was especially popular in the suburbs. Clement Walker spoke of 'Skippon's secret listing of schismatics in the City amongst the congregations of Mr. Goodwin, Mr. Patience and others, with power given him to kill and slay.' The radical complexion of this force in the eyes of conservatives was evident in Walker's echo of Thomas Edwards, that Skippon was 'listing servants against their masters' and granting commissions 'to divers schismatical apprentices to raise men underhand.'[8] The fact that members of Thomas Patience's congregation were sufficiently prominent to attract Walker's attention suggests that despite the reservations of their leaders the Particular Baptists normally participated in the activities of the radical Independents.

Walker also reported that early in July 'counter petitions against a personal treaty are sent about by Alderman Gibbs, Foukes, Estwicke, Wollaston, Andrews, Nye the Independent priest and others. . .to be subscribed even by apprentice boys.'[9] These petitions of the uppermost Independents were not presented, because the manoeuvres of the political Independents in Parliament had to take into account the larger forces unleashed by the second civil war. The radicals, however, were able to move closer together to petition for more limited purposes. On 1 August a petition with ten thousand hands was presented to the Commons on Lilburne's behalf, and on 15 August Levellers and Independents cooperated in a petition against the Scottish invasion to counter the intemperate petition from the Common Council of the 8th, which had asked for an immediate cessation of arms and the release of the King from his restraint. Mrs Hutchinson reported a story that Cromwell was accompanied at his departure from London for the north by 'the chief of these Levellers,' who left Cromwell with great satisfaction until they heard that a 'coachful of Presbyterian priests' followed after them.[10] The spirit of the story is confirmed by Walker, who linked the uppermost Independents and the Presbyterian Stephen Marshall in efforts to placate Argyle and the clergy in Scotland in order to undermine Hamilton's invasion of England. Cromwell's victory over the Scots at Preston in mid August, Walker reported in another story, worked like 'bottled ale' with the republicans in the House of Commons who thought that they could bring proceedings in the personal treaty to an end; but a tie vote in the Commons was broken by Speaker Lenthall, 'though at this time the foreman of Oliver's shop,' in favour of continuing with the treaty. In the Lords, Lord Say said, 'God forbid that any man should take advantage of this victory to break off the treaty.'[11] The reasoning behind this attitude was explained to Ludlow by Ireton at Colchester, 'that it was best to permit the King and the Parliament to make an agreement, and to wait till they had made a full discovery of their intentions, whereby the people becoming sensible of their own danger, would willingly join to oppose them.' The effect of these 'jugglings,' as Lilburne called them, undertaken in the parliamentary context, was to muzzle the Independents in the popular context in London at the very time that the religious radicals at large sought an outlet for their feelings against the disastrous trend of the personal treaty.[12]

The result was to throw the initiative once again into the hands of the Levellers. By initiating a popular demonstration against the personal treaty in the 'humble' petition of 11 September, the Levellers were able to present their reform programme in a context that commanded the support of virtually the whole of the radical interest in the nation, far beyond the confines of the Leveller organization. The tactic was basically a repetition on a larger scale of the circumstances of the March petition of 1647 when the 'Independents' in Parliament – no Levellers certainly – and the City Independents were forced to rally to the Leveller petition. When the Leveller petition of 11 September is viewed as a popular demonstration against the personal treaty with the King that Parliament was about to launch in earnest despite the victories of the contrary-minded New Model Army in the second civil war, its very considerable success in London, the counties, and the Army need not be attributed to an exclusively Leveller organization.

Once again the Levellers were marching in the vanguard of a movement they did not really control.

H. N. Brailsford has convincingly demonstrated the impact of the 11 September petition in rallying the 'revolutionary minority' in the country at large, an impact enhanced by the opening of the Newport negotiations in mid September.[13] The petition was reported to have been signed by forty thousand people, and it was immediately endorsed by a second petition presented on 13 September by Army officers and citizens urging the House to give priority to the 'humble' petition over the personal treaty. In the following weeks, as the Newport negotiations continued, petitions poured in from the countryside and from the Army to support, not the 'Leveller' petition, but the petition against the personal treaty. Whitelocke described an Oxfordshire petition presented on 30 September thus: 'A petition in the name of many thousands of Oxfordshire, agreeing with the large petition of the city against the treaty.' Mrs Hutchinson said that

> many petitions had been brought to the parliament from thousands of the well-affected of the city of London and Westminster and borough of Southwark, and from several counties in England, and from the several regiments of the army. . .all urging them. . .to make inquiry for the guilt of the blood that had been shed in the land in both wars, and to execute justice.[14]

In Roger Howell's book on Newcastle we can see the local context that gave rise to the Newcastle petition to the same effect, which arrived at the House of Commons on 10 October along with petitions from York, Hull, and another place unnamed; the Newcastle petition had the support of its city government and represented the sentiments of the 'well-affected' or what might be loosely termed the Independents, and not a Leveller faction of the well-affected.[15]

The situation in London, as usual, was more complex simply because the political structure of the radicals was more complex. Brailsford remarked that 'the Independent divines in the City were hostile' to the 'humble' petition, with the implication that the London petition was a Leveller petition. He interpreted as referring to the Independent divines Lilburne's comment in *Legal Fundamental Liberties* in 1649, that at the time of the September petition Cromwell's 'churchmen, now my chiefest adversaries, durst not join in it, nor own it for very fear.'[16] But the reference is specifically to the authors of *Walwins Wiles*, especially John Price, Edmund Rosier, and William Kiffin, and it does not provide a basis for concluding that the London Independents stood aloof from the September petition. The evidence points instead towards a deep emotional unity among all of the radicals in those late August days when it seemed that their common cause was to be blasted by the personal treaty with the King. This new unity can be detected in a pamphlet published on 1 September by David Brown of Chidley's church, who often delivered Lilburne's manuscripts to the printer. With Walwyn's assistance, Brown undertook to defend Cromwell and Ireton against the charges of Major Robert Huntington delivered to Parliament a month earlier, when the Presbyterians had released Lilburne from his imprisonment in the vain hope that he would endorse Huntington's attack upon Cromwell. Brown's pamphlet expressed relief that 'all jars and scars are healed, all are hearty true and real friends, no by-names nor scandalous distinctions are mentioned amongst them.'[17] Thomas Brooks, one of the men behind the joint Congregational–Baptist *Declaration* of 1647, preached Colonel Rainsborough's funeral sermon at a great Leveller demonstration in mid November 1648. Walwyn, answering John Price's charge that he had divided the 'honest party,' replied that on the contrary the September petition had 'the greatest power of uniting as ever was' and asked, 'I wonder of what honest party this author reckons himself to be.' Price's personal animosity to Walwyn was confirmed by his refusal to serve with him on a joint committee in mid November, at a time when Walwyn was on intimate terms with other uppermost Independents in London.[18] The *Second Part of Englands New-Chaines*, published by the Levellers in 1649, lamented that 'many good and well disposed people, both soldiers and others,' who supported the September petition, remained loyal to the Army thereafter and refused to follow the Levellers once again into opposition. Three such people can be identified: David Brown and Samuel Chidley, who came from the very heart of the Leveller organization itself, and the prominent Particular Baptist Samuel Richardson, of whom Lilburne could say that he was 'one we judged honest and our friend' when Richardson came to see the four imprisoned Levellers in the Tower in March 1649.[19]

The success of the September initiative of the Levellers explains why the London Independents, perhaps at Cromwell's suggestion, invited the Levellers in early November to join their meetings at the Nag's Head tavern to discuss future tactics. A 'large debate' ended with a victory for the Leveller contention that the establishment of principles for a permanent settlement must have priority over bringing the King to justice and purging or dissolving Parliament as desired by the Independents. The Army grandees accepted the principle of an Agreement of the People, and in the press of events the Levellers accepted the idea of a commission of sixteen, four each nominated by the Army, Parliament, London Independents, and Levellers, to serve as a kind of constituent assembly to draft the second Agreement, which the Levellers understood was to be binding upon all parties as the basis of settlement. At various stages of these negotiations, the Levellers were represented by Walwyn, Lilburne, Wildman, Petty, and Lieutenant-Colonel William Wetton, with Samuel Highland serving on occasion as their messenger to the Army. The London Independents were represented by Lieutenant-Colonel Tichborn, Colonel John White, Dr William Parker, Samuel Moyer, and three members of John Goodwin's congregation, John Price, Daniel Taylor, and Richard Price.[20]

The London members of this commission were far from being representative of London radicalism as a whole, and this must in part explain the failure of the second Agreement. These negotiations went on over the heads of the sectarians, except in the very limited sense in which the Levellers might be understood to represent the sectarian interest; as a result the London sectarian community had no direct involvement in, or identification with, the second Agreement. As for the Independents, the large role of the members of John Goodwin's congregation indicates clearly enough that they represented the more radical Independents who since 1646 had been prepared on occasion to work with the Levellers. Quite apart from the complicated problem of the political Independents, the conservative wing of the religious Independents in London was also not directly represented. The omission was important, for the more conservative of the religious Independents led by Philip Nye had not yet given up all hope of accommodation with the moderate Presbyterians led by Nye's father-in-law Stephen Marshall, and they were left free to support Ireton when he challenged the Levellers by reopening the debate on the second Agreement in the Council of the Army.

The premises of the second Agreement were violated immediately from the Leveller point of view, first, in the Army's march on London and Pride's Purge of Parliament on 6 December before the commission of sixteen had completed the Agreement, intended to provide a moral sanction for such moves, and second, in the submission of the completed Agreement to the Council of the Army at Whitehall for discussion and reconsideration instead of for acceptance and subscription. Although on both questions, and especially on the latter in view of the unrepresentative character of the commission of sixteen, the Leveller position was unrealistic, it was fundamentally on these issues that the Levellers again broke with their allies, rather than over the issue of substance debated at Whitehall, religious toleration. In resisting the restrictive power of the magistrate, that is, his power to regulate idolatry and blasphemy, the Levellers had solid support from sectarian officers and from such radical Independents as John Goodwin and Dr Parker. They were opposed by Ireton and Philip Nye, who had one eye on the moderate Presbyterian clergy hovering in the wings and whose support the grandees were anxious to have.[21] Lilburne, however, chose to base his opposition to Ireton on another ground. Personally offended at what he regarded as Ireton's breach of faith in not accepting as binding the version of the Agreement produced by the commission of sixteen, he withdrew from the Council of the Army and on 15 December published the Agreement arrived at by the commission, altering the clause on religious toleration to eliminate the compromise reached within the commission with Ireton.[22]

Lilburne's move was precipitate, taking the rest of the Levellers by surprise and angering their allies among the London Independents. Since Walwyn and Wildman did not withdraw from the Council at the same time there was no concerted action by the Leveller organization as a whole.[23] Lilburne was henceforth isolated, with the support of only a section of the Leveller party. His supporters can be identified from the list of fifteen men who accompanied him on 28 December to deliver to General Fairfax a protest against the proceedings of the Council of the Army. Apart from Overton, Prince, Major Robert Cobbet, a member of the Walwyn–Prince circle and one of the mutineers at Ware, and John Harris the Leveller printer, the names are obscure and undoubtedly represent a selection of the rank and file of the Leveller following. Three of the four who can be identified, Edward Tench, Thomas Daffern, and Andrew Dednam, were General Baptists, and there may have been more members of this sect in the list. The fourth was Samuel Blacklock, the 'teacher' associated with Richard Blunt in the formation of the early Particular Baptist congregations in 1641; he had probably become a Seeker in the break-up of one of these congregations soon afterwards.[24]

Walwyn and Wildman hesitated to follow Lilburne's initiative, and although they both withdrew from the Army Council on 18 December they also ceased to meet with the London agents or to contribute further to the leadership of the Leveller organization. Wildman's break with the movement was permanent, but Walwyn, in fundamental agreement with Lilburne's principles if not with his tactics, was thrown together again with the Leveller leaders in the crisis that overtook the movement in March 1649. Equally significant was the defection of men like Samuel Highland and Samuel Chidley, whose contribution to the Levellers had been largely organizational. Writing in 1652, Chidley said that he accepted the Army's purge of the Commons, the removal of the King and the Lords, and the establishment of the Commonwealth, 'and have owned them ever since, and have done them faithful service, and offices of love in endeavouring to make reconciliation betwixt party and party, and to persuade them that they may sit down quietly under this present government.'[25] The absence of Chidley and other separatists from Lilburne's supporters on 28 December signifies the dissolution of the inner core of leadership in the Leveller organization. Lilburne recognized the realities of the moment. Having delivered his protest to Fairfax, he left London for the north on his personal affairs and was absent from the scene during the trial and execution of the King and the establishment of the Commonwealth.

The Particular Baptists reject the Levellers

In the weeks following Pride's Purge and the execution of the King, the Particular Baptist leaders demonstrated that, however much they sympathized with the practical reforms desired by the Levellers, they were completely insensitive to the constitutional principles that drove Lilburne to demand a secular state based upon popular sovereignty and the Agreement of the People. A few days before the execution of the King, Samuel Richardson had roundly condemned the Presbyterian clergy of London for their attack on the Army, whose purge of Parliament he defended by appealing to the natural law of self-preservation, that it was right to save themselves 'and others' from an intolerant settlement. Richardson had no illusions that the Army and its friends were more than a 'small part' of the nation, but 'they were the better part, wise and faithful'; even if the people 'declared against what they have done, yet it is to be justified, to be necessary, good, and lawful.'[26] In February the provincial Particular Baptist leader Thomas Collier echoed Richardson's arguments in more explicitly providential terms, and he placed upon the new godly magistrate the responsibility to bring forth 'righteousness,' which he defined as 'reducing magisterial power to its primitive institution, viz. to be for the punishment of evil doers, and for the praise of them who do well.'[27] Neither man was a doctrinaire republican nor a doctrinaire theocrat, but they were practising theocrats in their defence of a godly minority imposing toleration upon a reluctant nation.

Despite these statements by prominent Particular Baptists, it had not yet registered with the Levellers that the Baptist congregations were infertile ground for an attack upon the new regime. On Sunday, 25 March, Leveller agents attended the meetings of the Particular Baptist congregations in London where they read out a paper, *The Second Part of Englands New-Chaines Discovered*, in an effort to secure signatures to the latest indictment in the mounting Leveller campaign against the Commonwealth and the Army. Lilburne's tactic in appealing to the Baptist congregations, a revival of the techniques of 1646 and early 1647 in circularizing the 'generality of congregations,' was undoubtedly forced on him by the breakdown of the autonomous and secular Leveller organization in December. Even in this disarray, the Levellers alarmed the government. *The Second Part of Englands New-Chaines* was condemned by Parliament, and on Wednesday, 28 March, Lilburne, Walwyn, Overton, and Prince were arrested, the latter two by Lieutenant-Colonel Daniel Axtell of Kiffin's church. On Friday or Saturday, Samuel Richardson visited the Leveller leaders in the Tower, probably with Cromwell's connivance, to persuade them on behalf of the Baptists to give up their campaign against the government. The conversation was an extended one, in which the Baptist said that the Levellers 'would centre no where, but merely laboured to pull down those in power.' The Levellers were not to be persuaded out of their 'defiance,' although they offered terms for mediation which both they and Richardson knew would not be met.[28]

The outcome of the conference with Richardson caught the imprisoned Levellers by surprise. On Sunday the Baptist pastors appeared in their congregations with copies of their own petition to Parliament for subscription. It was short and to the point. It recited the attempt the previous Sunday to raise subscriptions for the Leveller paper, and it expressly dissociated the Baptists from 'the framing, contriving, abetting or promoting of the said papers.' Their motive in presenting the petition was stated in the familiar phraseology: 'well weighing how through the injustice of historians, or the headiness of some unruly men formerly in Germany called Anabaptists, our righteous profession heretofore hath been and now may be made odious, as if it were the fountain and source of all disobedience, presumption, self-will, contempt of rulers, dignities and civil government whatsoever,' the Baptists testified 'that our meetings are not at all to intermeddle with the ordering or altering civil government. . .but solely for the advancement of the Gospel.' The petition concluded with a request to Parliament to speedily undertake the 'settling of the Commonwealth, the relieving of the oppressed, removing all the grievances of the people, and providing for the languishing condition of the poor of this nation,' as well as for the 'making, and due execution of sufficient laws against whoredoms, drunkenness, cheating, and all such like abominations (of civil cognizance) in whomsoever.'[29]

On Monday the leading Particular Baptists of London appeared at the bar of the House of Commons to present their petition, and Kiffin briefly addressed the House. Through the Speaker, the House gave the Baptists the assurance they had long awaited: 'That for yourselves and other Christians walking answerable to such professions as in this petition you make, they do assure you of liberty and protection, so far as God shall enable them, in all things consistent with Godliness, honesty and civil peace.'[30] For the Baptists a long campaign was over, the stigma of 'Anabaptism' removed, and they rested securely in the bosom of the new Commonwealth.

These events shocked and angered the Levellers in the Tower, who saw the Baptists purchasing toleration at the price of their own blood on charges of high treason. Their dismay is evident in the accounts written by Lilburne and Overton two days later. Lilburne professed himself to be at a loss to account for such an 'unnatural' petition: 'I have much wondered with myself, what should make most of the preachers in the Anabaptist congregations so mad at us four.' Both Lilburne and Overton described Kiffin as the moving spirit behind the petition and said that a member of Kiffin's congregation told them that Kiffin had openly confessed in his church that the petition had been drawn up to please some members of the Commons. Lilburne thought he detected a second motive in a recent rumour that 'some of the Congregational preachers are very mad. . .and therefore out of revenge might petition against us' because of the earlier appearance of Walwyn's *Vanitie of the Present Churches*. He also accused the Baptist pastors of deleting a clause in the petition asking for mercy for the imprisoned Levellers before they presented it to Parliament. Overton remarked that 'the generality of the people dissented from their petition against us. . .they had scarce ten in some congregations to sign it, in some not above 2 or 3, in some none; and in the main they had not the tithe of the people.' A little later Walwyn said of this 'pharisaical' petition that 'most of their own people abhorred the practice, as un-Christian.' Overton added that until those 'well-minded Christian people of those several churches' who disagreed with the 'bloody petition' publicly disavowed it, 'they will be sharers in the public guilt of our imprisonment, yea, and of our blood.'[31] The petition of the seven churches, Walwyn said, was 'an ill requital for our faithful adherence unto them in the worst of times, and by whose endeavours under God they attained that freedom they now enjoy.'[32]

The Baptist petition signified the end of the Leveller role as political spokesman for the sects or the godly, well-affected people of the nation. Walwyn confessed that though the friends of the Levellers had prepared a petition for the speedy trial of the four men, 'the Seven Churches were got before them, and had so much respect, that our friends found none at all.'[33] Overton saw the danger when members of the House and friends of the government were able to 'negotiate with the principal leaders of several congregations of religious people about the town,' thus intercepting the Leveller claim to speak for 'the generality of congregations'; 'for could they by their delusions overwhelm us once in the odium of religious people. . .then they think they may with ease and applause cut us off.'[34] John Price also appreciated this point and went to some effort to secure what might be described as interdenominational sponsorship for his indictment of Walwyn's religious views which was published as *Walwins Wiles* later in the month. This work, although undoubtedly Price's, appeared over the names of seven men headed by William Kiffin and including the separatist pastor Edmund Rosier as well as several members of Price's faction within John Goodwin's congregation.[35] Neither Price nor the Baptist pastors had undergone a change of heart towards the Levellers; the former had always opposed Walwyn and the latter had pursued an independent, if circumspect, policy in the background during the two preceding years. It was their public disavowal of Leveller aims and tactics that seriously impaired the Leveller movement and dismayed the Leveller leaders in the early months of 1649. The failures of the spring throw into strong relief the earlier dependence of the Levellers on the political base of the 'generality of congregations' which they could not, in the end, control.

'*Mock churches*'

Walwyn was the first of the Levellers to realize what had happened to the movement. He had not followed Lilburne's lead on 15 December in turning against the Army Council, but almost immediately afterwards abandoned both the Council and the Leveller organization itself. His assessment of the political realities must have been confirmed in his mind by the version of the Agreement presented to Parliament on 20 January by the Army officers. This futile document, which the Rump simply ignored, provided for a commission of twelve men, named in the text of the Agreement, to supervise the establishment of constituencies and the collection of signatures to the Agreement. This commission was controlled by the former allies of the Levellers, including three members of John Goodwin's congregation, Daniel Taylor, Mark Hildesley, and Richard Price, as well as Colonel John White, Samuel Moyer, and William Hawkins, the 'sagamore of the Independents.'[36] The membership of this commission symbolized the final alienation of the radical Independents from the Levellers and their collaboration with the Army, but they were not mere tools of the grandees; they were experienced political leaders among the London radicals whose most fundamental assumptions were now clearly and permanently at variance with the political principles of the Levellers. This point was carefully analysed by Walwyn in *The Vanitie of the Present Churches*, the fruit of his gloomy reflection upon the destruction of the political base of the Levellers, published anonymously at the end of February. This work was the first explanation by one of the Levellers for the collapse of their party, and it was offered several weeks before the full extent of the collapse was evident.

Walwyn's basic insight was that the members of the gathered churches, despite their professions of toleration, had failed to make the distinction between church and state or to accept the secular state as the sphere of moral action in its own right. As Walwyn saw it, 'all men going in their several ways of serving God, whether public or private [whether in parochial or gathered churches], may nevertheless be free to communicate in all civil offices of love and true friendship, and cordially join with any for a public good.' But this is not what happened, and who 'could have suspected what since hath been discovered?' Men puffed up with 'vain thoughts that they are in a way well pleasing to God, because they are in a [gathered] church way, as they call it. . .are for the most part regardless of storing their minds with truth's real Christian virtue, little or nothing caring either for public justice, peace, or freedom amongst men.'[37] Instead, he said, they will 'neither stir nor undertake anything of any nature, civil or natural, but as they are prompted thereunto (as they imagine) by the Spirit.' It is hard to believe 'the infinite evils which comes to the world by this false supposition and assumption of these churches of having the spirit of God, or being taught immediately thereby'; for – an allusion to the execution of the King – in 'these ecstacies, as they call them (but indeed feverish distempers), they have been bid, as they thought, to do such things as the holy Scriptures abhor, and yet could never rest till they had done them.' Yet if you enquire 'what at any time the Spirit immediately hath made known unto them, they cannot tell one syllable, but recite some place of Scripture'; or if you demand 'a real demonstration of the Spirit, they can give you none, but (peradventure) will tell you, that you must await God's time, and he will enlighten you.'[38]

This deadly arrogance and obscurantism was in Walwyn's view inherent in the very nature of the gathered churches, or, as he now called them, 'imaginary churches,' 'mere mock churches,' 'tottering imaginary structures.'[39] For the gathered churches, no less than the churches of the Pope, the bishops, or the Presbyterians, were instruments of power and privilege, not of Christian virtue. Like the 'man in

Peter's chair,' they assumed their own infallibility, 'a power of life and death over all opinions and ways not owned by them,' and buttressed this with revelations of the Spirit of God. They 'daily spit their venom privately and publicly' against those who, like Walwyn himself, do not join with them or those who, like Clement Wrighter and Samuel Blacklock, 'out of conscience have separated from them.' They have 'scummed the parish congregations of most of their wealthy and zealous members' so that ministers and 'pretended [lay] preachers' might 'maintain themselves and families in wealth, plenty, and honour.' Usurers were tolerated in the congregations without reproach, and many members made, bought and sold 'baubles and toys such as serve only to furnish out the pride, luxury and fantasticalness of the world.' No programme of reform to enable men to live 'in peace and quietness one with another' could ever prevail 'until the mock churches are overturned and laid flat.'[40]

Yet these very gathered churches had presented, during the dominance of the Presbyterian conservatives, an apparent alternative in 'professing the meekness of the very lambs of Christ, and humility towards all men' as well as in supporting the political organization of the Levellers.[41] Walwyn's conclusion became yet more pessimistic. If the performance of the gathered churches fell so far short of their profession, then there were no churches, no communion, and no ministry in the world worthy of the name of Christian. Walwyn was not a Seeker, he did not believe in a future age of the Spirit, and he did not expect or feel the need of a future revelation to understand the basic doctrine 'very plain and easy to be understood,' 'that it is the blood of Christ which cleanseth us from all sin.' But he was deeply influenced by the Seeker view that there were no longer 'men having authority' to administer the sacraments or to provide an authoritative exposition of the Bible, and hence, by implication, no true churches and no true ministry. Walwyn was especially hostile to the sermons of the clergy, 'making merchandise of the blessed word of truth.' The Bible alone was sufficient for the Christian, and beyond that he suggested there might be 'conferences and mutual debates, one with another, the best way for attaining a right understanding, far excelling that which is called preaching.'[42]

Walwyn was as individualistic a Christian as Roger Williams or John Milton. Experience had taught him that churches, gathered no less than parochial, stood in the way of a humane society where the Christian religion should serve as the very foundation of a compassionate and tolerant society. Lilburne saw this failure, as usual, in terms of personal betrayal, but Walwyn seems to have faced the conclusion that he had made a mistake in attempting to fashion a political movement out of the saints. The bitterness of this realization explains his vehemence in denouncing the gathered churches as 'mere mock churches.'

The triumph of the saints

Walwyn's analysis provides an invaluable clue to what had happened in the separate churches of London between November and January. His diatribe was not directed against the Army grandees who had stage-managed Pride's Purge and the trial and execution of the King; this theme of military dictatorship was taken up in the two parts of *Englands New-Chaines* and other Leveller pamphlets. Rather it was directed against those London churches whose very existence had been a central preoccupation of Walwyn's whole political career in London. This suggests that at this critical period these churches had found a unity and a sense of purpose from which Walwyn was excluded, that they had finally become what John Price had always wanted, a political party of saints.

This is difficult to prove, because there is so little direct evidence for the thoughts and feelings of the members of the separate churches at this period. The indirect evidence tends to confirm Walwyn's testimony. George Cokayn, the pastor of the church originally gathered by Nicholas Lockyer, preached before the Commons a few days before Pride's Purge on the theme of imposing God's justice even on kings, for which Rowland Wilson, a member of his church, conveyed to him the thanks of the House.[43] The Rump secured a radical victory in the Common Council elections on 21 December by disenfranchising not only royalists but also Presbyterian or conservative supporters of the personal treaty in the previous summer. It was Robert Tichborn of Cokayn's church who, with the help of Owen Rowe, a parochial Independent of St Stephen Coleman Street, organized the new Common Council in mid January to petition for equal justice on the King. The royalist Lord Mayor was replaced in April by Thomas Andrewes of Sidrach Simpson's church. In the Common Council itself there was a rising tide of religious radicals for the next year or so: John Fenton, Thomas Pride, John Bolton, Praise-God Barbone, Edmund Rosier, Samuel Eames, and the ubiquitous members of John Goodwin's church, Henry Brandriff, John Price, Daniel Taylor, Mark Hildesley, and Nathaniel Lacy, the last three of whom were also appointed to the judicial commission to try five royalist peers in February 1649.[44] Members of gathered churches in London were not prominent enough to figure very largely in the more important High Court of Justice that tried the King, although their interests were well represented by the military members of the Court. Of the prosecuting lawyers, however, the active John Cook was certainly a member of a gathered church, and the silent John Aske, a former exile, was probably a member of Sidrach Simpson's church.

The most important single political element in the experience of the separate churches was the physical presence of the Army in London. The real initiative in December and January was in the hands of the Army grandees and their organ, the General Council of the Army. Henry Ireton and a large group of his supporters in the Army were determined to eliminate the King because of his guilt for the second civil war. They were able to secure the support of the religious radicals in London not by the clumsy machinery of the commission of sixteen set up to review the Agreement of the People but by direct access to the whole range of separate churches. One of the most important grandees, Colonel Sir William Constable, could in his leisure moments in London in those early days of December talk over with Thomas Goodwin and Philip Nye the old days in Arnhem. According to Professor Underdown, Constable is one of the strongest candidates for membership in the tiny informal subcommittee of six, three officers and three MPs, who made the final decision in favour of purging rather than dissolving Parliament.[45] Colonel Edward Whalley, another grandee, was a member of Thomas Goodwin's gathered church.[46] Colonel Pride, a stronger candidate than Constable for membership in the vital sub-committee, might have spent his off-duty hours in London in his circle of friends in Duppa's separatist church. Here Samuel Chidley could explain to Pride why men should not be executed 'merely for stealing' or be pressed to death for refusing to plead in courts of law. They may even have agreed that a reform in these matters might be secured by a new Common Council and a more Christian Lord Mayor; such an interview might explain how Chidley's loyalty was won away from John Lilburne. When Thomas Andrewes failed to respond to Chidley's plea for reform, Chidley turned to Pride again in 1651 to have the issue discussed in the General Council of the Army.[47] Colonel Okey, another Londoner, met with Henry Jessey and his friends. Here Jessey's stories about Seekers may have reinforced Okey's own concern, leading him to harass Captain Francis Freeman out of his regiment of dragoons for the latter's presumptuous conviction that he had passed above ordinances.[48] Lieutenant-Colonel Daniel Axtell was a member of Kiffin's church. He was not, however, restrained by Kiffin's scruples, and his behaviour as the commander of the guard at the King's trial earned his eventual execution as a regicide. Axtell was also the loyal servant of the Council of State in arresting the Levellers Thomas Prince and Richard Overton in March 1649; it is impossible to tell if his unnecessary brutality towards Overton arose from the doctrinal rivalry of the two kinds of 'Anabaptists.'[49] Captain Richard Lawrence, another Particular Baptist and Marshall-General of horse in the New Model, acted as military policeman in dealing with some of the more dangerous Members secluded from the House of Commons by Colonel Pride's soldiers.[50] Henry Ireton himself may have had direct contact with one of the gathered churches if his brother John was already a member of Cokayn's church.[51] There were undoubtedly many other Londoners present among the soldiers who came with the Army to London; such men as Robert Barrow, Edmund Chillenden, Henry Denne, and John Spencer can be identified by their attendance at the meetings of the General Council of the Army in Whitehall.[52]

As a result, the political leadership of the separate churches in London at this period was directly in the hands of the Army grandees. The separate churches gave the Army leaders a solidly loyal party in the City which was able to organize significant minority support from the old radical party for the Army's course of action. The separate churches seem to have entirely accepted the tactics and the strategy of the Army leaders, and they were represented at the King's trial by men like Constable, Pride, and Okey.[53] Faced with this solidarity between the Army leaders and the separate churches, the Leveller leaders in their attendance at the General Council of the Army at Whitehall represented nobody but themselves. It is this realization that inspired *The Vanitie of the Present Churches.* Up to the climax of the revolution, the religious radicals of the separate churches had remained clients of larger political forces and members of larger political coalitions, and this had given the Leveller leaders significant opportunities to seize important political initiatives in the complex political life of London. In December 1648 the religious radicals became a force in their own right as saints; they cooperated with the saints in the Army to seize the initiative in the revolution, and the execution of the King became the symbol of their triumph as saints.

It was an inadvertent triumph. Providence had thrust a sword into the hands of the saints and the head of a defenceless king onto the block before them. They followed the lead of Providence blindly, as saints should, without clear secular political principles to guide their sword. It was this that so infuriated Walwyn. Yet the saints had arrived at an achievement they had not foreseen. In 1644 in *Theomachia*, John Goodwin had said clearly: 'The Kingdoms and powers of this world need not fear either the numbers or power of the saints for taking away their crowns or breaking the sceptres of their rule and government, until the world that now is be translated into that which is to come.'[54] For many years after Goodwin wrote these words the saints had adhered to a great radical political coalition whose fundamental principle was that the power of government came from the people. At the last moment the saints swerved aside, tempted by Providence, to take away a crown and to break a sceptre, even although all but the simpler enthusiasts among them were perfectly clear that Goodwin's condition, the translation of the world, went unfulfilled. Not a new eschatological insight but practical expediency led the saints to accept the principle that the power of government resided in the saints of the New Model Army and in the Rump. What John Goodwin said after Pride's Purge was: 'If the people be incapable in themselves of the things of their peace, it is an act of so much the more goodness and mercy in those who, being fully capable of them, will engage themselves accordingly to make provision for them.'[55] The 'plain man' of Wapping had already made the point more plainly: if the wicked majority won't leave the saints alone, then the saints had better look after themselves.[56]

The execution of the King was the climax of the revolution for members of the separate churches, because it marked both literally and symbolically the moment of the liberation of the saints in their separate churches. Originally the notion of King Jesus had no implication whatever for the worldly magistrate in his own sphere, even by analogy. Yet when Providence placed a guilty king at the mercy of the saints, the notion appeared in a new light: Jesus was the only divine king, and the hedges of divinity were removed from earthly kings to leave them mortal and guilty men, vulnerable in person and office to the headsman's axe. For the saints, the King's execution was beyond human agency, embedded in the providences of God. The 'wonderful hand of God,' said a typical letter from several General Baptist congregations to Oliver Cromwell, was manifest in 'bringing down the proud and haughty ones, making them to drink the wine of the cup of his fury, staining the pride of all their glory and pouring shame, judgement and contempt upon them.'[57] The saints thus became republicans, but theological and emotional rather than secular republicans. Their republicanism never transcended the limitations of its origin in the expedient decisions of December 1648 and January 1649. Tied to the Rump and to the New Model Army, it lacked any intellectual depth and any clear conception of institutional form, even of a theocratic kind. The institutions of parliamentary monarchy proved too strong for these republican saints because they had no firmly conceived vision of the secular state which might have prevented the Restoration.[58]

The lasting political achievement of the saints was negative, the end of divine right monarchy. Their positive achievement was religious and social, the creation of English nonconformity. The brief period of freedom that followed the execution of the King permanently changed the meaning of religious liberty in England. It permitted that luxuriant growth of 'notionists' so vividly described by Christopher Hill in *The World Turned Upside Down*: Seekers, Familists, True Levellers, Diggers, Ranters, and Quakers. Most of these new radicals had probably been members of separate churches before 'falling away' or 'rising above ordinances,' and they became the most pressing problem faced by the separate churches in the 1650s; the London Particular Baptists expressed it in the very title of their official *Heart-Bleedings for Professors Abominations* in 1650. Although the separate churches fought this threat with a flood of pamphlets and with personal encounters, they did not seek to revive the coercive power of the state in spiritual matters, and they firmly resisted the attempts of others to do so against Socinians and Quakers.[59] The pluralism of English nonconformity therefore was based on the spiritual liberty of the individual against not only the state and the state church but also against the claim to universality of any church at all. The Christian community was no longer conceived as universal.

APPENDIX A

SAMUEL EATON AND HIS CONGREGATION

At two points in the institutional development of the Jacob circle of churches – the nature of Samuel Eaton's rebaptism, and the fate of his congregation after his death in August 1639 – I have presented conclusions in this book at variance with the traditional Baptist interpretation, best stated in Dr B. R. White's recent articles, 'Samuel Eaton (d. 1639), Particular Baptist Pioneer' (*BQ*,* xxiv, 10–21, where several of the relevant documents are printed), and 'How did William Kiffin join the Baptists?' (*BQ*, xxiii, 201–7). My argument is given here.

The principal evidence concerning Eaton's rebaptism takes the form of statements in the Jessey and Kiffin memorandums. The Jessey memorandum, written by Jessey in 1641 several years before he was converted to believer's baptism, added to the report of the 1633 secession from the Jacob church the words, 'Mr. Eaton with some others receiving a further baptism.' In 1638, when six members of the Jacob church withdrew to join the congregation of John Spilsbury, Jessey gave as the reason that they were 'of the same judgement with Sam. Eaton,' meaning that they also sought a further baptism (Burrage, ii, 299). There is no evidence here as to the motive for rebaptism, but at this time (1641) Jessey would attach little importance to the distinction between ultra-separatist rebaptism and believer's baptism, as compared with the act of rebaptism in itself. To make any other inference would be to attribute to Jessey an insight that did not come to him until several years later.

The Kiffin memorandum (misleadingly named, since Kiffin was not a principal in these events) covers the same ground in reviewing the secessions from the Jacob church, but it was written several years later by a Particular Baptist for the purpose of reconstructing the events culminating in Richard Blunt's great immersion ceremony in January 1642. Since some members of Eaton's former church were involved in this ceremony, the Kiffin memorandum reported the 1633 secession from the Jacob church, but it did so without mentioning the rebaptism of Samuel Eaton and others. Since there is no reason to doubt the fact of Eaton's rebaptism, this omission in the Kiffin memorandum suggests that the Baptist author did not recognize it as believer's baptism. In dealing with the six dissidents who withdrew from the Jacob church to join Spilsbury in 1638 the Kiffin

* For abbreviations see p. 197.

memorandum remarked explicitly that they were 'convinced that baptism was not for infants, but professed believers' (Burrage, II, 302). This is the first recognition, by the Baptist author, of believer's baptism in the secessions from the Jacob church. The implication is that Eaton's rebaptism was not believer's baptism but ultra-separatist rebaptism.

Baptist historians have traditionally read the remark in the Jessey memorandum about 1638 in the light of what is said in the Kiffin memorandum about the same event, improperly construing their reading as evidence; thus, Dr White expressly 'collates' the two versions (*BQ*, vol. XXIV, p. 21, n. 25). The two memorandums are entirely distinct, and each is internally consistent in its own point of view. Thus the Jessey memorandum does not say or imply that Eaton practised believer's baptism. Neither does the Kiffin memorandum, nor does this latter associate Eaton in any way with the 1638 dissidents. Jessey could mention Eaton's name in connection with the 1638 dissidents because in 1641 he would not distinguish betwen believer's and ultra-separatist rebaptism. The silence of the Baptist author of the Kiffin memorandum about Eaton's rebaptism is a compelling argument against its being true believer's baptism.

A second consideration telling against Eaton's rebaptism as believer's baptism is the behaviour of the six dissident members who left the Jacob church seeking believer's baptism in 1638. Had they truly shared Eaton's judgement they could have joined his church. Their formal dismissal from the Jacob church, which occurred after their actual withdrawal and joining with Spilsbury, is dated 8 June 1638 (Burrage, II, 299). Samuel Eaton at this date was almost certainly at liberty and in active leadership of his congregation. Eaton's widow later claimed that he was in Newgate 'one whole year' before his death in late August 1639 (*BQ*, XXIV, 19). This makes it very unlikely that he was imprisoned in early June 1638, but even had this been the case his church continued in existence and Eaton discharged some of his pastoral functions in prison (ibid., pp. 16–17). The six dissidents, however, are said in both memorandums to have joined John Spilsbury (Burrage, II, 299, 302). The possibility that Spilsbury had taken over the leadership of Eaton's congregation upon Eaton's imprisonment, unlikely in any case in view of the timing, raises too many other difficulties to be acceptable. For instance, this would place in Eaton's congregation in 1638 four men, Richard Blunt (Burrage, II, 299), William Kiffin (ibid., p. 302), Thomas Shepard (ibid.), and John Spilsbury, each of whom in subsequent years was at the head of his own distinct Baptist congregation. Had this occurred, surely the Eaton church, under its successive (and unknown) pastors, rather than Jessey's church would have formed the focal point for the Kiffin and Knollys memorandums which give us a glimpse of the events lying behind the formation of the Baptist congregations of London. The evidence, slight as it is, will not bear this interpretation. In joining Spilsbury, the six dissidents from the Jacob church were avoiding the more closely related congregation under Eaton, presumably because they could not secure believer's baptism in the latter.

Other evidence about Eaton's rebaptism is too ambiguous to be conclusive. Eaton is reported to have preached in prison 'that baptism was the doctrine of devils and its original was an institution from the devil' (*BQ*, XXIV, 16); the latter phrase might be construed as a reference to a false church, as would be expected from an ultra-separatist. The statement of John Taylor the water-poet that Spilsbury rebaptized Eaton (ibid., p. 12), if it is not poetic license (linking two names known to have been involved in rebaptisms), does not prove Eaton was a Baptist because, as I have argued in the text (pp. 24–5), it is plausible for other reasons to conclude that Spilsbury practised an ultra-separatist rebaptism before arriving at believer's baptism.

There is no direct evidence for the fate of Eaton's congregation after his death in 1639, but the presence of two members, Richard Blunt and William Kiffin, in Jessey's congregation in subsequent years, raises the possibility that Eaton's congregation dissolved at his death; this is adopted in my text as the most likely explanation for the total silence surrounding this church after 1639. Blunt is identified as a member of the Eaton church in the Jessey memorandum, Kiffin in the Kiffin memorandum (Burrage, II, 299, 302). The author of the Kiffin memorandum, reviewing the successive divisions of the Jacob church, describes that of 1640 in these terms: 'The church became two by mutual consent just half being with Mr. P. Barebone, and the other half with Mr. H. Iessey Mr. Richard Blunt with him being convinced of baptism' (Burrage, II, 302). The words 'with him' can refer only to the immediately preceding Mr H. Jessey; Blunt joined the parent Jacob church after Eaton's death and remained with Jessey's branch when the church divided in 1640.

The case of William Kiffin is more ambiguous and also more important, for his presence in Jessey's church in 1643 provides, in part at least, the key to the formation of the Particular Baptist denomination and the issuing of the *Confession* of the seven churches in October 1644. The principal evidence is the Knollys memorandum, where 'B. Ki', almost certainly Brother Kiffin, is credited with an important speech in the controversy that broke out within the congregation when Hanserd Knollys refused to have his child baptized in 1643 (*TBHS*, I, 242). In my reconstruction of this difficult and obscure memorandum (pp. 55–6), Kiffin was the spokesman for the Baptists within Jessey's congregation, the leader of the group that decided that a true church must be based on believer's baptism, the pastor of the exclusively Baptist congregation formed by this group after their withdrawal from Jessey's church, and the main mover in the issuing of the *Confession* of the seven closed communion Baptist churches in October 1644. This interpretation presupposes that Kiffin had become a member of the Jessey church sometime after Eaton's death in 1639. The alternative interpretation, that Kiffin appeared as an outside consultant in the course of the baptism controversy in Jessey's church, raises too many difficulties to be acceptable. To suppose that Kiffin was a continuing member of Eaton's church at this date is purely conjectural, for there is no independent contemporary evidence for the existence of such a congregation. The Knollys memorandum expressly describes outside consultants as such, but does not place 'B. Ki' in this category. The most serious difficulty is that this conjecture makes it impossible to identify the leading Baptist spokesman within Jessey's congregation, or the leader and subsequent pastor of the group that withdrew from Jessey's church to form an exclusively Baptist congregation; nor would it be possible to identify this important new church among the seven churches signing the Baptist confession in 1644. William Kiffin fulfils these roles so adequately on the basis of the surviving documentation that there is no reason to adopt a purely conjectural alternative.

The view of Kiffin's career presented in this book is not incompatible with his reminiscences written down fifty years later. In his memoirs Kiffin was not concerned with our formal and analytical distinctions among the congregations of Eaton, Jessey, and Kiffin. He must have been more aware of the continuities, especially if a few individuals moved with him through these three associations; and undoubtedly his strongest recollection must have been his constant presence through all of his early career in a community of Christians larger than the individual congregations. His memories are accordingly stated in round figures, 'these forty years' (*BQ*, XXIII, 205), 'more than fifty years' (Kiffin, *Remarkable Passages*, p. 45), 'sixty years' (ibid., p. 89), which lack the precision necessary for a close analysis of his early career. The difference between the 'sixty years since it pleased the Lord to give me a taste of his rich grace and mercy in Jesus Christ,' and 'the congregation with whom I have walked for more than fifty years' is sufficient to accommodate his experience in the Eaton and Jessey churches before forming his own congregation at the end of 1643 or early 1644. The passage in his memoirs relating to 1643, although vaguely worded, amply conveys the atmosphere of crisis evident in the Knollys memorandum when Kiffin reports that he abandoned his successful business career to spend 'my time chiefly in studying the word of God' (ibid., p. 22). The sense of continuity in these memories reflects a reality of Kiffin's experience in London at this time, but there is no reason to believe, and no independent evidence to confirm, that this took the form of membership in a single congregation, originally Eaton's, which 'evolved' into the close communion Baptist congregation of William Kiffin (cf. Dr White, *BQ*, XXIII, 207).

APPENDIX B

BASTWICK'S ACCOUNT OF AN INDEPENDENT COVENANT

Buried in his verbose book of 1646, *The Utter Routing of the Whole Army of Sectaries*, Dr John Bastwick gave a description of the covenant of an Independent church dating from the time of the anti-episcopal alliance of 1641 and 1642. The passage is worth quoting in full as a rare account of an Independent church covenant of this period. That it is Independent rather than separatist is evident in the exalted position of the pastor in the first clause; the reference to a 'new light' suggests the covenant of Thomas Goodwin's church. The most surprising feature is the degree of control over the lives of members implied by the second and third clauses, since this has usually been associated with more radical sectarian congregations.

> I have been informed by some of them, when in familiar manner, and in the time of our friendship, I desired to know the method of admitting of their joint members, and especially what the Covenant imported, and what they promised in it, and what by it they were tied unto, and for answer they replied, 'that three things were contained in this their holy explicit Covenant.'
>
> First, 'That they promise and by this Covenant bind themselves to each other in all church fellowship, as to be helpful one to another in all things, and especially to their pastors, and to stand by one another without desertion of each other, and that in the greatest dangers and difficulties, and to yield obedience and willing subjection and conformity not only to those truths that are now embraced and entertained amongst them, but also willingly to submit themselves to all such New Light for the future, that God shall by his Word and by the ministry of their pastors discover unto the church.' This as I have been informed by the Independents, is the first thing they require of those that are to be admitted as members, and which they promise and covenant to perform.
>
> The second thing contained in the Covenant is, 'That if they be single persons either bachelors or maidens, widows or widowers, they may not marry without the consent of the church.'
>
> The third thing contained in this their holy Covenant is, 'That they may not remove their habitations and dwellings, though ever so advantageous unto them for their traffic and tradings, into any remote place from them, without the consent of the congregation,' and some other things there are comprised under this Covenant, which they keep among themselves as *arcana regni* as secrets of their kingdom. [pp. 306–7]

ABBREVIATIONS

Acts and Ordinances	C. H. Firth and R. S. Rait, *Acts and Ordinances of the Interregnum*, 3 vols. (1911)
Baillie	*Letters and Journals of Robert Baillie*, ed. David Laing, 3 vols. (Edinburgh, 1841–2)
BQ	*Baptist Quarterly*
Burrage	Champlin Burrage, *The Early English Dissenters*, 2 vols. (Cambridge, 1912)
CJ	*Journals of the House of Commons*
Clarke Papers	*The Clarke Papers*, ed. C. H. Firth, 4 vols., The Camden Society (1891–1901)
CSPD	*Calendar of State Papers, Domestic*
DNB	*Dictionary of National Biography*
EHR	*English Historical Review*
Gang. I	Thomas Edwards, *Gangraena* (1646) (several editions with varying pagination). The copy cited here is British Museum pressmark E. 323 (2)
Gang. II	Thomas Edwards, *The Second Part of Gangraena* (1646)
Gang. III	Thomas Edwards, *The Third Part of Gangraena* (1646)
LJ	*Journals of the House of Lords*
Shaw	W. A. Shaw, *A History of the English Church 1640–60*, 2 vols. (1900)
TBHS	*Transactions of the Baptist Historical Society*
TCHS	*Transactions of the Congregational Historical Society*
Whitelocke	Bulstrode Whitelocke, *Memorials of the English Affairs*, 4 vols. (Oxford, 1853)

NOTES

Preface

1 William Haller, *Liberty and Reformation in the Puritan Revolution* (New York, 1955), p. 203.

Introduction

1 B. R. White, *The English Separatist Tradition* (Oxford, 1971), pp. xii, xiv, 84.

1 The Jacob Church

1 Burrage, I, 281–326; John von Rohr, 'The Congregationalism of Henry Jacob,' *TCHS*, XIX (1962), 106–17, and '*Extra Ecclesiam Nulla Salus*: An Early Congregational Version,' *Church History*, XXXVI (1967), 107–21; Robert S. Paul, 'Henry Jacob and Seventeenth-Century Puritanism,' *The Hartford Quarterly*, VII (1967), 92–113. Cf. Geoffrey F. Nuttall, *Visible Saints: The Congregational Way 1640–1660* (Oxford, 1957), pp. 10–11. For the Elizabethan John Field, see Patrick Collinson, *The Elizabethan Puritan Movement* (1967), *passim.*

2 At the moment of separation from the Church of England, Henry Barrow and John Smyth were in their mid thirties, Robert Browne, Francis Johnson, and John Robinson were about thirty, Robert Harrison in his late twenties, Henry Ainsworth and John Greenwood in their early twenties.

3 Henry Jacob, *A Defence of the Churches and Ministry of Englande* (Middelburg, 1599), p. 38. The statement in the *DNB* life of Jacob that he went to Holland with the Brownists in 1593 cannot be substantiated.

4 Stuart Barton Babbage, *Puritanism and Richard Bancroft* (1962), pp. 52–3, 57, 70–1, 140–2; Collinson, *Elizabethan Puritan Movement*, pp. 452–63; [Henry Jacob], *A Christian and Modest Offer of a Most Indifferent Conference* ([Middelburg], 1606), pp. 28–30; Oliver Ormerod, *The Picture of a Puritane* (1605), sig. C4^{r} (I owe this last reference to the kindness of Richard Tyler).

5 Henry Jacob, *Reasons Taken Out of Gods Word* ([Middelburg], 1604); Burrage, II, 148–53, 165–6.

6 [Henry Jacob], *Christian and Modest Offer*, and *To the right High and mightie Prince, James.. .An humble Supplication for Toleration* ([Middelburg], 1609), p. 48. In 1605, before leaving England, Jacob had been associated with another request for toleration, Burrage, II, 161–5. His authorship of the *Modest Offer* is stated in *Supplication*, p. 43; his authorship of both is disguised in a later book, probably because Jacob wished to preserve the corporate character of these works (*An Attestation of many Learned Divines* [Middelburg], 1613, pp. 98, 137, 196).

7 Jacob, *Reasons*, pp. 4–5, 27–8.

8 Burrage, II, 163; White, *Separatist Tradition*, p. 112. In 1606 Jacob warned that if the bishops' persecutions continued, 'both the ministers and many of the people will be forced to leave their ordinary standing in these [parish] churches' (*Modest Offer*, p. 39).

9 Jacob, *Supplication*, pp. 8, 28.

10 Henry Jacob, *The Divine Beginning and Institution of Christs true Visible. . .Church* (Leyden, 1610), sigg. A8ff. and *passim*. This was a new emphasis rather than a novel idea; see *Reasons*, pp. 52–4.

11 See for instance Leland H. Carlson, ed., *The Writings of Henry Barrow 1587–1590* (1962), pp. 71–3, 509–12. For an expression of the idea in its mature Independent form, see Thomas Goodwin, *The Government of the Churches of Christ*, in *The Works of Thomas Goodwin*, 12 vols. (Edinburgh, 1861–6), XI, 303–8.

12 Both of Jacob's works that year, *A plaine and cleere Exposition of the Second Commandment*, and *Divine Beginning*, were published in Leyden, the latter expressly dated by Jacob at Leyden on 20 December 1610. This indicates the date of his well known conferences in Leyden with Robinson, Ames, and Parker. Burrage (I, 292) believed that this contact occurred after *Divine Beginning*, but in my judgement this work incorporates one of the main points on which Robinson probably influenced Jacob.

13 Henry Jacob, *A Declaration and Plainer Opening of Certain Points* ([Leyden], 1612), p. 18; *Attestation*, pp. 204, 209.

14 Ibid., pp. 164, 298–300.

15 Jacob, *Exposition*, sig. E6v; *Divine Beginning*, sig. A1v.

16 Ibid., sig. A4v.

17 Jacob, *Reasons*, pp. 35–7, 51–2.

18 Jacob, *Exposition*, sig. E6v; *Attestation*, p. 17.

19 I agree with Dr White's observation (*Separatist Tradition*, p. 167) that Robinson's influence on Jacob has been underestimated, but this does not mean that Jacob became a separatist. On the other hand, Jacob's influence on Robinson has been exaggerated; for while Robinson moderated his separatism in the matter of listening to sermons and in admitting members without a formal renunciation of the Church of England, he drew the line at intercommunion with the parish churches. This was a fundamental difference from Jacob's

position. Jacob permitted intercommunion because he took an essentially congregational view of the parish churches; Robinson could not accept it because he remained fundamentally true to his separatist view of the Church of England.

20 *A Confession and Protestation of the Faith of Certaine Christians in England* ([Middelburg], 1616), article 15.

21 Ibid., sig. E2^{r}.

22 Ibid., sig. A4^{v}; *A Collection of sundry matters* ([Middelburg], 1616), sig. A6^{v}.

23 *Confession*, sigg. A3–4, D5, E3.

24 A. T., *A Christian Reprofe against Contention* ([Amsterdam?], 1631), p. 17; Larzer Ziff, *The Career of John Cotton: Puritanism and the American Experience* (Princeton, 1962), p. 49.

25 *Confession*, article 4.

26 Ibid., article 8, and title page.

27 Ibid., article 11.

28 G. W. Prothero, *Select Statutes...of Elizabeth and James I* (Oxford, 1949), pp. 89–92; the act was continued through the reign of James I.

29 The Jessey memorandum forms part of a collection of documents known as the Stinton Repository which has been discussed critically by Burrage, I, 336–56, and by W. T. Whitley, *TBHS*, I, 197–205. Four items in the collection are relevant to the development of separate churches in London: (1) the Jessey memorandum, an account of the Jacob church from its foundation to 1641; (2) the Kiffin memorandum, an account of the introduction of believer's baptism by immersion in London in January 1642; (3) the Knollys memorandum, a set of jottings relating to the baptism controversy in Jessey's church between 1643 and 1645; (4) the How–More memorandum, a late seventeenth-century account of the separatist congregation led by Samuel How and Stephen More. These documents are printed by Whitley in *TBHS*, I, 203–45; II, 31–52; Burrage, II, 291–308, prints documents 1, 2, and excerpts from 4.

30 Burrage, II, 293. In view of Jacob's ostentatious connection with the silenced ministers there is no reason to doubt that it was the well known puritans Walter Travers and John Dod intended in the memorandum, both of whom may have been in London at this period; see *DNB*, John Dod, and S. J. Knox, *Walter Travers: Paragon of Elizabethan Puritanism* (1962), pp. 143–4. Richard Mansell or Maunsell was deprived of a living in Gloucestershire and was the subject of a celebrated legal case, Babbage, *Bancroft*, pp. 215, 272.

31 Burrage, II, 294; William Bradford, *Of Plymouth Plantation*, ed. S. E. Morison (New York, 1952), p. 9.

32 Staresmore also knew Sir Edward Coke, whose assistance he sought when arrested in 1618 at a conventicle, and in whose circle he perhaps first came to know the young Roger Williams: Bradford, *Of Plymouth Plantation*, pp. 354–9; Ola E. Winslow, *Master Roger Williams* (New

York, 1957), pp. 43–5; John Cotton, *A Reply to Mr. Williams his Examination*, in *The Complete Writings of Roger Williams*, 7 vols. (New York, 1963), II, 10.

33 Massachusetts Historical Society, *Collections*, 2nd series, V, 187–8; John Winthrop, *Winthrop's Journal*, ed. J. K. Hosmer, 2 vols. (New York, 1908), I, 66, 71–2.

34 John Bellamie, *A Justification of the City Remonstrance and its Vindication* (1646), pp. 20–9.

35 See Brown's letter of 12 February 1651 to Oliver Cromwell, in John Nickolls, ed., *Original Letters and Papers of State...of Mr. John Milton* (1743), pp. 58–60. This anonymous letter is endorsed as Mr. Chidley's letter, but Brown's authorship is clear from a comparison with his pamphlet, *To the Supream Authority of England* (1652).

36 *CSPD 1635–36*, p. 504.

37 Bellamie, *Justification*, p. 23; Burrage, II, 299.

38 David D. Hall, 'John Cotton's Letter to Samuel Skelton,' *William and Mary Quarterly*, 3rd series, XXII (1965), pp. 480–1. Of the remaining members of the early Jacob church nothing more than their names is known: David Prior, Andrew Almey, William Throughton, Mr Gibs, Edward Farre, Henry Goodall (Burrage, II, 294); and Daniel Ray of St Saviour's, Southwark (Bellamie, *Justification*, p. 23).

39 Ibid., p. 22; Shaw II, 130. Roborough was one of the scribes of the Westminster Assembly of Divines.

40 A. T., *Christian Reprofe*, p. 6; see also *Collection of Sundry Matters*, sig. B3ᵛ, where there is a reference to communicating 'once amongst the open wicked.'

41 Ibid., sig. A5, where it is said that each Christian is to keep God's ordinances 'for his own part so far as each one's part requireth.'

42 Bellamie, *Justification*, p. 23, gives instances in which children of members were baptized not merely in a parish church but specifically in the territorial parish church of the parents.

43 A. T., *Christian Reprofe*, p. 20. Burrage, I, 177, 321, at an important point in his argument interpreted this passage to mean that Staresmore had his child baptized in a parish church, but both the passage itself and the general argument of the Barrowist author make it perfectly clear that it was the Jacob church in which the Staresmore baptism occurred, probably in 1619 (see Bradford, *Of Plymouth Plantation*, p. 359).

44 *Confession*, articles 18, 25, 26.

45 *Collection*, sigg. A2ᵛ, B1ʳ, C5ᵛ.

46 Burrage, I, 172–7; II, 294; A. T., *Christian Reprofe*, *passim.* John Robinson's church at Leyden recognized the Jacob church as a true church, but this embroiled Robinson with the older Barrowist congregations, and the controversy embittered his later years at Leyden; see Walter H. Burgess, *John Robinson* (1920), pp. 140–1, 290–7.

47 A. T., *Christian Reprofe*, p. 5; Bellamie, *Justification*, p. 23.

48 Ibid., pp. 22–8.

49 Sabine Staresmore, *The Unlawfulnes of Reading in Prayer* ([Leyden], 1619), p. 6.

50 Ibid., p. 47.

51 Burrage, II, 295; Paul, *Hartford Quarterly*, VII, 98.

52 Burrage, II, 296; Bellamie, *Justification*, pp. 23–4; Samuel E. Morison, *The Founding of Harvard College* (Cambridge, Mass., 1935), p. 388. Lathrop may have left behind him at Egerton the rudimentary organization of a separatist church led by John Fenner; see *The Works of William Laud*, 7 vols. (Oxford, 1847–60), V, 336, 347–8.

53 This reconstruction of the episode is based upon the jumbled account in the Jessey memorandum, Burrage, II, 299, 301–2.

54 Burrage, II, 299; *CSPD 1635–36*, p. 86.

55 Burrage, II, 296–9, 313–14. The transcripts of the court appearances of the separatists are printed in full in S. R. Gardiner, ed., *Reports of Cases in the Courts of Star Chamber and High Commission*, Camden Society, 1886, with excerpts in Burrage, II, 311–22.

56 Elizabeth Milborne's petition states that she and her husband were imprisoned for a year and a half (*CSPD 1641–43*, p. 529); the Jessey memorandum says that the church suffered for 'the space of some two years, some only under bail, some in hold' (Burrage, II, 297).

57 Ibid., II, 298, 322; *TBHS*, I, 218–19; *CSPD 1641–43*, p. 518.

58 Burrage, II, 298–9; Winthrop, *Journal*, I, 136; Edmund S. Morgan, *Visible Saints: The History of a Puritan Idea* (New York, 1963), p. 86, n. 42.

59 Burrage, II, 306.

60 Ibid., II, 299.

61 *D.N.B.*, Henry Jessey; E[dward] W[histon], *The Life and Death of Mr. Henry Jessey* (1671), pp. 1–9; 'Letters of Henry Jacie', Massachusetts Historical Society, *Collections*, 3rd series, I, 235–46; 4th series, VI, 452–66.

62 Whiston, *Life of Jessey*, pp. 9–10; Geoffrey F. Nuttall, *The Welsh Saints* (Cardiff, 1957); Thomas Richards, *A History of the Puritan Movement in Wales 1639 to 1653* (1920), pp. 24ff. and *passim*.

63 Burrage, II, 302; Whiston, *Life of Jessey*, p. 11; John Taylor, *New Preachers, New* [1641], p. 6; J. C. Jeaffreson, ed., *Middlesex County Records*, III (1888), 170.

64 See Appendix A.

65 David Brown, *Two Conferences between...Separatists and Independents* (1650); the conferences of the title took place in 1645 and 1648.

66 Katherine Chidley, *The Justification of the Independent Churches of Christ* (1641), pp. 33, 36, 50.

67 Ibid., pp. 3–9, 22–3, 59, 69. This church also used the office of teacher (p. 3).

68 *Tub-preachers overturn'd* (1647); Burrage, II, 299, 301; Brown, *Two Conferences*, p. 1; *Milton State Papers*, pp. 60, 64.

69 *CSPD 1636–37*, p. 487; R[ice] B[oy], *The Importunate Beggar* (1635), p. 29, and *A Just Defence of the Importunate Beggars Importunity* (1636), preface; Edward Norice, *A Treatise* (1636), preface, and *The New Gospel* (1638), p. 51.

70 John Taylor, *A Swarme of Sectaries* (1641), p. 4; *Milton State Papers*, p. 64.

71 Pauline Gregg, *Free-born John: A Biography of John Lilburne* (1961), p. 326; D. Brown, *The Naked Woman* (1652), p. 14, remarks that women were not permitted to speak in this congregation.

72 Ibid., p. 14.

73 Brown, *Two Conferences*, pp. 9–10; *Milton State Papers*, pp. 60, 64, where the references to Pride are ambiguous, but Pride cannot be linked with any other London church.

74 Burrage, II, 299, 302; William Kiffin, *Remarkable Passages in the Life of William Kiffin*, ed. W. Orme (1823), pp. 14–15.

75 White, 'Samuel Eaton, Particular Baptist Pioneer,' *BQ*, XXIV, 10–21, where several of the relevant documents are printed in full. I do not agree with Dr White's conclusion that Eaton was a Baptist; see Appendix A.

76 Joseph Hall, *The Works of Joseph Hall*, IX (Oxford, 1863), 25; Thomas Wynell, *The Covenants Plea for Infants* (Oxford, 1642), preface.

77 *Writings of Barrow 1587–1590*, pp. 422–52; White, *Separatist Tradition*, pp. 142–9.

78 P[raise-God] B[arbone], *A Discourse Tending to prove the Baptisme* (1642). See also Samuel Chidley, *The Separatists Answer* (1651). In the same spirit the separatists in 1645 republished Francis Johnson's 'oddly tangential' arguments in *A brief Treatise* (1645).

79 The memorandum traditionally called the 'Kiffin manuscript' was not written by either Jessey or Kiffin but by a former member of the Jacob church who participated in the immersion ceremony of the Particular Baptists in January 1642, in which neither Jessey nor Kiffin was involved. It was probably prepared for use in the series of conferences among the Independents in 1645 which considered the later baptism crisis in Jessey's church; thus it has the sketchy character of the Jessey memorandum, which the author may have used in preparing his own notes. The Kiffin memorandum is printed in Burrage, II, 302–305, and in *TBHS*, I, 230–6.

80 Taylor, *Swarme of Sectaries*, p. 6.

81 John Spilsbury, *A Treatise Concerning the Lawfull Subject of Baptisme* (1643), preface, pp. 38–41. Spilsbury did not revise these opinions for the second edition of this work in 1652.

82 Samuel Chidley, *Separatists Answer*, preface, where Chidley said in 1651 that his answer to Spilsbury 'hath been of about ten years standing.'

83 The dissolution of Eaton's church is suggested by the presence of members like Richard Blunt and William Kiffin in Jessey's church at a later date; see Appendix A.

84 Burrage, II, 299, 304; *Gang.* III, 249.
85 Burrage, II, 302–5.
86 Spilsbury, *Treatise*, preface.
87 Daniel Featley, *The Dippers Dipt* (1645), pp. 3–18; William Kiffin, *A Sober Discourse of Right to Church Communion* (1681), 'To the Christian Reader,' where Kiffin said he had been a Baptist for forty years; see also Appendix A.

2 *'These Broken Times'*
London Separatism on the Eve of the Revolution

1 Kiffin, *Remarkable Passages*, pp. 11–12.
2 Ibid., pp. 14–15.
3 Edward Terrill, *The Records of a Church of Christ Meeting in Broadmead, Bristol*, ed. N. Haycroft, The Bunyan Library (1865), pp. 6–10.
4 Ibid., pp. 13–19; Champlin Burrage, 'Was John Canne a Baptist?' *TBHS.*, III (1912–13), 212–46; John F. Wilson, 'Another Look at John Canne,' *Church History*, XXXIII (1964), 34–48; A. E. Trout, 'Nonconformity in Hull,' *TCHS*, IX (1924–6), 29–43. While Burrage is undoubtedly correct that Canne was not a Baptist, his argument that Canne's visit to Bristol occurred in 1648 rather than 1641 seems to me to be going too far, for it would render Terrill's account of the visit totally unintelligible. It is not unlikely that Canne visited England in 1641 only to leave again in view of the continuing persecution of Brownists.
5 Terrill, *Broadmead Records*, pp. 24–9.
6 Taylor, *New Preachers, New*, title page; *CSPD 1640*, pp. 405, 416, 426, 430; *CSPD 1640–41*, p. 384; Roger Quatermayne *Quatermayns Conquest over Canterburies Court* (1642), pp. 19, 23.
7 Ibid., pp. 13, 24.
8 Ibid., pp. 28–9.
9 Collinson, *Elizabethan Puritan Movement*, pp. 84–91, 208–21, 372–82. See also Patrick Collinson, 'Towards a Broader Understanding of the Early Dissenting Tradition,' in C. Robert Cole and Michael E. Moody, eds., *The Dissenting Tradition: Essays for Leland H. Carlson* (Athens, Ohio, 1975), pp. 3–38.
10 Wilbur C. Abbott, *The Writings and Speeches of Oliver Cromwell*, 4 vols. (Cambridge, Mass., 1937–47), I, 95–6; Violet A. Rowe, *Sir Henry Vane the Younger* (1970), p. 7.
11 John Bunyan, *Grace Abounding to the Chief of Sinners* (Oxford, 1962), pp. 15ff.; *The Church Book of Bunyan Meeting 1650–1821*, p. 1, quoted in Nuttall, *Visible Saints*, p. 48.
12 *Gang*, I, 111–12.
13 Ziff, *John Cotton*, p. 49.
14 Bellamie, *Justification*, p. 29.

15 Christopher Hill, *Society and Puritanism in Pre-Revolutionary England* (1964), chapter 13.

16 For an example, see below p. 36 for the household of Thomas Hewson, John Lilburne's master.

17 Quatermayne, *Conquest*, p. 29.

18 Hill, *Society and Puritanism*, p. 467.

19 For examples, see below, pp. 44–5, 106.

20 Christopher Hill, *Economic Problems of the Church* (Oxford, 1963), p. 297.

21 Haller, *Liberty and Reformation*, p. 115.

22 Kiffin, *Remarkable Passages*, p. 3; Valerie Pearl, *London and the Outbreak of the Puritan Revolution* (1961), pp. 163–5.

23 *CSPD 1635–36*, pp. 242–3.

24 *CSPD 1648–49*, pp. 425–6.

25 *DNB*, John Everard; William Haller, *The Rise of Puritanism* (New York, 1957), pp. 206–12.

26 Norice, *Treatise*, pp. 156–64, and *New Gospel*, p. 8; C. E. Whiting, *Studies in English Puritanism from the Restoration to the Revolution, 1660–1688* (1931), pp. 314–16; B. R. White, 'John Traske (1585–1636) and London Puritanism,' *TCHS*, XX (1968), 223–33; *BQ*, XXIV, 18.

27 *The Brownists Synagogue* (1641), pp. 2–5. See Burrage, I, 205–8.

28 *Gang.* III, 248; John Spencer, *The Spirituall Warfare* (1642) was preached in the pulpit of St. Michael Crooked Lane.

29 Burrage, II, 296, 320–2.

30 *TBHS*, II, 36–52; *LJ*, IV, 133–4. John Canne was briefly pastor of this church in 1630, but he moved to Amsterdam with some of the members. He remained in communication with How's church; a member, Benjamin Pratt, a silkweaver living in Old Street in Holborn, was arrested in June 1634 when he tried to collect twenty copies of Canne's *Necessitie of Separation* from the Customs House, *CSPD 1634–35*, p. 119.

31 *Leveller Tracts*, p. 383. This sermon at the Nag's Head Tavern probably gave rise to the term 'tub-preacher.'

32 Kiffin contributed a postscript to the 1655 edition in which he recalled his acquaintance with How. See Haller, *Rise of Puritanism*, pp. 267–8.

33 *Leveller Tracts*, p. 408.

34 Ibid., p. 404; Massachusetts Historical Society, *Collections*, 3rd ser., I, 235, 240.

35 *Leveller Tracts*, pp. 401–8; Gregg, *Free-Born John*, pp. 52–6, 62; Samuel Chidley, *The Dissembling Scot* (1652), p. 4.

36 John Lilburne, *Copy of a Letter*, in *Innocency and Truth Justified* (1645), pp. 15–17, quoted in Haller, *Rise of Puritanism*, p. 275.

37 For Canne's role in printing Lilburne's early pamphlets, see Wilson, *Church History*, XXXIII, 38–41. For Lilburne's early pamphlets and the extensive range of his separatist contacts at this date, see Haller, *Rise of Puritanism*, pp. 432–40.

38 Burrage, I, 205–8; *The Brothers of the Separation* (1641), sig. A2; *CSPD 1637*, p. 49.

39 John Nalson, *An Impartial Collection of the Great Affairs of State*, II (1683), 265, 270; *Middlesex County Records*, III, 113.

40 Katherine Chidley, *Justification*, pp. 64–5, conceded that the Independent churches were 'narrow'; Barbone preached to a congregation of a hundred in 1641 (Taylor, *New Preachers, New*, p. 6); How's church may have had as few as thirty members in 1638, and only about eighty people were apprehended when the church was caught in Southwark in 1641 (*CSPD 1638–39*, pp. 186–7; Burrage, II, 323–4; *LJ*, IV, 133–4).

41 Burrage, II, 300–1, 314; Kiffin, *Remarkable Passages*, p. 15; Whiston, *Life of Henry Jessey*, pp. 10–11; Taylor, *New Preachers, New*, p. 6.

42 *TBHS*, II, 40; Kiffin, *Remarkable Passages*, p. 15; Katherine Chidley, *Justification*, p. 64; *Middlesex County Records*, III, 170.

43 Taylor, *New Preachers, New*, p. 6.

44 Katherine Chidley, *Justification*, p. 59.

45 The identification of these trades comes from the enemies of the lay pastors and cannot always be confirmed by other evidence.

46 Hill, *Society and Puritanism*, pp. 124 ff.

47 Karl S. Bottigheimer, *English Money and Irish Land* (Oxford, 1971), p. 181; Burrage, II, 303.

48 T. C. Dale, *The Inhabitants of London in 1638*, 2 vols. (1931), I, 173; Pearl, *London*, pp. 191–2.

49 Dale, *Inhabitants*, I, 144.

50 Ibid., I, 47; *TBHS*, II, 41.

51 Dale, *Inhabitants*, I, 38.

52 Ibid., I, 125.

53 Burrage, II, 301.

54 Dale, *Inhabitants*, I, 183, 109, 112.

55 *TBHS*, I, 243; *Clarke Papers*, I, 153; C. H. Firth and Godfrey Davies, *The Regimental History of Cromwell's Army*, 2 vols. (Oxford, 1940), II, 572–3.

56 [John Redmayne], *A True Narrative of the Proceedings in Parliament* (1659), p. 65; *Acts and Ordinances*, II, 1294. In 1654, William Puckle of Bread Street was a member of the committee for the ejection of scandalous ministers in London (ibid., II, 973), but this would not necessarily preclude his membership in Jessey's church; Jessey himself was one of the Triers.

57 Katherine Chidley, *Justification*, pp. 43–4.

58 Ibid., pp. 56–8.

59 The broader significance of popular anti-clericalism and the development of a lay religious leadership is assessed in James Fulton Maclear, 'The Making of the Lay Tradition,' *The Journal of Religion*, XXXIII (1953), 113–36.

60 Barbone, *Discourse*, pp. 10–11.

61 Burrage, II, 298.
62 Kiffin, *Remarkable Passages*, pp. 2–14.
63 Burrage, II, 300.
64 Kiffin, *Remarkable Passages*, p. 14; Morison, *Founding of Harvard College*, pp. 255, 344–5, 378–80; Bradford, *Of Plymouth Plantation*, p. 284. A warrant was issued in January 1637 for the arrest of Glover the elder and Glover the younger dwelling in Aldgate (*CSPD 1636–1637*, p. 360).
65 William Kiffin, ed., *The Life and Death of...Mr. Hanserd Knollys* (1692), preface, p. 16; Kiffin states that at Knolly's death in 1691 he had known him above fifty-four years.
66 Jeremiah Burroughes, *A Vindication of Mr Burroughes* (1646), pp. 20–2; Kiffin, *Remarkable Passages*, p. 14.
67 Benjamin Brook, *The Lives of the Puritans*, 3 vols. (1813), III, 299; *DNB*, Thomas Goodwin.
68 Massachusetts Historical Society, *Collections*, 3rd ser., I, 235–40, 246; 4th ser., VI, 460.
69 Ibid., VI, 459; J. T. Cliffe, *The Yorkshire Gentry From the Reformation to the Civil War* (1969), p. 273.
70 A. P. Newton, *The Colonising Activities of the English Puritans* (New Haven, 1914), pp. 177–86; Cliffe, *Yorkshire Gentry*, pp. 306–8.
71 Burrage, II, 291; G. Lyon Turner, 'Williamson's Spy Book,' *TCHS*, V (1911–12), 251.
72 Thomas Edwards, *Antapologia* (1644), pp. 22–3.
73 *The Apologeticall Narration* (1643), p. 6.
74 For Thomas Goodwin's authorship, see John F. Wilson, 'A Glimpse of Syons Glory,' *Church History*, XXXI (1962), 66–73.
75 Laud, *Works*, III, 389–91.
76 Lord Brooke, *A Discourse...of Episcopacie* (1642), p. 92.
77 *CSPD 1636–37*, pp. 427, 487.
78 *CSPD 1637*, p. 49. The books and papers of Burton and Prynne were siezed by virtue of a general warrant against separatists (*CSPD 1635–1636*, pp. 242–3). Henry Jessey was familiar with the terms of the indictment in 1637 (Massachusetts Historical Society, *Collections*, 4th series, VI, 461). Judith Manning was rebaptized by Blunt in January 1642 (Burrage, II, 304); a William Jackson belonging to Jessey's church was caught importing bibles in 1638 (*TBHS*, I, 253).
79 Massachusetts Historical Society, *Collections*, 4th series, VI, 460–4; Brown, *Two Conferences*, p. 2.
80 Laud, *Works*, III, 391; *BQ*, XXIV, 16.
81 Gregg, *Free-born John*, pp. 64–7; Haller, *Rise of Puritanism*, pp. 277–280.
82 Laud, *Works*, V, 337, 347; *CSPD 1636–37*, p. 341.
83 Burrage, II, 300–1; *Quatermayns Conquest*, pp. 20–1, 23–7. Quatermayne said (p. 20) that there had been a similar tumult a week earlier, on the Court's first day of term at St Paul's.

84 *CSPD 1640–41*, pp. 192, 384.
85 Laud, *Works*, III, 237; VI, 586; S. R. Gardiner, *History of England 1603–1642*, 10 vols. (1884), IX, 215.
86 *Leveller Tracts*, p. 406.
87 John Taylor, *The Anatomy of the Separatists* (1642), p. 6.
88 Edwards, *Antapologia*, p. 241.
89 *Life and Death of Hanserd Knollys*, p. 18; Kiffin, *Remarkable Passages*, p. 18; *Milton State Papers*, p. 60.
90 Gardiner, *History of England*, X, 179–82.
91 Brown, *To the Supream Authority*, pp. 4–7, 11, where Brown says that Sir Henry Vane junior was sent to him with the thanks of the House.

3 *Particular Baptists and Separatists*

1 Kilcop, *A short Treatise of Baptisme* [1642], To the Christian Reader.
2 Featley, *Dippers Dipt*, p. 9.
3 See Morgan, *Visible Saints*, pp. 125–38.
4 Winthrop, *Journal*, I, 297.
5 Thomas Patience, *The Doctrine of Baptism* (1654), Epistle to the Reader.
6 *Gang.* II, 16; III, 100.
7 [Henry Lawrence], *Of Baptisme* ([Rotterdam], 1646); Robert Baillie, *A Dissuasive from the Errours of the Time* (1646), p. 76; John E. Bailey, 'President Henry Lawrence and his Writings,' *Notes and Queries*, June, 1879, pp. 501–3; Perez Zagorin, *The Court and the Country* (1969), pp. 103–4.
8 Richard Baxter, *Plain Scripture Proof of Infants Church-membership and Baptism* (1651), preface, 'The true History of the Conception and Nativity of this Treatise.'
9 John Tombes, *An Apologie or Plea for the Two Treatises* (1646), p. 6.
10 Lucy Hutchinson, *Memoirs of the Life of Colonel Hutchinson*, ed. C. H. Firth, 2 vols. (1885), II, 101–3.
11 *Gang.* II, 16.
12 Barbone, *Discourse*, pp. 3–11.
13 Winthrop, *Journal*, I, 309.
14 *Gang.* III, 112–13; Francis Bampfield, *A Name, an After-one;. . .or, An Historical Declaration of the Life of Shem Archer* (1681), p. 16. Edwards' informant was a woman who had married a member of Thomas Lambe's General Baptist congregation, suggesting that Blunt's church was hurt by the rivalry of the Arminian Baptists as well as by the Seekers.
15 Kilcop, *Baptisme*, pp. 9–11; Robert Barrow, *A Briefe Answer to A Discourse* (1642).
16 Spilsbury, *Treatise*, pp. 40–1.

17 John Spilsberie, *Gods Ordinance, The Saints Priviledge* (1646), especially p. 37; Thomas Killcop, *Seekers Supplyed* (1646); R[obert] B[arrow], *A Briefe Answer to R. H.* (1646).

18 The first edition of the Particular Baptist confession of faith is printed in William L. Lumpkin, *Baptist Confessions of Faith* (Philadelphia, 1959), pp. 153–71.

19 *TBHS*, I, 239–45. The memorandum was perhaps written by Jessey.

20 Ibid., I, 240; *Gang*, I, 97.

21 *TBHS*, I, 240–3. See also Appendix A.

22 *TBHS*, I, 243–4.

23 *Gang.* I, 97; John Lightfoot, *The Whole Works*, XIII: *The Journal of the Proceedings of the Assembly of Divines*, ed. J. R. Pitman (1824), 302; *Life of Knollys*, pp. 30–1; *TBHS*, I, 244.

24 Stephen Marshall, *A Sermon of the Baptizing of Infants* (1644), p. 5.

25 Lumpkin, *Baptist Confessions*, p. 155.

26 See Table 2.

27 Spilsbury, *Treatise*, preface.

28 *TBHS*, I, 234. Shepard had earlier been a member of Samuel Eaton's church along with Richard Blunt (ibid., I, 220, 230).

29 Ibid., I, 234; *LJ*, IV, 133.

30 *TBHS*, II, 44.

31 Ibid., I, 235.

32 *A Confession of Faith of seven Congregations or Churches of Christ in London, which are commonly (but unjustly) called Anabaptists*, Second Impression corrected and enlarged (1646). This edition is reprinted in E. B. Underhill, ed., *Confessions of Faith...of the Baptist Churches of England*, Hanserd Knollys Society (1854), pp. 11–48.

33 *TBHS*, I, 244–5; Henry Jessey, *A Storehouse of Provision* (1650), p. 80.

34 *TBHS*, I, 244–5; Jessey, *Storehouse*, pp. 15, 80.

35 Whiston, *Life of Jessey*, pp. 83, 87–8; *TBHS*, I, 245. See also a pamphlet published by 'an ancient member of that long ago gathered congregation, whereof Mr. Henry Jacob was an instrument of gathering it,' *To Sions Virgins: or A Short Forme of Catechisme of the Doctrine of Baptisme*, dated by Thomason 4 November 1644, in which one of the older members of the Jacob church strenuously opposed the new practice of believer's baptism.

36 He was perhaps Trooper Thomas Shepherd of Ireton's regiment who was examined before the House of Commons on 30 April 1647. Although the soldier described himself as from Shropshire, this was not inconsistent with his having been a Londoner through most of his mature life; William Allen of Cromwell's regiment, examined at the same time, first described himself as a Warwickshire man, but on more detailed examination it came out that he had been a feltmaker of Southwark (*Clarke Papers*, I, 430–1).

37 *Gang.* III, 251–2, 254.

38 The parent congregation published a protest against the schismatics

(*Complainte de l'Eglise Francoise de Londres*, [London], 1645) and complained to the Westminster Assembly, which set up a committee to investigate the matter (Lightfoot, *Works*, XIII, 89).

39 *Gang.* I, 98.

40 *Gang.* I, 91.

41 Jessey, *Storehouse*, preface, p. 127.

42 *Leveller Tracts*, pp. 213, 229.

43 William Kiffin, *To Mr. Thomas Edwards* (1644).

44 Samuel Richardson, *Some brief Considerations on Doctor Featley his Book* (1645).

45 *A Declaration concerning the Publike Dispute which should have been in the Publike Meeting-House of Alderman-Bury...Concerning Infants-Baptisme* (1646); *The Lord Mayors Farewell...sent him in a Letter, by one of those who are usually (but unjustly) called Anabaptists* [1646]; *An Answer to A scandalous Paper, lately sent to...the Lord Mayor* (1646).

46 Martin Blake, *The Great Question* (1645), preface, pp. 2–3; Baxter, *Plain Scripture Proof*, preface; *Gang.* I, 95–6; Benjamin Cox, *An After-Reckoning with Mr. Edwards* (1646).

47 For Cox's preoccupation with Calvinist doctrine, see his letter, 'To the Reader,' in Spilsbury, *Gods Ordinance*, and his pamphlets, *Some Mistaken Scriptures Sincerely explained* (1646); *An Appendix to a Confession of Faith* (1646).

48 Tombes, *Apologie*, pp. 5–11; *Two Treatises and an Appendix to them concerning Infant-Baptisme* (1645).

49 Among those to whom Tombes found it necessary to reply within months of the publication of his *Two Treatises* in December 1645 were Stephen Marshall, Nathaniel Homes, Edmund Calamy, Richard Vines, John Geree, Thomas Bakewell, John Ley, William Hussey, and Thomas Blake (Tombes, *Apologie*, *passim*).

50 Tombes, *Two Treatises*, p. 19. For Tombes's later career, see A. J. Klaiber, *Bewdley Baptists 1649–1949* (1949), pp. 2–3.

51 Samuel Richardson, *Justification by Christ Alone* (1647); Thomas Kilcop, *Ancient and Durable Gospel*, (1648), pp. 20, 31.

52 Paul Hobson, *Christ the Effect not the cause of the love of God* (1645), p. 7.

53 Paul Hobson, *Practicall Divinity* (1646), pp. 86–7; *A Discovery of Truth* (1645); *A Garden Inclosed* (1647).

54 Hobson, *Practical Divinity*, p. 92.

55 Hobson, *Garden Inclosed*, p. 14. See also *A Testimony to the Truth of Jesus Christ* (1648), p. 9; H. John McLachlan, *Socinianism in Seventeenth-Century England* (Oxford, 1951), p. 222.

56 *CJ*, IV, 420–1.

57 Featley, *Dippers Dipt*, p. 184.

58 See article 21.

59 *Gang.* I, 184.

60 Robert Baillie, *Anabaptism the True Fountaine of Independency* (1646), pp. 48–52, 93–4.

61 Stephen Marshall, *A Defence of Infant-Baptism* (1646), pp. 75–6.

62 *Gang.* III, 65–6.

63 Not one of the important lay pastors of London appears in Dr. Nuttall's *Visible Saints*, the most authoritative history of the Congregationalists of this period.

64 'The Eschatology of Praise-God Barbone,' *TCHS*, IV, 64–78; James E. Farnell, 'The Usurpation of Honest London Householders: Barbone's Parliament,' *EHR*, LXXXII, 36–46.

65 Ibid., 36.

66 *Milton State Papers*, pp. 60, 64. In addition to the books and pamphlets listed under the names of members of this church in Wing, *STC*, David Brown was the author of the anonymous *Two Conferences* as well as *A Back-Blow to Major Huntington* [1648]; Sabine Staresmore was probably responsible for the broadsheet by S. S., *A Looking-Glasse, or Paralel, opposing The Prophane, Carnal Professor and true Believer* [n. d.]; and this church was probably responsible for another anonymous broadsheet, *A Confession of Faith, Of the Holy Separated Church of God* [n. d.].

67 Brown, *Two Conferences*, p. 2. For the connection of this church with the separatist Independent church at Bury St Edmunds in Suffolk, see 'The Bury St. Edmund's [sic] Church Covenants,' *TCHS*, II (1905–6), 333–4; *Gang.* III, 170–1; John Lanseter, *Lanseters Lance* (1646).

68 Katherine Chidley, *A New-Yeares-Gift* (1645), p. 0.

69 Henry Ainsworth used this as a separatist argument against John Paget in 1611, Alice Carter, *The English Reformed Church in Amsterdam in the Seventeenth Century* (Amsterdam, 1964), p. 56.

70 *Gang.* I, 79; Brown, *Two Conferences, passim; TCHS*, II, 33, and Nuttall, *Visible Saints*, p. 49; Samuel Chidley, *To His Highness the Lord Protector* [1656].

71 *TBHS*, II, 42–5. The only man who can be further identified, Peter Row, soon became a Baptist: Joseph Ivimey, *A History of the English Baptists* (1811), pp. 238–40, 247.

72 *Leveller Tracts*, p. 401.

73 *Gang.* III, 248–9.

74 *A Declaration of several of the Churches of Christ concerning the Kingly Interest of Christ* (1654); Daniel Featley, *Spongia or, Articles exhibited by certain Semi-separatists* (1643), pp. 23–6; *Acts and Ordinances*, I, 1010.

75 *Tub-preachers overturn'd* (1647); separatists: Duppa, Wilkins, and Barbone; Particular Baptists: Kiffin, Patience, and Hobson; General Baptists: Lambe, Tew, Oates, Ives, and Bulcher (presumably Fulcher); the unidentifiable names: Wiet a cobbler, Robine a saddler, Sammon a shoe-maker, Barde a smith, Fletcher a cooper, Parvis a goldsmith, Bignall a porter, Henshaw a confectioner, and Hawes a broker.

76 *Gang.* I, 111–12.

77 *Declaration of several Churches* (1654); Farnell, *EHR*, LXXXII, 30–3.

78 *Middlesex County Records*, III, 113; Nalson, *Impartial Collection*, II, 265. Banks cannot be traced further.

79 *TBHS*, I, 245. Jackson also appears as a radical in Major Butler, *The Fourth Paper* (1652), in Roger Williams, *Complete Writings*, VII, 119.

80 Farnell, *EHR*, LXXXII, 33–4.

4 *Anabaptists: the General Baptists*

1 The early General Baptists fall outside the scope of this book, but they have been well served by historians. See W. T. Whitley, ed., *The Works of John Smyth*, 2 vols. (Cambridge, 1915), Introduction; W. H. Burgess, *John Smyth The Se-Baptist, Thomas Helwys and the First Baptist Church in England* (1911); Benjamin Evans, *The Early English Baptists*, 2 vols., The Bunyan Library (1862–4); Burrage, I, 221–80; II, 172–259; *TBHS*, III, 18–30; White, *English Separatist Tradition*, chs. 6, 7, 8. For the writings of the early General Baptists, see W. T. Whitley, *A Baptist Bibliography*, I (1916). The brief account here is based on these works.

2 *Writings of Barrow 1587–1590*, pp. 424, 443, 445.

3 Thomas Helwys, *A Short Declaration of the mistery of iniquity* ([Amsterdam], 1612), pp. 211–12.

4 *CSPD 1639–40*, pp. 286, 426; *CSPD 1640*, pp. 379, 385, 389, 391, 421, 426, 430, 432, 434; *CSPD 1640–41*, p. 384.

5 Cox, 'To the Reader,' in Spilsbury, *God's Ordinance*.

6 Luke Howard, *A Looking-Glass for Baptists* (1672), p. 5.

7 Lambe's authorship of this pamphlet can be inferred from his views expressed in other works; it is also asserted by Thomas Crosby, *A History of the English Baptists*, 4 vols. (1738–40), III, 56.

8 *Fountaine of Free Grace*, pp. 13–14.

9 See the case of Samuel Fisher, a former General Baptist, in Hill, *World Turned Upside Down*, p. 209.

10 See especially Henry Denne, *Grace, Mercy, and Peace* (1645), *passim.*

11 Collinson, *Elizabethan Puritan Movement*, p. 37.

12 Edward Barber, *A Small Treatise of Baptisme, or Dippin* (1641), preface.

13 Edward Barber and Thomas Nutt, *The humble request of certain Christians reproachfully called Anabaptists* [1643].

14 *LJ*, IV, 135, 138; *Middlesex County Records*, III, 113; Nalson, *Impartial Collection*, II, 265.

15 Peter Chamberlen, *Master Bakewells Sea of Absurdities...Calmely Driven back* (1650), p. 3; *CSPD 1640*, pp. 379, 385, 389, 391, 432, 434.

16 *CSPD 1640–41*, p. 384; Featley, *Dippers Dipt*, sig. B4v. Thomas Seeles signed the General Baptist confession of 1660, where his name appears immediately after Clayton's.

17 Edward Dobson, *XIV Articles of Treason and other Misdemeanors* (Oxford, 1643), p. 3.

18 Historical Manuscripts Commission, *Sixth Report* (1877), Appendix, p. 46; *LJ*, VII, 97, 142, 185; H. R. Plomer, 'Secret Printing During the Civil War,' *The Library*, New series, v (1904), pp. 375–81.

19 *Gang.* I, 92; I. E., *The Anabaptists Groundwork for Reformation* (1644), preface.

20 *Gang.* I, 92–5.

21 Wynell, *Covenants Plea*, p. 70.

22 Ibid., preface, p. 70; John Stalham, *The Summe of a Conference at Terling in Essex* (1644); *Gang.* I, 92–3, 181; III, 30.

23 *DNB*, Henry Denne; E. B. Underhill, ed., *Records of the Churches of Christ, Gathered at Fenstanton, Warboys, and Hexham, 1644–1720*, Hanserd Knollys Society (1854), pp. 251–4, 266–9, 283–4; Henry Denne, *The Doctrine and Conversion of John Baptist* (1643); Reginald L. Hine, *History of Hitchin*, 2 vols. (1927–9), I, 184; *Gang.* I, 76–7, 181–2; Firth and Davies, *Regimental History*, I, 110–14.

24 The earliest contemporary reference to Oates is in John Lightfoot's journal of the Westminster Assembly in 1643, where he is described as a notorious Anabaptist 'about Norwich' and distinguished from a clergyman of the same name (*Works*, XIII, 81). Oates subsequently based his authority to evangelize upon his lawful call from the congregation at Norwich (John Drew, *A Serious Addresse to Samuel Oates*, 1649, pp. 10–12).

25 *Gang.* I, 92–4, 182, Appendix; II, 3–4, 10, 146–8; III, 105–6, Edward Drapes, *A Plain and Faithfull Discovery* (1646), p. 13; *The Diary of the Rev. Ralph Josselin*, Camden Society, 3rd ser. (1908), p. 33; John Stalham, *Vindiciae Redemptionis* (1647), preface; *LJ*, IX, 570–3, 619, 673; X, 258, 259.

26 Edward Barber, *A Declaration and Vindication of the carriage of Edward Barber* (1648).

27 *Gang.* I, 104–5.

28 Henry Danvers, *A Treatise of Laying on of Hands* (1674), p. 58. Danvers cited 'an eye and ear-witness' who placed this event in 'that baptized congregation then meeting in the Spittle Bishopsgate Street,' at the opposite end of Bishopsgate Street from Barber's church; this was certainly Lambe's church. Cornewell's appearance must have occurred between the move of Lambe's church from Bell Alley to the Spital, sometime in the second half of 1645, and the ceremony in Barber's church on 12 November 1645; the division in Lambe's church occurred slightly later, early in 1646.

29 Ibid., pp. 58–9; Walter Wilson, *The History and Antiquities of Dissenting Churches. . .in London*, 4 vols. (1808–14), II, 175–9. The dating of this division to 1646 is confirmed in Griffith's funeral sermon in 1700, where he was said to be 'about fifty-four years a pastor' and 'devoted to the Lord' for three-score years (ibid., II, 176); this suggests

that he may have been a General Baptist and presumably a member of Lambe's church from about 1640.

30 *Gang.* II, 9; III, 110.

31 Samuel Loveday, *The hatred of Esau* (1650); *To the King of these Nations, The Humble Representation of several Societies, commonly called...Anabaptists* (1660). It seems unlikely that this was the Samuel Loveday listed as a householder in the parish of St Thomas the Apostle (Dale, *Inhabitants*, I, 182) in 1638, when the future Baptist pastor was nineteen years old, or the author of *The Answer to the Lamentation of Cheapside Crosse* in 1642.

32 *Gang.* III, 88.

33 *DNB*, William Kiffin; Bodleian MS. Rawl. A 38, fol. 487.

34 *Gang.* I, 84, 88–9, Appendix; II, 24–5, 105–6; III, 14, 113. Even the forceful Katherine Chidley was debarred by her sex from the senior offices of her congregation (Brown, *Naked Woman*, p. 14), although she engaged in public disputes (*Gang.* I, 79–80). See also Keith Thomas, 'Women and the Civil War Sects,' *Past and Present*, no. 13 (1958), pp. 42–62.

35 *Gang.* I, 84–8, Appendix.

36 *LJ*, IX, 572–3; A. G. Matthews, *The Congregational Churches of Staffordshire* [1924], p. 34; Howard, *Looking-Glass for Baptists*, p. 5; Robert Purnell, *Good Tydings for Sinners* (1649), p. 61; *Gang.* I, 82; III, 36–7, 110.

37 *Gang.* II, 17–18.

38 R[ichard] O[verton], *Mans Mortalitie* (Amsterdam [London], 1644), pp. 17, 23, and *passim*. See also P. Zagorin, 'The Authorship of *Mans Mortallitie*,' *The Library*, 5th ser., V (1950), 179–83; H. N. Brailsford, *The Levellers and the English Revolution* (1961), pp. 51–2; Norman T. Burns, *Christian Mortalism from Tyndale to Milton* (Cambridge, Mass., 1972).

39 *Gang.* I, 81–2.

40 *Gang.* I, 81, 83–4. See also Hill, *World Turned Upside Down*, p. 213.

41 Luke Howard, *Love and Truth in Plainness Manifested* (1704), pp. 5–8. In 1642, when he was 21, Howard lived briefly in Coleman Street and attended John Goodwin's ministry, where, he said, 'I was as it were received as a member.' Both Howard's qualifying phrase and the date 1642 make it clear that he was not a member of Goodwin's gathered church.

42 Ibid., pp. 9–11.

43 Thus Lawrence Clarkson spoke of his long career as a Ranter as 'notional worship' (*The Lost sheep found*, 1660, p. 34). See also the descriptions of Richard Farnworth and Isaac Penington the younger, cited in Richard T. Vann, *The Social Development of English Quakerism* (Cambridge, Mass., 1969), pp. 24, 26–7.

44 Howard, *Love and Truth*, pp. 11–15; it was among such 'shattered

Baptists' that George Fox found his earliest converts (*The Journal of George Fox*, ed. John Nickalls, Cambridge, 1952, p. 25).

45 Clarkson, *Lost Sheep*, p. 10.

5 *King Jesus and the gathering of Independent Churches in London*

1 Thomas Goodwin, *Works*, XII, 63; Wilson, *Church History*, XXXI, 66–73.

2 Henry Burton, *The Protestation Protested* (1641), sigg. A4v, B3r. See also Katherine Chidley, *Justification*, p. 11; William Sedgewick, *Scripture a Perfect Rule for Church-Government*, pp. 37–8, cited in John F. Wilson, *Pulpit in Parliament* (Princeton, 1969), p. 51, and placed by Wilson in mid 1641. Sedgewick was closely linked with the Independents at this period and became chaplain of Sir William Constable's regiment in 1642; but his development in the 1640s took him in a Seeker direction akin to that of William Dell and John Saltmarsh rather than to the gathered church (*DNB*, William Sedgewick).

3 Quoted in David Underdown, *Pride's Purge* (Oxford, 1971), p. 37.

4 There is no trace of millenarianism in Jacob's writings, but he shared his exile in Middelburg for half a dozen years with Hugh Broughton, whose *A Revelation of the Holy Apocalyps* was published in 1610. For Broughton, who died in 1612, see *DNB;* Wilson, *Pulpit in Parliament*, p. 215, suggests Broughton's influence was strongest on the expatriates in the Netherlands.

5 A. S. P. Woodhouse, *Puritanism and Liberty* (1951), pp. 234, 237, 240–1. Woodhouse (pp. 233–41) prints excerpts from the sermon, which is also reprinted in Thomas Goodwin, *Works*, XII, 61–79. The famous reference to 'common people' cannot be used to determine the social standing of Goodwin's audience because he was speaking ironically, with the lordly bishops and their lofty attitude to the vulgar multitude in mind, as the rest of the passage shows; the irony was heightened if Sir William Constable, Sir Richard Saltonstall, Sir Matthew Boynton, and Henry Lawrence were among his audience (Burrage, II, 291). At the same time Goodwin intended to encourage those of genuinely humble rank by reminding them of the maidservants' riot at St Giles's in Edinburgh in 1637 (Gardiner, *History of England*, VIII, 314).

6 Wilson, *Pulpit in Parliament*, pp. 207–35. See also Tai Liu, *Discord in Zion: The Puritan Divines and the Puritan Revolution 1640–1660* (The Hague, 1973), chapters 1, 2.

7 According to Thomas Edwards, *Antapologia* (1644), pp. 23, 187, Archer was the pastor of the Arnhem church from his arrival there in 1637. Edwards also states that he died there, being one of the men described in the *Apologeticall Narration* as a victim of life in exile, and the *Personalle Raigne* was perhaps published posthumously.

8 Thomas Goodwin, *A Sermon of the Fifth Monarchy* (1654), and *The World to Come* (1655).

9 Wilson, *Pulpit in Parliament*, p. 227; Nuttall, *Visible Saints*, pp. 146–148; Henry Burton, *The Sounding of the Two Last Trumpets* (1641); Nicholas Lockyer, *Christs Communion with his Church Militant* (1644, 1st edn. 1641).

10 Louise Fargo Brown, *The Political Activities of the Baptists and Fifth Monarchy Men in England During the Interregnum* (Washington, 1912), *passim*. This work substantially exaggerates Baptist involvement in the Fifth Monarchy movement by mistakenly identifying as Baptists a large number of Independents, including William Steele, William Dell, Samuel Moyer, John Barkstead, John Canne, and George Cockayne, as well as the Independent or separatist congregations of Praise-God Barbone, Samuel Highland, and John Fenton.

11 Thus there is no hint of millenarianism in Thomas Goodwin's authoritative statement of the kingship of Christ in 1645, in his *Works*, XI, 303 ff. Cf. Wilson, *Pulpit in Parliament*, p. 229.

12 Edwards makes this charge in *Antapologia*, p. 217.

13 For this, see the important book by Michael Fixler, *Milton and the Kingdoms of God* (1964), pp. 74, 77–8, 99, 103, and *passim*.

14 Edwards, *Antapologia*, pp. 240–1. See also John Vicars, *The Schismatick Sifted* (1646), pp. 15–16; Baillie, I, 311. Vicars placed the meeting about November 1641.

15 William M. Lamont, *Marginal Prynne 1600–1669* (1963), pp. 59–64. See also Lamont, *Godly Rule, Politics and Religion 1603–60* (1969), p. 51; Wilson, *Pulpit in Parliament*, pp. 215–23; Fixler, *Milton*, ch. 1; Christopher Hill, *Antichrist in Seventeenth-Century England* (1971), pp. 26–7, 99.

16 Baillie, II, 313; *Dissuasive*, pp. 224 ff.

17 William Haller, *Foxe's Book of Martyrs and the Elect Nation* (New York, 1963), ch. 7.

18 Nuttall, *Visible Saints*, pp. 9–14. Dr Nuttall quite rightly emphasizes the diffuseness of the development of Congregationalism in England; my point here is limited to his failure also to give due weight to those events that occurred between 1641 and 1643 in London.

19 Perry Miller, *The New England Mind: The Seventeenth Century* (Cambridge, Mass., 1954), p. 434; S. R. Gardiner, *History of the Great Civil War*, 4 vols. (1901), I, 264, 268.

20 Nuttall, *Visible Saints*, pp. 14–17, comments upon Cotton's influence.

21 Perry Miller, *Orthodoxy in Massachusetts 1630–1650* (Boston, 1959), *passim;* Ziff, *John Cotton*, *passim*.

22 Philip Nye quoted from Jacob's *Attestation* (p. 115) of 1613 in a work written in the decade after the Restoration, *The Lawfulness of the Oath of Supremacy* (1683), cited in D. Nobbs, 'Philip Nye on Church and State,' *Cambridge Historical Journal*, V (1935), 55. It is

typical of the extreme reticence of the Independent leaders to express themselves in print on church government that Nye's work was published posthumously.

23 John Bastwick, *The Utter Routing of the Whole Army of Sectaries* (1646), p. 297. Bastwick had lived with William Ames for two years when he was studying at the University of Franeker, *The Second Part of...Independency Not Gods Ordinance* (1645), preface, sig. A3v.

24 Thomas Goodwin, *Works*, XI, 536.

25 Jeremiah Burroughes, *Vindication*, p. 15; cf. Jacob, *Confession*, article 11.

26 Burton, *Protestation Protested*, sigg. B3r–C1v. Burton also said that the pastors of such gathered churches eschewed tithes and would be content with the 'competent maintenance' allowed them 'freely, without any compulsion,' by their congregations (sig. C3r).

27 Woodhouse, *Puritanism and Liberty*, p. 241.

28 For an explicit expression of a similar argument, see William Kiffin, *A Briefe Remonstrance of The Reasons and Grounds of those People commonly called Anabaptists* (1645), p. 6: 'our congregations were erected and framed as now they are, according to the rule of Christ, before we heard of any Reformation, even at that time when Episcopacy was in the height of its vanishing glory...and we hope you will not say, we sinned in separating from them whose errors you now condemn.'

29 Edwards, *Antapologia*, pp. 222–3.

30 *A Copie of two writings sent to the Parliament, The one intituled Motions for reforming of the Church of England...The Other A Humble Petition* ([Amsterdam], 1641), sig. C2r. That this was an Independent rather than a strict separatist petition is evident in the request (sig. B1v) 'that some zealous and godly ministers who have been forced to fly out of the realm by reason of the prelates' persecution may be called home' to attend any 'committee or convocation and meeting of some divines to treat of the thing [church government].'

31 Thomas Edwards, *Reasons against the Independent Government of Particular Congregations* (1641), preface, introduction, p. 39. See Appendix B.

32 Edwards, *Antapologia*, p. 222; *Gang.* II, 16; Brook, *Puritans*, III, 312. Symonds was in England in mid 1641 when he preached before Parliament (Wilson, *Pulpit in Parliament*, pp. 48, 276), but he returned to Rotterdam where he remained until late 1646 (ibid., p. 248).

33 Edwards, *Reasons*, p. 39.

34 Wilson, *Pulpit in Parliament*, pp. 48, 276; Brook, *Puritans*, III, 39–40. Of the returned exiles, Jeremiah Burroughes, John Bachelor, and William Sedgewick took neither parish nor gathered churches under their pastoral charge.

35 Lord Brooke, *Discourse of Episcopacie*, p. 100–4.
36 Thomas Goodwin, *Works*, XI, 5.
37 Burton, *Protestation Protested*, sig. B4.
38 *Mercurius Aulicus*, 9–16 April 1643, p. 184; Anthony Wood, *Athenae Oxoniensis*, ed. P. Bliss, 4 vols. (1815–20), III, 1168–9.
39 Terrill, *Broadmead Records*, p. 26.
40 *A Secret Negotiation*, pp. 5–6, in *The Camden Miscellany*, vol. VIII, Camden Society (1883).
41 Lightfoot, *Works*, XIII, 46; Edwards, *Antapologia*, pp. 253, 307; John Vicars, *The Picture of Independency* (1645), p. 9.
42 Baillie, II, 111, 193.
43 Edwards, *Antapologia*, pp. 253, 307; A. T. Jones, *Early Days of Stepney Meeting* [1887], pp. 4, 11.
44 *Gang.* II, 16.
45 Baillie, II, 211–12. Edwards suggested that Sidrach Simpson's congregation especially suffered from Seekers (*Antapologia*, p. 295; *Gang.* II, 16).
46 See above p. 88.
47 Wilson, *Church History*, XXXI, 68–9. The Independent clergy cited Mrs. Chidley's arguments with approval: John Goodwin, *Anapologesiates Antapologias* (1646), pp. 12, 168–9, 181; John Bastwick, *Independency Not Gods Ordinance* (1645), p. 110.
48 Lightfoot, *Works*, XIII, 56–7, 62; Edwards, *Antapologia*, p. 5; Baillie, II, 111.
49 Edwards' protest in *Antapologia* has been ignored by historians, for example, Nuttall, *Visible Saints*, pp. 11–14; George Yule, *The Independents in the English Civil War* (Cambridge, 1958), pp. 10–11; Gardiner, *Great Civil War*, I, 261–9, especially p. 268, where Gardiner stated his belief that the apologetical narrators rejected the intention 'to form separate congregations unconnected with the principal Church of the nation.'
50 Thomas Goodwin *et al.*, *An Apologeticall Narration* (1643 [Thomason's date, 3 January 1644]), p. 24. Goodwin and Nye repeated their dedication to the 'middle-way' in their introduction to John Cotton's *The Keyes of the Kingdom of Heaven* (1644), reprinted in Woodhouse, *Puritanism and Liberty*, p. 296.
51 *Apologeticall Narration*, p. 16.
52 Except ibid., p. 6–7, where visitors from England were said to be admitted to communion in the exiled churches on the strength of their parochial church membership in England.
53 Baillie, II, 145–6. Nye's arguments upon this occasion are undoubtedly those given in Thomas Goodwin, *Works*, XI, 465–6.
54 A. F. Mitchell and J. Struthers, eds., *Minutes of the...Westminster Assembly of Divines* (Edinburgh, 1874), pp. 132–3; Baillie, II, 266–7, 271, 291, 296, 306, 315; Vicars, *Schismatick Sifted*, p. 19.
55 Thomas Goodwin, *The Government of the Churches of Christ*, in

Works of Thomas Goodwin, vol. IV (1697), reprinted in *Works*, vol. XI. It is clear both from the subjects considered and from references to the accommodation committee that this important work was mostly if not completely written during the period when the Independents still hoped to influence the Assembly in 1645.

56 Thomas Goodwin, *Works*, XI, 303; John Goodwin, *Anapologesiates*, p. 137; Brown, *Two Conferences*, p. 3.

57 Wilson, *Pulpit in Parliament*, *passim;* Paul S. Seaver, *The Puritan Lectureships* (Stanford, 1970), p. 281.

58 Henry Burton, *Truth still Truth, Though Shut out of Doores* (1645), p. 29; Brown, *Two Conferences*, p. 4; Edwards, *Antapologia*, p. 51; Baillie, *Dissuasive*, pp. 174–6.

59 Thomas Goodwin, *Works*, XI, 352, 370.

60 John Goodwin, *Innocencies Triumph* (1644), p. 15.

61 *Gang.* I, 79–80.

62 Baillie, *Dissuasive*, p. 123.

63 Edwards, *Antapologia*, pp. 51, 217, 222, 243–4, 268.

64 Ibid., p. 51; Baillie, *Dissuasive*, p. 105; John Goodwin, *Anapologesiates*, pp. 158–9.

65 Edwards, *Antapologia*, pp. 49–50; *Gang.* II, 13.

66 Woodhouse, *Puritanism and Liberty*, p. 296; Baillie, *Dissuasive*, pp. 118, 175–6. On this point the English Independents differed from Cotton.

67 Thomas Goodwin, *Works*, XI, 294, 352. Cf. Katherine Chidley, *Justification*, pp. 5–6, 20–1; *A New-Yeares-Gift*, pp. 14–16.

68 Thomas Goodwin, *Works*, XI, 377–88.

69 Ibid., pp. 468–9; Shaw, II, 147–8.

70 John Goodwin, *Anapologesiates*, p. 185; *Theomachia* (1644), p. 25. See also [Edmund Calamy], *The Door of Truth Opened* (1645), p. 14; *Papers Given in to the Honorable Committee. . .For Accommodation* (1648), *passim;* Thomas Goodwin, *Works*, XI, 462–72; Burroughes, *Vindication*, p. 15.

71 Baillie, II, 307.

72 As Dr Nuttall seems to suggest, *Visible Saints*, pp. 133–7. Dr Nuttall was perhaps influenced by the later concern of Richard Baxter to find common ground between Independents and Presbyterians. See also Lamont, *Godly Rule*, pp. 113, 119–20, 127, 144–50; and Lamont's article, 'Richard Baxter, The Apocalypse and the Mad Major,' *Past and Present*, no. 55 (1972), pp. 86–8.

73 C. Gordon Bolam, Roger Thomas, *et al.*, *The English Presbyterians* (1968), pp. 21, 53–7.

74 Thomas Goodwin, *Works*, XI, 307–8. See also Bolam, *English Presbyterians*, p. 57, where Roger Thomas observes, 'There was and in fact could be no middle way or compromise between these conflicting religious ideals' of the gathered church and the parish church.

75 Bastwick, *Independency Not Gods Ordinance*, p. 99; Nuttall, *Visible Saints*, chapter 4; Morgan, *Visible Saints*, *passim*.

76 Baillie, *Dissuasive*, p. 106.

77 Thomas Goodwin, *Works*, XI, 353.

78 Ibid., 353–8.

79 *Leveller Tracts*, p. 258; Bastwick, *Independency*, pp. 142–3; Edwards, *Antapologia*, p. 222; *Gang.* II, 17; Vicars, *Picture of Independency*, p. 10; Lord Clarendon, *The History of the Rebellion and Civil Wars in England*, ed. W. D. Macray, 6 vols. (Oxford, 1888), IV, 311.

80 *Gang.* II, 16–17.

81 A. G. Matthews, *Calamy Revised* (Oxford, 1934), p. 326; Wilson, *Pulpit in Parliament*, pp. 128–9, 248, 253, 254; Abbott, *Cromwell*, II, 379, 415, 477, 568; T. G. Grippen, 'Nicholas Lockyer: A Half-forgotten Champion of Independency,' *TCHS*, IX (1924–6), 64–77.

82 Lockyer held a regular parochial lectureship in London, perhaps at St Pancras Soper Lane, for Edmund Calamy said in 1645 (*Door of Truth Opened*, p. 15) that Lockyer had engaged to the minister of the parish where he lectured not to preach on Independency.

83 Lightfoot, *Works*, XIII, 46; Edwards, *Antapologia*, pp. 253, 307; *Gang.* II, 16. John Bachelor, a clergyman who had been in exile in Rotterdam (*Antapologia*, pp. 48, 185), an army chaplain (*Gang.* III, 266) and one of the licensers of the press appointed by Parliament (*Gang.* III, 102–5), may have been a member of Lockyer's church. He was linked ambiguously with Lockyer in *Antapologia* (p. 253), he was said to be 'no minister' (*Gang.* II, 139), and he shared Lockyer's appointment as preacher at Windsor Castle in 1649 (Shaw, II, 524).

84 Vicars, *Picture of Independency*, p. 9; John Goodwin, *Anapologesiates*, pp. 108, 139–44.

85 *A Second Narrative*, reprinted in *The Harleian Miscellany*, VI (1810), 501.

86 *Leveller Tracts*, pp. 417, 421, 424; *A Paire of Spectacles for The Citie* (1648), p. 9.

87 Matthews, *Calamy Revised*, p. 124; *DNB*, George Cokayne; C. Bernard Cockett, 'George Cokayn,' *TCHS*, XII (1933–6), 225–35; Underdown, *Pride's Purge*, pp. 234, 261; H. R. Trevor-Roper, *Religion, the Reformation and Social Change*, 2nd edn. (1972), pp. 330–1.

88 Yule, *Independents*, p. 141, following Matthews, *Calamy Revised*, p. 124, dates Cokayn's appointment at St Pancras to 1646, but the living was vacant in October 1648 (Shaw, II, 103) and his appointment was probably made after that date.

89 Tichborn lived in the parish of St. Michael Le Querne (H. A. Dillon, 'On a MS. List of Officers of the London Trained Bands in 1643,' *Archeologia*, LII (1890), 136; Dale, *Inhabitants*, I, 152); Rowland Wilson in the parish of St Lawrence, Old Jewry (ibid., I, 84).

90 Edwards, *Antapologia*, p. 222; *A Secret Negotiation*, p. 34.

91 Daniel Neal, *The History of the Puritans*, ed. Dr Toulmin, 5 vols. (1882), II, 288.

92 J. C. Whitebrook, 'Sir Thomas Andrewes, Lord Mayor and Regicide, and his Relatives,' *TCHS*, XIII (1937–9), 151–65 (the problem of Andrewes' residence raised by Whitebrook, p. 155, seems to be settled by Dale, *Inhabitants*, I, 102, which establishes the moderated rent of Andrewes' house next to his shop at £30); Pearl, *London*, pp. 309–11 and *passim;* Seaver, *Puritan Lectureships*, p. 257–8; Brook, *Puritans*, III, 311–13; Neal, *Puritans*, II, 288, where Neal gives a list of exiles from an unknown source, which is, in part at least, correct. This is the only source for Andrewes' exile.

93 Edwards, *Antapologia*, pp. 35, 143; John Goodwin, *Anapologesiates*, p. 239; Neal, *Puritans*, II, 288; *Leveller Tracts*, pp. 415–21. After the Restoration there was a Colonel White in exile in Rotterdam again (*TCHS*, v, 255, 312).

94 Neal, *Puritans*, II, 288; C. V. Wedgwood, *The Trial of Charles I* (Fontana edn. 1967), pp. 118–19, 146.

95 *DNB*, Sidrach Simpson; Nuttall, *Visible Saints*, p. 12 (both confuse Sidrach with John Simpson in reporting the former as being imprisoned under the Protectorate); Edwin Freshfield, *Some Remarks upon the...History of the parish of St. Stephen, Coleman Street* (Westminster, 1887), p. 11; Shaw, II, 109, 269; *TCHS*, XIII, 160–1.

96 Cliffe, *Yorkshire Gentry*, pp. 306–8, 332–3, 337, 346–7, 351, 353 and *passim*; Firth and Davies, *Regimental History*, II, 399–402; *TCHS*, IX, 32.

97 Baillie, *Dissuasive*, p. 76; Alexander Forbes, *An Anatomy of Independency* (1644), p. 25; *DNB*, Henry Lawrence.

98 The meeting place of Thomas Goodwin's gathered church has traditionally been placed in the parish of St Dunstan's in the east, but there does not seem to be any contemporary evidence for this; the tradition may have arisen from the fact that Goodwin's successor as pastor, Thomas Harrison, held a lectureship in this parish. See Nuttall, *Visible Saints*, p. 13; Yule, *Independents*, p. 142; Walter Wilson, *Dissenting Churches*, I, 212–22.

99 Edwards, *Antapologia*, p. 144; Thomas Goodwin, *Works*, XI, 529; *TBHS*, I, 243; *Leveller Tracts*, pp. 388, 415–16; Woodhouse, *Puritanism and Liberty*, pp. 145, 163.

100 Edwards, *Antapologia*, pp. 222–3. Samuel Moyer's later membership in this congregation is attested in his will (Prerogative Court of Canterbury 1683), and he was a well known radical in London from the beginning of the revolution (Pearl, *London*, pp. 310, 331).

101 Seaver, *Puritan Lectureships*, p. 281; Shaw, II, 130–2.

102 Wilson, *Dissenting Churches*, I, 221–5, Thomas Goodwin organized another gathered church in London after the Restoration (ibid., III, 427–34).

103 Neal, *Puritans*, IV, 416, remarks that Nye left 'behind him the

character of a man of uncommon depth, and of one who was seldom if ever outreached.'

104 A. E. Trout, 'Nonconformity in Hull,' *TCHS*, IX, 31–2. Nuttall, *Visible Saints*, p. 33 n. 4, doubts that Nye had a gathered church in the neighbourhood of Hull, but Nye's presence at or near Hull and his activity there in association with Boynton is undoubted, on Trout's evidence, and also hinted at pretty clearly by Edwards, *Antapologia*, p. 217.

105 *DNB*, Philip Nye; Matthews, *Calamy Revised*, pp. 369–70; Shaw, II, 315.

106 Edwards, *Antapologia*, p. 217.

107 Baillie, II, 306.

108 Newton, *Colonizing Activities*, pp. 178, 184. For Jeremiah Burroughes' familiarity with the circle, see his *Vindication*, pp. 19–21.

109 Gardiner, *Great Civil War*, I, 228–35; *Secret Negotiation*, pp. 5–6.

110 Nuttall, *Visible Saints*, p. 137.

111 Shaw, II, 132–4, 268–70.

112 Burroughes himself makes this point in his *Vindication*, p. 13; cf. Nuttall, *Visible Saints*, p. 12.

113 *DNB*, Jeremiah Burroughes; Seaver, *Puritan Lectureships*, p. 281, where Burroughes' significance as a lecturer is under-estimated; Edwards, *Antapologia*, p. 216; Burroughes, *Vindication*, pp. 22–4; Nuttall, 'Identification,' *TCHS*, XVI, 156.

114 Shaw, II, 300; Jones, *Stepney Meeting*, p. 15 and *passim;* G. W. Hill and W. H. Frere, eds., *Memorials of Stepney Parish* (Guildford, 1890–1), p. 198.

115 Wilson, *Pulpit in Parliament*, p. 119; Brook, *Puritans*, III, 299; *The Reasons of the Dissenting Brethren against the Third Proposition* (1645), p. 42; Mitchell and Struthers, *Westminster Assembly*, pp. 17, 19, 46, 47, 191, 231, 293, 297; *TBHS*, I, 245.

116 *Gang.* II, 13, 16; *Antapologia*, pp. 253, 307; John Goodwin, *Anapologesiates*, pp. 108, 121, 139; Jessey, *Storehouse of Provision*, p. 127.

117 *Gang.* II, 16; Matthews, *Calamy Revised*, pp. 32–3; Nuttall, *Visible Saints*, p. 53 and *passim*. Bartlet returned to London at the Restoration, *TCHS*, V, 246.

118 *To the Officers and Souldiers of the Army...a sober admonition from some sighing Souls* [1656], p. 3; Brook, *Puritans*, II, 501–3; Whitelock, *Memorials*, I, 36–7, 44.

119 Shaw, II, 309; Yule, *Independents*, pp. 134, 148; Edmund Calamy, *An Abridgment of Mr. Baxter's History* (1702), p. 204.

120 Ana Trapnel, *The Cry of a Stone* (1654), p. 3; *DNB*, Ralph Venning; Shaw, II, 568, where Venning was said to be minister of the chapel in the Tower of London in 1649; Calamy, *Abridgment*, p. 196.

121 *Gang.* II, 16; III, 162 (misnumbered 163); Terrill, *Broadmead Records*, p. 26.

122 Nuttall, *Welsh Saints*, pp. 1–36; Nuttall, *Visible Saints*, pp. 35–6;

Trapnel, *Cry of a Stone*, p. 3; *DNB*, Walter Cradock; Dale, *Inhabitants*, I, 10–12; Shaw, II, 329, 540; Mitchell and Struthers, *Westminster Assembly*, pp. 266, 293, 296, 476.

123 John Simpson, *The Perfection of Justification maintained* (1648), preface; John Graunt, *A right Use by a Stander by at the two Disputations at Great All-hollowes between Mr. Goodwin and Mr. Sympson* [1649]; *TBHS*, III, 121 ff.; Shaw, II, 302; J. A. Dodd, 'Troubles in a City Parish under the Protectorate,' *EHR*, X (1895), 41–54. An official letter of Jessey's church in 1653 remarked that about two hundred members 'of the church meeting at Great Allhallows, London,' had been baptized in the last three years, *Records of the Churches of Christ Gathered at Fenstanton, Warboys, and Hexham*, p. 346.

124 Trapnel, *Cry of a Stone*, p. 3; *The Failing & Perishing of Good Men* (1663), preface, quoted in Nuttall, *Visible Saints*, p. 165. John Proud, elder, and Caleb Ingold, deacon, signed a prefactory epistle to Anna Trapnel's *A Legacy for Saints* (1654) in the name of 'The Church of God usually meeting in Great Al-Hallows, London, (whereof Mr. John Simpson is Teacher).'

125 Vicars, *Schismatick Sifted*, pp. 26–7; *Picture of Independency*, p. 9; Edwards, *Antapologia*, pp. 301, 307; Shaw, II, 301; *DNB*, Nathaniel Holmes.

126 *DNB*, Henry Burton; Baillie, II, 279, 296, 299; Henry Burton, *Truth Shut out of doores* (1645); *Truth still Truth;* Calamy, *Door of Truth Opened*, p. 13.

127 Nuttall, *Visible Saints*, p. 105 n. 2; *TBHS*, I, 243.

128 *Gang.* III, 244, 247.

129 Brown, *Two Conferences*, pp. 1–7.

130 John Goodwin, *Innocencies Triumph*, pp. 15, 19; Edwards, *Antapologia*, p. 48; Dorothy Ann Williams, 'London Puritanism: The Parish of St. Stephen, Coleman Street,' *The Church Quarterly Review*, CLX (1959), 464–82.

131 Shaw, II, 102.

132 The reconstruction that follows is based upon Goodwin's fairly specific comments in 1644 in his *Innocencies Triumph*, pp. 14–19, and in 1646 in his *Anapologesiates Antapologias*, pp. 53–4, 227–8, and upon the parish records reported in Freshfield, *Remarks*. See also Shaw, II, 134–6, 143–4, 346.

133 John Goodwin, *Innocencies Triumph*, p. 18.

134 Ibid., p. 15.

135 Ibid., p. 19.

136 Edwards, *Antapologia*, pp. 53–4.

137 Goodwin, *Innocencies Triumph*, pp. 15–19.

138 Goodwin, *Anapologesiates*, pp. 227–8; Freshfield, *Remarks*, p. 8.

139 Goodwin, *Anapologesiates*, p. 54.

140 *Gang.* I, 70, said that Goodwin made 'his house a meeting for the

sectaries,' and Goodwin explicitly defended the practice of church meetings in houses in *Anapologesiates*, pp. 106–7, 131.

141 Freshfield, *Remarks*, p. 11; Shaw, II, 135–6. In October 1647 some of the parishioners of St Stephen Coleman Street had petitioned unsuccessfully to have Goodwin restored as lecturer (ibid., p. 346), and Goodwin in 1649 sought to establish a Sunday afternoon lecture without success (Seaver, *Puritan Lectureships*, p. 282).

142 Ibid., p. 282.

143 Bottigheimer, *English Money and Irish Land*, pp. 184, 191; *Leveller Tracts*, pp. 351, 369; *Acts and Ordinances*, I, 1007. The names of sixteen members of the gathered church are appended to *An Apologeticall Account, of some Brethren of the Church, Whereof Mr. Goodwin is Pastor* (1647), p. 11.

144 *Leveller Tracts*, p. 392.

145 Ibid., pp. 391, 396; J. E. Farnell, 'The Navigation Act of 1651, the First Dutch War, and the London Merchant Community,' *EcHR*, 2nd series, XVI (1964), 447; Farnell, *EHR*, LXXXII, 28–9, although certainly James Russell and probably Owen Roe belonged to the parish congregation of St Stephen rather than to the gathered church; *CSPD 1652–53*, pp. 67, 336; *CSPD 1653–54*, p. 83.

146 *Leveller Tracts*, pp. 192, 355, 439–40; *Secret Negotiation, passim.*

147 *Leveller Tracts*, pp. 361, 368–9, 421, 423; Pearl, *London*, pp. 260–261.

148 *Leveller Tracts*, pp. 290, 351, 374, 376, 390, 395, 415, 421.

149 Massachusetts Historical Society, *Collections*, 3rd series, I, 246; 4th series, VI, 460; *Gang.* II, 9. Overton's shop was rated at two pounds annual rent in 1638 (Dale, *Inhabitants*, I, 145).

150 *Gang.* III, 160.

151 Freshfield, *Remarks*, p. 9. Shaw, II, 143–4.

152 Bastwick, *Independency Not Gods Ordinance*, p. 7. Yule, *Independents*, p. 12, in citing Bastwick's distinction, strangely overlooks the rest of Bastwick's definition of the difference between Independents and Presbyterians: 'There is a twofold question between us, they call the Presbyterians, and our brethren they term Independents. The first is concerning the government of the Church, viz. whether it be Presbyterian Dependent, or Presbyterian Independent. The second question is, concerning the gathering of churches.' For a useful modern definition of 'Presbyterian Independent,' see Underdown, *Pride's Purge*, p. 234.

153 Vann, *Social Development of English Quakerism*, p. 22.

154 Baillie, II, 110.

155 Shaw, II, 401, 425; Mitchell and Struthers, *Westminster Assembly*, pp. 81, 231; Nuttall, *Visible Saints*, pp. 17, 26, 79. Caryl was appointed Rector of St Magnus in April 1645, and Phillip was restored to his rectory at Wrentham, Suffolk, in 1642. Peter Sterry's career in London is completely obscure at this period.

156 Phillip reorganized his congregation at Wrentham with a church covenant in 1650 (Nuttall, *Visible Saints*, p. 79).

157 Shaw, II, 102–4.

158 Shaw, II, 102.

159 Nuttall, *Visible Saints*, pp. 20–4.

160 Clarendon, *History*, IV, 311, where the Independents are described as 'more learned and rational' than the Presbyterians in the 'pulpit-skirmishes' of London in the late 1640s.

161 *TCHS*, IX, 269–70.

162 Shaw, II, 147–9.

163 John Goodwin, *Anapologesiates*, pp. 176–7.

6 *Accommodation or toleration?*

1 Perry Miller, *The New England Mind: From Colony to Province* (Cambridge, Mass., 1953), pp. 8–9; Gardiner, *Great Civil War*, I, 264.

2 Baillie, II, 343; *Dissuasive*, p. 76. Lawrence cannot be linked with a Baptist congregation despite his Baptist views.

3 Clarkson, *Lost Sheep*, p. 12; Howard, *Love and Truth*, pp. 7–8; *TBHS*, I, 245.

4 Baillie, *Dissuasive*, p. 120. Baillie also remarked that Thomas Goodwin denied the 'federal holiness' of children (ibid., p. 119; *Letters*, II, 218), which Lucy Hutchinson described as the 'main buckler' of the paedobaptists (*Memoirs of Col. Hutchinson*, II, 102).

5 Thomas Goodwin, *Works*, XI, 471–2.

6 *The Ancient Bounds* (1645), reprinted in Woodhouse, *Puritanism and Liberty*, p. 253.

7 Edwards, *Antapologia*, p. 224.

8 *TBHS*, I, 243, 245.

9 Brown, *Two Conferences*, p. 21.

10 *Gang.* III, 244.

11 *Gang.* I, 14–15, 83.

12 Baillie, II, 111; John Goodwin, *The Remedie of Unreasonableness* (1650); Graunt, *A right Use;* William Hartley, *Good News to all People* (1650), p. 32.

13 Nathaniel Homes, *A Vindication of Baptizing Beleevers Infants* (1646); *Gang.* III, 244–7.

14 Such conferences continued to be important in the next decade; see the detailed account of meetings in 1656 and 1657 in B. S. Capp, *The Fifth Monarchy Men* (1972), Appendix *iii*.

15 Lightfoot, *Works*, XIII, 9, 12–13, 37, 40, 163, 186, 262, 299, and *passim; CJ*, III, 584–5.

16 Lightfoot, *Works*, XIII, 56–7, 62; Baillie, II, 111; Ephraim Pagitt, *Heresiography* (5th edn, 1654), p. 75.

17 *Certaine Considerations to Dis-swade Men* [1643], pp. 3, 5.

18 Forbes, *Anatomy of Independency*, p. 13; Baillie, II, 118, 121. Lightfoot, *Works*, XIII, 92, said that 'it was urged that they [the Independents] should lay down and resign the churches they had already gathered; but when that could not be obtained' *Certaine Considerations* was instead 'accepted and ordered' with the consent of most of the Independents.

19 Thomason dated his copy of the *Apologeticall Narration* 3 January, but Edwards is quite explicit in saying that it appeared in December 1643 (*Gang.* II, 62).

20 Shaw, II, 37; Gardiner, *Great Civil War*, II, 30, 75.

21 Baillie, II, 230, 235–6.

22 Ibid., 236; *Papers Given in to the Honorable Committee...For Accommodation* (1648), pp. 1–9; Shaw, II, 37–44.

23 Baillie, II, 218.

24 Shaw, I, 328–33; *CJ*, III, 697; IV, 123; *LJ*, VII, 337; *Acts and Ordinances*, I, 677; Gardiner, *Great Civil War*, II, 193.

25 *Gang.* I, 95.

26 *Gang.* I, 90–1; III, 42; William Prynne, *A Fresh Discovery of some Prodigious New Wandring-Blasing-Stars* (1645), preface, p. 13; H. G. Tibbutt, ed., *The Letter Books of Sir Samuel Luke 1644–45*, Historical Manuscripts Commission (1963), pp. 328, 582–4, 622, where it appears that General Fairfax was very sympathetic to the two Baptists who, he said, had already left their commands at their own request. See also Drapes, *Plain and Faithful Discovery*, pp. 21–25.

27 Baillie, II, 236.

28 Mitchell and Struthers, *Westminster Assembly*, pp. 70–87, 132–3.

29 *Gang.* II, 87; Burroughes, *Vindication*, pp. 4, 9, 25; *Mercurius Aulicus*, 17–23 September 1643, p. 561.

30 John Price, *The City-Remonstrance Remonstrated* (1646), pp. 17–18; Bellamie, *Justification*, pp. 20–9. John Lilburne described Bellamie as 'kinsman to the weather cock' in *The Charters of London* (1646) p. 2, quoted in Farnell, *EHR*, LXXXII, 29.

31 *CJ*, IV, 280; *Perfect Passages*, Numb. 48, 17–23 September 1645, p. 380; *The Moderate Intelligencer*, Numb. 30, 18–25 September 1645, p. 138; *The true Informer*, Numb. 23, 27 September 1645, p. 179; Katherine Chidley, *Good Counsell, to the Petitioners for Presbyterian Government* [1645], reprinted in *TCHS*, IV, 325–9; *Dictated Thoughts Upon the Presbyterians late Petitions* [1646]; Burroughes, *Vindication*, pp. 23–6; Burton, *Truth Shut out*, sig. A2^{r}, where it appears that it was Burton's sermon against the citizens' petition, in his lecture at St Mary's Aldermanbury on 23 September, which led Edmund Calamy's parishioners to lock him out of the church henceforth. A printed version of the citizens' petition in the Thomason Collection (B. M. Pressmark 669.f.10, 37) bears a manuscript note that it was 'sent to Mr. Geo. Thomason to get hands to it

about 20 September 1645.' *Gang.* I, 40, 65, 109–11; III, 2nd unnumbered page following p. 240.

32 Baillie, II, 326–50; *Papers for Accommodation*, pp. 16–17, and *passim.*

33 *Gang.* I, 14–15, 83–4.

34 Baillie, *Anabaptism*, p. 49.

35 Baillie, II, 343, 346.

36 *Gang.* I, 83–4.

37 *CJ*, IV, 348; Gardiner, *Great Civil War*, III, 11; Whitelocke, I, 537–8.

38 *Mercurius Civicus*, Numb. 136, 24 December 1645 – 1 January 1645/1646, pp. 1186–7; *To the Right Worshipfull, the Alderman, and Common Counsell-men of the Ward of Farrington within* (1645/6); *Gang.* I, 105.

39 *A Letter of the Ministers of the City of London...Against Toleration* (1645/6); *A true copy of a Letter from divers Ministers about Colchester...against a Toleration* (1645/6); Mitchell and Struthers, *Westminster Assembly*, p. 174.

40 Whitelocke, I, 559; *CJ*, IV, 407; *LJ*, VIII, 104–5; *Gang.* II, 37; *The humble Petition of the Lord Mayor, Aldermen, and Commons of the City of London...concerning Church-Government...Presented to the House of Peers...the 16 of January 1645.*

41 *Gang.* II, 8–9.

42 Haller, *Liberty and Reformation*, pp. 223, 226–9; A. L. Morton, *The World of the Ranters* (1970), pp. 20–6; *Leveller Tracts*, p. 352.

43 Baillie, II, 215–16. Another possible source for Edwards' implacable hostility to the Independents goes back to 1627, when Thomas Goodwin, then curate of St Andrew's, Cambridge, and William Bridge were among the witnesses against Edwards when he was in serious trouble for a sermon preached at St Andrew's (Brook, *Puritans*, III, 82–3); but there seems to be no hint of this ancient quarrel in the pamphlets of the forties.

44 *Gang.* I, 2.

45 Shaw, I, 279–312.

46 *Gang.* I, 89.

47 *Gang.* I, 55 (second page so numbered).

48 *Gang.* I, 104.

49 *Gang.* I, 105. For the conservative reaction in the City, see Valerie Pearl, 'London Puritans and Scotch Fifth Columnists: A Mid-Seventeenth-Century Phenomenon,' in A. E. J. Hollander and William Kellaway, eds., *Studies in London History* (1969), pp. 317–31; Valerie Pearl, 'London's Counter-Revolution,' in G. E. Aylmer, ed., *The Interregnum: The Quest for Settlement 1646–1660* (1972), pp. 29–56.

50 Baillie, II, 358, 361, 362, 365–6.

51 Whitelocke, II, 13; Shaw, II, 79; *CJ*, IV, 170, 184, 526.

52 *To the Honourable the House of Commons...The Humble Remonstrance and Petition of the Lord Mayor, Aldermen and Commons of*

the City of London (1646); *To the Right Honorable the Lords...The Humble Remonstrance and Petition...*(1646).

53 *LJ*, VIII, 331–4; *CJ*, IV, 555.

54 Whitelocke, II, 26.

55 Baillie, II, 393, 396, 398, 402–3; *CJ*, IV, 556, 659, 663, 665, 666, 670, 674.

56 *A Petition of Citizens of London Presented to the Common Council ...22 May 1646; The Humble Acknowledgement and Petition of Divers Inhabitants in, and about the Citie of London. Presented to the Honourable the Commons of England...the second of June 1646; The Weekly Account*, Numb. 22, 20–26 May 1646; Numb. 23, 27 May – 3 June 1646; *The Scottish Dove*, Numb. 136, 28 May – 3 June 1646, p. 676.

57 MS. note by George Thomason on BM 669.f.10, 58; *The True Copy of a Petition Delivered to the Right Honourable the Mayor...on Tuesday the 23 of June 1646; The spirit of Persecution Again broken loose* (1655), p. 7.

58 For the Independents: *A Moderate Reply to the Citie-Remonstrance* (1646); *A New Petition...Declaring the danger of the said New Petition* (1646); *The Interest of England Maintained* (1646); *Conscience caution'd, & so set at libertie* (1646); Price, *City-Remonstrance Remonstrated*. For the Remonstrance: *A Glasse for Weak ey'd Citizens* (1646); [Captain Jones], *Plain English: or, The Sectaries Anatomized* (1646); *A Vindication of the London Remonstrance* (1646); John Bellamie, *A Vindication of the Humble Remonstrance* (1646), *A Justification of the...Vindication* (1646). For the spread of the controversy outside London: *Vox Populi...Containing the Rise Progresse Ruine of Norwich Remonstrance* (1646), answered by S. T., *Truth Vindicated From The unjust accusations of the Independent Society, in the City of Norwich* (1646); *A New birth of the City Remonstrance* (1646), answered by John Tilsley, *A true Copie of the Petition of Twelve thousand five hundred and upwards of the Well-affected Gentlemen, Ministers, Free-holders and others of the County Palatine of Lancaster* (1646).

59 Whitelocke, II, 91–2; Baillie, II, 412.

60 *CJ*, V, *20–1, 24–5; LJ*, VIII, 617–18, 621; *To the Honourable The House of Commons...The Humble Petition of the Lord Mayor, Aldermen and Commons of the City of London...Together with an humble Representation...of the well-affected Freemen, and Covenant-engaged Citizens of the City of London* (1646).

61 *LJ*, VIII, 621, 630–1; *CJ*, V, 22, 25, 31, 33.

62 *CJ*, V, 34–5; Gardiner, *Great Civil War*, III, 186; *A Declaration of the Commons...against all such Persons as shall take upon them to Preach...except they be Ordained* (2 January 1646/7).

63 On 15 January the Commons debated a schedule of penalties ranging from one month imprisonment for the first offence to exile for the

fourth offence for those convicted of lay preaching; a week later they were discussing corporal punishment for this offence. To suggest the enormous difficulties encountered in defining a lay preacher: a week later still, a captain or officer who preached to his company, troop, or regiment was to be exempted from punishment. The best account of these debates is given in the *Moderate Intelligencer* Numbs. 96–102, 31 December 1646 – 18 February 1647.

64 *The Humble Petition of many well-affected Freemen, and Citizens of the City of London...To the Right Honorable the Lord Mayor... January 25, 1646; CJ*, v, 66; *Acts and Ordinances*, I, 913–14; *Gang.* I, 168, where Edwards made the initial suggestion for such a national fast day.

65 Lucy Hutchinson, *Life of Colonel Hutchinson*, II, 95.

66 *Leveller Tracts*, pp. 354–5.

67 *Hinc Illae Lachrymae, Or The Impietie of Impunitie* (1648), pp. 3–10; *Clarke Papers*, I, 4; *Life of Knollys*, pp. 22–3, where Knollys says merely 'and so I went away, and ceased not to teach and preach Jesus Christ'; Kiffin was still involved with the committee of examinations in late March and tried to secure an interview with a committee of divines of the Assembly (Mitchell and Struthers, *Westminster Assembly*, pp. 340–1); *The Anabaptists late Protestation* (Printed in the happy Yeare/When Sectaries durst not appear [1647]).

68 For this Remonstrance, see Pearl, *London*, pp. 260–1.

69 *Leveller Tracts*, p. 361.

70 Ibid., pp. 355, 365; *Secret Negotiation, passim;* Gardiner *Great Civil War*, I, 264–9.

71 John Bastwick, *A Just Defence of John Bastwick* (1645), p. 20 and *passim;* William Prynne, *The Lyar Confounded* (1645), pp. 6, 22; *Calendar of the Committee for Advance of Money, 1642–1656*, I, 150; *Cal. St. Pap. Ireland 1633–1647*, pp. 368, 405; *Cal. St. Pap. Ireland 1647–1660*, p. 419 and *passim;* Bottigheimer, *English Money*, pp. 95, 155, 183, 204; Don M. Wolfe, *Leveller Manifestoes of the Puritan Revolution* (New York, 1944), p. 344. Hawkins was perhaps the 'Master H. a great Independent' mentioned by Edwards (*Gang.* I, 183) who was in trouble at the Common Council in February 1646 for remarking that 'the King, the Scots and the Common Council did drive on one design.'

72 Pearl, *London*, pp. 172, 174, 252–61, 282–3, 310.

73 Shaw, II, 402.

74 Technically his offence lay in attributing the threat to an MP (Whitelocke, II, 93); Bottigheimer, *English Money*, pp. 73, 194, 212.

75 *A Declaration of divers Elders and Brethren of Congregationall Societies* [1651], p. 8.

76 Samuel Richardson, *Divine Consolation*, (1649), Part III, epistle; Hill and Frere, *Memorials of Stepney Parish*, pp. 189–95, 204, 207, 240. For the wider significance of Thompson's important career, see

Farnell, 'The Navigation Act of 1651,' *EcHR*, 2nd series, XVI, 443–6.

77 See Underdown, *Pride's Purge*, *passim.*

78 *Mercurius Aulicus*, 17–23 September 1643, p. 561; *Cal. of the Com. for Advance of Money*, I, 1–2; Pearl, *London*, pp. 137, 152, 274n.

79 *Gang.* I, 52, 53, 65, 67–8, 105, Appendix, p. 121.

7 *'The Generality of Congregations' and the Levellers*

1 Brailsford, *Levellers*, is the most comprehensive account of the Levellers, but there are many other good books: W. Schenk, *The Concern for Social Justice in the Puritan Revolution* (1948); Haller, *Liberty and Reformation;* Joseph Frank, *The Levellers* (Cambridge, Mass., 1955); M. A. Gibb, *John Lilburne* (1947); and Pauline Gregg, *Free-born John.*

2 William Haller, ed., *Tracts on Liberty in the Puritan Revolution 1638–1647*, 3 vols. (New York, 1933–4), III, 324.

3 Pearl, *London*, pp. 260, 267–73.

4 *Acts and Ordinances*, I, 406, 408; *The Weekly Account*, 17–23 September 1645; *Leveller Tracts*, p. 351.

5 *Gang.* I, 83–4; III, 161.

6 Haller, *Tracts on Liberty*, III, 325.

7 *CSPD 1641–43*, pp. 506–7; Haller, *Tracts on Liberty*, III, 66, 97–101.

8 *Gang.* I, Appendix, 121–2.

9 *Gang.* III, 146; *CJ*, IV, 561; Whitelocke, II, 28; *Works of Darkness Brought to Light* (1647), p. 9.

10 *Leveller Tracts*, p. 352; *Gang.* I, Appendix, 121–2.

11 John Lilburne, *Jonahs Cry out of the Whales belly* [1647], pp. 5–6.

12 *Leveller Tracts*, p. 343.

13 Gregg, *Free-born John*, chapter 9.

14 *Gang.* I, 40.

15 *Gang.* I, 68; William Walwyn referred to Prynne's earlier association with 'the Separation' in his anonymous *A Helpe to the right understanding of a Discourse concerning Independency* (1644), p. 5.

16 John Batswick, *The Storming of the Anabaptists Garrisons* (1647), preface; *Just Defence*, pp. 16–17.

17 *Gang.* I, 68; John Lilburne, *Innocency and Truth Justified* (1646), p. 29.

18 *Leveller Tracts*, pp. 408–9.

19 *The Picture of the Good Old Cause* (1660); *CSPD 1655–56*, p. 335; J. T. Rutt, ed., *Diary of Thomas Burton*, 4 vols. (1828), I, 308–10.

20 Lilburne, *Jonahs Cry*, p. 5.

21 *Gang.* III, 161.

22 In May 1646 Goodwin's congregation contributed fifty shillings towards the printing of ten thousand copies of Walwyn's pamphlet, *A Word in Season* (*Leveller Tracts*, p. 393).

23 *Gang.* III, 160–1; *Leveller Tracts*, pp. 352–4; J[ohn] P[rice], *A Spirituall Snapsacke for the Parliament Souldiers* (1643); *Honey out of the Rock* (1644); *Unity our Duty* (1645); *Independency accused . . .and Acquitted* (1645).

24 *Leveller Tracts*, pp. 353, 391–2. Although Walwyn named his detractor as 'master Husbands, a linen-draper in Cornhill,' Humphrey Brooke's more detailed account of this episode in *The Charity of Church-men* (in *Leveller Tracts*, p. 343) named him as Mr. Woolaston, who can plausibly be placed in this circle (*A Declaration of divers Elders and Brethren*, p. 8).

25 *Leveller Tracts*, p. 288.

26 Ibid., p. 230.

27 Hist. MSS. Comm., *Sixth Report*, Appendix, pp. 46, 130–1; *LJ*, VII, 91, 92, 97, 142, 185, where Thomas Lambe 'an oilman' (p. 97) was linked with the distribution of pamphlets from this press in December 1644; Plomer, 'Secret Printing,' *The Library*, new series, V, 374–403. It seems unlikely that Walwyn's *Compassionate Samaritane* was printed on this press in mid 1644, as Plomer suggests.

28 *Gang.* II, 9. Henry Overton, a member of John Goodwins' church, and the radical Giles Calvert also handled this pamphlet.

29 *Gang.* III, 110.

30 *Leveller Tracts*, pp. 307–8.

31 Ibid., p. 355.

32 Ibid., pp. 307–8.

33 *CJ*, V, 112; *Perfect Diurnall*, Numb. 190, 15–22 March 1646/7, p. 1519.

34 Ibid., p. 1525; Whitelocke, II, 121; *Leveller Tracts*, pp. 355–6.

35 *Clarke Papers*, I, 3.

36 *Leveller Tracts*, p. 356; *Gold tried in the fire* (1647); the printed petitions belonging to the copy of this pamphlet in the Thomason collection, E. 392 (19), have become separated and are bound between E. 392 (20) and (21); Whitelocke, II, 151; *Clarke Papers*, I, 117; *CJ*, V, 119, 162, 179, 195; Gardiner, *Great Civil War*, III, 254–7.

37 *Leveller Tracts*, p. 356; *CJ*, V, 179.

38 *Clarke Papers*, I, 118, 152 ff.; Whitelocke, II, 132, 136, 138; *CJ*, V, 160–1.

39 *Leveller Tracts*, p. 356.

40 Ibid., p. 356; Whitelocke, II, 151; *CJ*, V, 195. See also *The poore Wise-mans Admonition unto All the plaine People of London* (1647).

41 Richard Baxter, *Reliquiae Baxterianae*, ed. Matthew Sylvester (1696), p. 53. For the military careers of the men discussed in this section, see Firth and Davies, *Regimental History*, *passim*.

42 *Gang.* III, 251–4.

43 John Vicars, *The Burning-Bush not Consumed* (1646), p. 336; Whitelocke, I, 555.

44 *Clarke Papers*, I, 430–1.

45 Ibid., 431. See above, p. 209, n36.
46 Brailsford, *Levellers*, pp. 506–7; *TBHS*, I, 234; Dale, *Inhabitants*, I, 207.
47 *Milton State Papers*, p. 64.
48 *Gang.* III, 46, 252–3. Hewson joined the congregation of John Rogers, the later Fifth Monarchy leader, in Ireland in 1651 (Edward Rogers, *The Life and Opinions of a Fifth-Monarchy-Man* (1867), p. 29). His daughter, who married Dr Philip Carteret, became a General Baptist (Thomas Ashton, *Satan in Samuels Mantle* (1659), pp. 4–5). His congregational affiliation in the 1640s is not known.
49 John Thurloe, *A Collection of State Papers*, ed. T. Birch, 7 vols. (1742), IV, 621; H. G. Tibbutt, *Colonel John Okey 1606–1662*, Pubs. of the Bedfordshire Hist. Record Soc., XXXV (1955), 50, 151.
50 *Leveller Tracts*, pp. 218, 228.
51 Ashton, *Satan in Samuels Mantle*, p. 4.
52 See C. H. Firth, 'The Raising of the Ironsides,' *Transactions of the Royal Historical Society*, New Series, XIII (1899), 17–73; 'The Later History of the Ironsides,' ibid., XV (1901), 1–45.
53 Abbott, *Cromwell*, I, 277–8; *The Quarrel between the Earl of Manchester and Oliver Cromwell*, Camden Society, New Series, XII (1875), 59.
54 John Lilburne, *The Upright Mans Vindication* (1653), p. 2.
55 Abbott, *Cromwell*, II, 378.
56 *Reliquiae Baxterianae*, pp. 53–4.
57 *Clarke Papers*, I, 430–1.
58 Edward Harrison, *Plain Dealing* (1649); *BQ*, VII, 214 ff.
59 Jane Turner, *Choice Experiences* (1653), preface, pp. 81 ff.; *A Remonstrance Sent from Colonell Lilburnes Regiment* (1647), p. 5; *Clarke Papers*, I, 208; John Rushworth, *Historical Collections*, 8 vols. (1721–2), VI, 471.
60 C. H. Firth, *Scotland and the Protectorate* (Edinburgh, 1899), p. 242; Turner, *Choice Experiences*, preface. Gough, not to be confused with his more famous namesake, was connected by marriage with William Kiffin's business partner George Gosfright (see will of George Gosfright jr, Prerogative Court of Canterbury 1685).
61 *Fenstanton Records*, pp. 307, 311, 318, 328, 329.
62 Richard Deane, *A Copy of a Brief Treatise* (1693), pp. 7–12.
63 *Clarke Papers*, I, 436–9; *Leveller Tracts*, p. 84.
64 Rushworth, *Historical Collections*, VI, 468, 474; *Clarke Papers*, I, 84–6, 100–1, 105–6. Firth thought the first of these letters might have been written by Sexby, but this seems unlikely both because the writer, as Firth himself points out, seems to have been an officer and because Sexby was among the agitators to whom it was addressed (ibid., I, 87–8).
65 Henry Cary, *Memorials of the Great Civil War*, 2 vols, (1842), I, 201–205; *Clarke Papers*, I, 430–1.

66 *Leveller Tracts*, p. 359.
67 *Clarke Papers*, I, 170–5, 183.
68 Ibid., I, 177–211.
69 Ibid., I, 213.
70 Ibid., I, xxxvii.
71 Gardiner, *Great Civil War*, III, 339–45. A group of Independents urging compromise upon the Common Council at the Guildhall on 2 August was 'cruelly hacked and hewed' by some of the conservative militia officers (Whitelocke, II, 187; *The Army Anatomized* (1647), p. 24).
72 Carter, *English Reformed Church in Amsterdam*, pp. 201–4.
73 Wolfe, *Leveller Manifestoes*, p. 187.
74 *Leveller Tracts*, p. 175.
75 Wolfe, *Leveller Manifestoes*, p. 42.
76 *Leveller Tracts*, pp. 176, 351; Whitelocke, II, 201–2.
77 *Leveller Tracts*, p. 359.
78 *Acts and Ordinances*, I, 1007, 1010, 1011, 1057; *CJ*, V, 318, 320; Whitelocke, II, 216; Clement Walker, *The Complete History of Independency*, 4 Parts (1661), I, 46, 83.
79 *Spectacles for The Citie*, p. 9 and *passim;* Walker, *Independency*, I, 75, 82–3; *The Army Anatomized*, p. 31; Firth and Davies, *Regimental History*, II, 572–3; *Clarke Papers*, I, 396.
80 *Leveller Tracts*, p. 175.
81 See Brailsford, *Levellers*, chapters 11, 12.
82 *The Tower of London Letter-Book of Sir Lewis Dyve, 1646–47*, ed. H. G. Tibbutt, Pubs. Bedfordshire Hist. Record Soc., XXXVIII (1958), 58, 64.
83 George Joyce, *A Letter or Epistle to All well-minded People* (1651), p. 3.
84 Dyve, *Letter-Book*, pp. 90, 92.
85 *Leveller Tracts*, pp. 177, 209.
86 Joyce, *Letter*, p. 4.
87 *Leveller Tracts*, p. 177.
88 Brailsford, *Levellers*, p. 222.
89 *Leveller Tracts*, p. 175; Whitelocke, II, 200–1, 204; Rushworth, *Historical Collections*, VII, 764–5.
90 Whitelocke, II, 222, 227–8, 231; Brailsford, *Levellers*, pp. 252–3; Gregg, *Free-born John*, p. 202.
91 Dyve, *Letter-Book*, pp. 90–2.
92 Brailsford, *Levellers*, pp. 260 ff.
93 *Clarke Papers*, I, 234; Whitelocke, II, 234–5.
94 *Clarke Papers*, I, 277–8.
95 Ibid., I, 372, 377, 379–80.
96 Ibid., I, 371; Rushworth, *Historical Collections*, VII, 943.
97 *Clarke Papers*, I, 231 n.; William Clarke, *A Full Relation of the Proceedings at...Corkbush field* (1647), p. 5; Brailsford, *Levellers*, pp. 296–7.

98 *Remonstrance Sent from Colonell Lilburnes Regiment*, p. 3. Most of the officers in 1647 were newly appointed to this regiment, which in any case appears to have had a reputation for making trouble (Robert Lilburne, *Col. Lilburnes Letter to a Friend*, 1645).

99 Rushworth, *Historical Collections*, VII, 943; *Clarke Papers*, I, 432–3.

100 Wolfe, *Leveller Manifestoes*, p. 77.

101 Walker, *Independency*, I, 40; Whitelocke, II, 218.

102 Wolfe, *Leveller Manifestoes*, pp. 237 ff.; *LJ*, IX, 572.

103 *Clarke Papers*, I, 156. Taylor's identity is obscure, but there was a meeting of General Baptists in Wapping after the Restoration (*Behold a Cry* (1662), p. 5), and a Thomas Taylor was imprisoned with other General Baptists in 1663 (*Middlesex County Records*, III, 329).

104 *Leveller Tracts*, p. 371.

105 *A Declaration by Congregational Societies* (1647), pp. 3–9.

106 *Leveller Tracts*, p. 372; Wolfe, *Leveller Manifestoes*, p. 238.

107 *Leveller Tracts*, pp. 372–3.

108 Thomas Brooks, *The Glorious Day of the Saints Appearance* (1648). See Rainsborough's contributions to the Putney debates, Woodhouse, *Puritanism and Liberty*, pp. 1–124.

109 *A Declaration of divers Elders and Brethren*, pp. 1, 8.

110 *Leveller Tracts*, p. 351.

111 Ibid., pp. 98–101; Samuel Chidley, *The Dissembling Scot* (1652), pp. 7–8.

112 Brailsford, *Levellers*, p. 247.

113 *Leveller Tracts*, p. 98.

8 *The triumph of the Saints*

1 Brailsford, *Levellers*, p. 302.

2 Walker, *Independency*, II, 46.

3 Wolfe, *Leveller Manifestoes*, p. 260; Walker, *Independency*, I, 71 (misnumbered 72); Brailsford, *Levellers*, pp. 326–7.

4 C. H. Firth, ed., *The Memoirs of Edmund Ludlow*, 2 vols. (Oxford, 1894), I, 184–6.

5 William Allen, *A Faithful Memorial of that Remarkable Meeting...at Windsor Castle, in the Year 1648* (1659), p. 5.

6 *Acts and Ordinances*, I, 1133–6; Whitelocke, II, 313, 315; Firth and Davies, *Regimental History*, II, 572–3.

7 Walker, *Independency*, I, 92, 108–11, 115–17, 121, 131–4; II, 37–8; Whitelocke, II, 308, 321, 343, and *passim; CJ*, V, 581, 617, 650, 673; *LJ*, X, 454; *Acts and Ordinances*, I, 1188–1215.

8 Walker, *Independency* I, 117, 121, 131–2; Whitelocke, II, 361, 385.

9 Walker, *Independency*, I, 116.

10 Lucy Hutchinson, *Life of Colonel Hutchinson*, II, 126; Gardiner, *Great Civil War*, IV, 172–5; Frank, *Levellers*, pp. 163–4; Whitelocke, II, 376; *LJ*, X, 427.

11 Walker, *Independency*, I, Appendix, p. 11; II, 11.
12 Ludlow, *Memoirs*, I, 204; *Leveller Tracts*, p. 414.
13 Brailsford, *Levellers*, pp. 349–56.
14 Whitelocke, II, 413; Lucy Hutchinson, *Life of Colonel Hutchinson*, II, 150–1.
15 Roger Howell, *Newcastle upon Tyne and the Puritan Revolution* (Oxford, 1967), pp. 203–4; Whitelocke, II, 419.
16 Brailsford, *Levellers*, p. 354; *Leveller Tracts*, pp. 388–9, 415.
17 [David Brown], *A Back-Blow to Major Huntington* [1648], p. 13. Brown's claim to have published such a work (*Milton State Papers*, p. 62) is confirmed by Walwyn's claim to have helped him to do so (*Leveller Tracts*, p. 384).
18 Ibid., pp. 388, 395, where Walwyn's tale of Colonel Tichborn's joke suggests his renewed intimacy with the Independents; Brailsford, *Levellers*, pp. 360–3.
19 *Leveller Tracts*, pp. 182–4, 210.
20 Ibid., pp. 415–23.
21 *Clarke Papers*, II, 71–132.
22 Wolfe, *Leveller Manifestoes*, pp. 291–303; *Leveller Tracts*, pp. 423–4.
23 *Clarke Papers*, II, 282. Lilburne appears to have been accompanied in his withdrawal by Richard Overton (Frank, *Levellers*, pp. 180, 317 n. 135), which would explain the strong support Lilburne received from the General Baptists on 28 December.
24 *Leveller Tracts*, pp. 423–4.
25 Samuel Chidley, *Dissembling Scot*, p. 8.
26 Samuel Richardson, *An Answer to the London Ministers Letter* (1649), p. 2.
27 Thomas Collier, *A Vindication of the Army-Remonstrance* (1649), preface, p. 4.
28 *Leveller Tracts*, pp. 209–10, 214, 228.
29 *The humble Petition and Representation of Several Churches of God in London, commonly (though falsly) called Anabaptists* (1649), pp. 4–6.
30 Ibid., pp. 7–8; *CJ*, VI, 177–8.
31 *Leveller Tracts*, pp. 213, 228–30, 374.
32 William Walwyn, *The Fountain of Slaunder Discovered* (1649), p. 19.
33 Ibid., p. 21.
34 *Leveller Tracts*, p. 228.
35 Ibid., p. 290.
36 Wolfe, *Leveller Manifestoes*, p. 344.
37 *Leveller Tracts*, pp. 257, 271, 274.
38 Ibid., pp. 258–60.
39 Ibid., pp. 255, 265, 275.
40 Ibid., pp. 258, 262, 264, 265, 271, 274.
41 Ibid., p. 257.
42 Ibid., pp. 263–73.

43 Trevor-Roper, *Religion, the Reformation and Social Change*, pp. 330–331; Underdown, *Pride's Purge*, p. 132; Wilson, *Pulpit in Parliament*, p. 94.

44 Farnell, *EHR*, LXXXII, 24–36. Owen Rowe and James Russell were not members of John Goodwin's gathered church, as Farnell suggests, but parishioners of St Stephen Coleman Street. Nor were Richard Shute, Samuel Moyer, John Fenton, William Steele, Praise-God Barbone, Christopher Feake, Thomas Brooks, Thomas Whalley or Thomas Harrison Baptists. Despite these mistakes in denominational affiliations, Farnell's article is valuable. William Steele, who was appointed Recorder of London in 1649, was perhaps a member of a gathered church at this date, since he was regarded as a trustworthy radical; he was a member of John Owen's church in London after the Restoration (*TCHS*, I, 27). See also Underdown, *Pride's Purge*, pp. 180, 304; Shaw, II, 402.

45 Underdown, *Pride's Purge*, p. 141.

46 *Second Narrative*, in *Harleian Miscellany*, VI, 499.

47 *Milton State Papers*, pp. 60, 64; Samuel Chidley, *A Cry Against a Crying Sin* (1652), in *Harleian Miscellany*, VI, 272–88.

48 Firth and Davies, *Regimental History*, I, 296–7; C. H. Firth, *Cromwell's Army*, 3rd edn. (1962), pp. 305–8.

49 *Leveller Tracts*, pp. 214–19, 228, 232–3; Wedgwood, *Trial of Charles I*, pp. 139, 175, 210, 246, 250–1.

50 Underdown, *Pride's Purge*, pp. 162–3.

51 Crockett, *TCHS*, XII, 226–7.

52 *Clarke Papers*, II, 270–82.

53 Walker, *Independency*, II, 103 (misnumbered 123).

54 Haller, *Tracts on Liberty*, III, 54.

55 John Goodwin, *Right and Might Well Met* (1649), in Woodhouse, *Puritanism and Liberty*, p. 216.

56 See above, p. 172.

57 *Milton State Papers*, p. 80.

58 For a lively discussion of the political and intellectual paradoxes resulting from the triumph of the saints as saints rather than secular political revolutionaries, see Lamont, *Godly Rule*, *passim*.

59 The line between spiritual liberty and indecency, sedition, and property rights was admittedly sometimes difficult to draw, but the generosity of members of separate churches to those who differed from them must be recognized. Some of the Independent clergy faltered in 1652 when they supported a proposal that would have made the pastors of separate churches subject to the approval of the triers who were to judge the parish ministers; Milton wrote an indignant sonnet addressed to 'Cromwell, our chief of men,' and the proposal was dropped (*TCHS*, IX, 25).

BIBLIOGRAPHY

This bibliography comprises works cited in the notes, with two important exceptions. Works in the List of abbreviations on page 197 are not repeated here. In the list of primary sources, works cited only once or in two or three consecutive notes (this is true of a large number of contemporary pamphlets) have been omitted, since full bibliographical details are provided at the first citation and readers will have complete information at the appropriate note. Subsequent citations are given in short form; such works are given here in full to permit easy identification. The list of secondary works includes all works cited and may serve as a select bibliography to the topics treated in this book.

PRIMARY SOURCES

Abbott, W. C., ed., *The Writings and Speeches of Oliver Cromwell*, 4 vols., Cambridge, Mass., 1937–47.

The Apologeticall Narration, 1643.

The Army Anatomized, 1647.

Ashton, Thomas, *Satan in Samuels Mantle*, 1659.

Baillie, Robert, *Anabaptism the True Fountaine of Independency*, 1646.

A Dissuasive from the Errours of the Time, 1646.

B[arbone]., P[raise-God]., *A Discourse Tending to prove the Baptisme*, 1642.

Barrow, Henry, *The Writings of Henry Barrow 1587–1590*, ed. Leland H. Carlson, 1962.

Bastwick, John, *Independency Not Gods Ordinance*, 1645.

A Just Defence of John Bastwick, 1645.

Baxter, Richard, *Plain Scripture Proof of Infants Churchmembership and Baptism*, 1651.

Reliquiae Baxterianae, ed. Matthew Sylvester, 1696.

Bellamie, John, *A Justification of the City Remonstrance and its Vindication*, 1646.

Bradford, William, *Of Plymouth Plantation*, ed. S. E. Morison, New York, 1952.

Brooke, Lord, *A Discourse. . .of Episcopacie*, 1642.

[Brown, David], *A Back-Blow to Major Huntington*, [1648].
Brown, David, *The Naked Woman*, 1652.
To the Supream Authority of England, 1652.
Two Conferences between...Separatists and Independents, 1650.
Burroughes, Jeremiah, *A Vindication of Mr. Burroughes*, 1646.
Burton, Henry, *The Protestation Protested*, 1641.
Truth Shut out of doores, 1645.
Truth still Truth, Though Shut out of Doores, 1645.
[Calamy, Edmund], *The Door of Truth Opened*, 1645.
Chidley, Katherine, *The Justification of the Independent Churches of Christ*, 1641.
A New-Yeares-Gift, 1645.
Chidley, Samuel, *The Dissembling Scot*, 1652.
The Separatists Answer, 1651.
Clarendon, Lord, *The History of the Rebellion and Civil Wars in England*, ed. W. D. Macray, 6 vols., Oxford, 1888.
Claxton [Clarkson], Lawrence, *The Lost sheep Found*, 1660.
A Collection of sundry matters [Middelburg], 1616.
A Confession and Protestation of the Faith of Certaine Christians in England [Middelburg], 1616.
Dale, T. C., *The Inhabitants of London in 1638*, 2 vols., 1931.
A Declaration of divers Elders and Brethren of Congregationall Societies [1651].
A Declaration of several of the Churches of Christ...concerning the Kingly Interest of Christ, 1654.
Drapes, Edward, *A Plain and Faithfull Discovery*, 1646.
Dyve, Sir Lewis, *The Tower of London Letter-Book of Sir Lewis Dyve, 1646–47*, ed. H. G. Tibbutt, Publications of the Bedfordshire Historical Record Society, XXXVIII (1958).
Edwards, Thomas, *Antapologia*, 1644.
Featley, Daniel, *The Dippers Dipt*, 1645.
Forbes, Alexander, *An Anatomy of Independency*, 1664.
Goodwin, John, *Anapologesiates Antapologias*, 1646.
Innocencies Triumph, 1644.
Goodwin, Thomas, *The Works of Thomas Goodwin*, 12 vols., Edinburgh, 1861–6.
Graunt, John, *A right Use by a Stander by at the two Disputations...between Mr. Goodwin and Mr. Sympson* [1649].
Haller, William, ed., *Tracts on Liberty in the Puritan Revolution 1638–1647*, 3 vols., New York, 1933–4.
The Harleian Miscellany, 12 vols., 1808–11.
Howard, Luke, *A Looking-Glass for Baptists*, 1672.
Love and Truth in Plainness Manifested, 1704.
Hutchinson, Lucy, *Memoirs of the Life of Colonel Hutchinson*, ed. C. H. Firth, 2 vols., 1885.
Jacob, Henry, *An Attestation of many Learned Divines* [Middelburg], 1613.

A Christian and Modest Offer of a Most Indifferent Conference [Middelburg], 1606.
The Divine Beginning and Institution of Christ true Visible...Church, Leyden, 1610.
A plaine and cleere Exposition of the Second Commandment [Leyden], 1610.
Reasons Taken Out of Gods Word [Middelburg], 1604.
To the right High and mightie Prince, James...An humble Supplication for Toleration [Middelburg], 1609.
Jessey, Henry, 'Letters of Henry Jacie,' Massachusetts Historical Society, *Collections*, 3rd series, I, 235–46; 4th series, VI, 452–66.
A storehouse of Provisions, 1650.
Joyce, George, *A Letter or Epistle to All well-minded People*, 1651.
Kiffin, William, *Remarkable Passages in the Life of William Kiffin*, ed. W. Orme, 1823.
Kilcop, Thomas, *A short Treatise of Baptisme* [1642].
Knollys, Hanserd, *The Life and Death of Hanserd Knollys*, ed. William Kiffin, 1692.
Laud, William, *The Works of William Laud*, 7 vols., Oxford, 1847–60.
Lightfoot, John, *The Whole Works*, vol. XIII: *The Journal of the Proceedings of the Assembly of Divines*, ed. J. R. Pitman, 1824.
Lilburne, John, *Jonahs Cry out of the Whales belly*, 1647.
Ludlow, Edmund, *The Memoirs of Edmund Ludlow*, ed. C. H. Firth, 2 vols., Oxford, 1894.
Lumpkin, William L., *Baptist Confessions of Faith*, Philadelphia, 1959.
Middlesex County Records, vol. III, ed. J. C. Jeaffreson, 1888.
Milton, John, *Original Letters and Papers of State...of Mr. John Milton*, ed. John Nickolls, 1743.
Mitchell, A. F., and J. Struthers, eds., *Minutes of the...Westminster Assembly of Divines*, Edinburgh, 1874.
Nalson, John, *An Impartial Collection of the Great Affairs of State*, 2 vols., 1683.
Norice, Edward, *The New Gospel*, 1638.
A Treatise, 1636.
A Paire of Spectacles for the Citie, 1648.
Papers Given in to the Honourable Committee For Accommodation, 1648.
Price, John, *The City-Remonstrance Remonstrated*, 1646.
Quatermayne, Roger, *Quatermayns Conquest over Canterburies Court*, 1642.
Records of the Churches of Christ, Gathered at Fenstanton, Warboys, and Hexham, 1644–1720, ed. E. B. Underhill, Hanserd Knollys Society, 1854.
A Remonstrance Sent from Colonell Lilburnes Regiment, 1647.
Rushworth, John, *Historical Collections*, 8 vols., 1721–2.
A Secret Negotiation, in *The Camden Miscellany*, vol. VIII, Camden Society, 1883.

Spilsbury, John, *Gods Ordinance, The Saints Priviledge*, 1646.
A Treatise Concerning the Lawfull Subject of Baptisme, 1643.
T., A., *A Christian Reprofe against Contention* [Amsterdam?], 1631.
Taylor, John, *New Preachers, New* [1641].
A Swarme of Sectaries, 1641.
Terrill, Edward, *The Records of a Church of Christ Meeting in Broadmead, Bristol*, ed. N. Haycroft, The Bunyan Library, 1865.
Tombes, John, *An Apologie or Plea for the Two Treatises*, 1646.
Two Treatises and an Appendix to them concerning Infant-Baptisme, 1645.
Trapnel, Ana, *The Cry of a Stone*, 1654.
Tub-preachers overturn'd, 1647.
Vicars, John, *The Picture of Independency*, 1645.
The Schismatick Sifted, 1646.
Walker, Clement, *The Compleat History of Independency*, 1661.
W[histon]., E[dward]., *The Life and Death of Mr. Henry Jessey*, 1671.
Whitley, W. T., ed., 'Debate on Infant Baptism, 1643' [Knollys Memorandum], *Transactions of the Baptist Historical Society*, I (1908–9).
'The Hubbard-How-More Church,' *Transactions of the Baptist Historical Society*, II (1910–11).
'Records of the Jacob-Lathorp-Jessey Church 1616–1641' [Jessey Memorandum], *Transactions of the Baptist Historical Sociey*, I (1908–9).
'Rise of the Particular Baptists in London, 1633–1644' [Kiffin Memorandum], *Transactions of the Baptist Historical Society*, I (1908–9).
Williams, Roger, *The Complete Writings of Roger Williams*, 7 vols., New York, 1963.
Winthrop, John, *Winthrop's Journal*, ed. J. K. Hosmer, 2 vols., New York, 1908.
Wolfe, Don M., *Leveller Manifestoes of the Puritan Revolution*, New York, 1944.
Wynell, Thomas, *The Covenants Plea for Infants*, Oxford, 1642.

SECONDARY WORKS

Babbage, Stuart Barton, *Puritanism and Richard Bancroft*, 1962.
Bailey, John E., 'President Henry Lawrence and his Writings,' *Notes and Queries*, June 1879.
Bolam, C. Gordon, Roger Thomas, *et al.*, *The English Presbyterians*, 1968.
Bottigheimer, Karl S., *English Money and Irish Land*, Oxford, 1971.
Brailsford, H. N., *The Levellers and the English Revolution*, 1961.
Brook, Benjamin, *The Lives of the Puritans*, 3 vols., 1813.
Brown, Louise Fargo, *The Political Activities of the Baptists and Fifth Monarchy Men in England During the Interregnum*, Washington, 1912.

Burgess, W. H., *John Smyth The Se-Baptist, Thomas Helwys and the First Baptist Church in England*, 1911.

John Robinson, 1920.

Burns, Norman T., *Christian Mortalism from Tyndale to Milton*, Cambridge, Mass., 1972.

Burrage, Champlin, 'Was John Canne a Baptist?,' *Transactions of the Baptist Historical Society*, III (1912–13).

Calamy, Edmund, *An Abridgment of Mr. Baxter's History*, 1702.

Capp, B. S., *The Fifth Monarchy Men*, 1972.

Carter, Alice, *The English Reformed Church in Amsterdam in the Seventeenth Century*, Amsterdam, 1964.

Cliffe, J. T., *The Yorkshire Gentry From the Reformation to the Civil War*, 1969.

Cockett, C. Bernard, 'George Cokayn,' *Transactions of the Congregational Historical Society*, XII (1933–6).

Collinson, Patrick, *The Elizabethan Puritan Movement*, 1967.

'Towards a Broader Understanding of the Early Dissenting Tradition,' in C. Robert Cole and Michael E. Moody, eds., *The Dissenting Tradition: Essays for Leland H. Carlson*, Athens, Ohio, 1975.

Crosby, Thomas, *A History of the English Baptists*, 4 vols., 1738–40.

Dillon, H. A., 'On a MS. List of Officers of the London Trained Bands in 1643,' *Archeologia*, LII (1890).

Dodd, J. A., 'Troubles in a City Parish under the Protectorate,' *English Historical Review*, X (1895).

'The Eschatology of Praise-God Barbone,' *Transactions of the Congregational Historical Society*, IV (1909–10).

Evans, Benjamin, *The Early English Baptists*, 2 vols., The Bunyan Library, 1862–4.

Farnell, James E., 'The Navigation Act of 1651, the First Dutch War, and the London Merchant Community,' *Economic History Review*, 2nd series, XVI (1964).

'The Usurpation of Honest London Householders: Barebone's Parliament,' *English Historical Review*, LXXXII (1967).

Firth, C. H., 'The Raising of the Ironsides,' *Transactions of the Royal Historical Society*, new series, XIII (1899).

'The Later History of the Ironsides,' *Transactions of the Royal Historical Society*, new series, XV (1901).

Cromwell's Army, 3rd edn., 1962.

Firth, C. H. and Godfrey Davies, *The Regimental History of Cromwell's Army*, 2 vols., Oxford, 1940.

Fixler, Michael, *Milton and the Kingdoms of God*, 1964.

Frank, Joseph, *The Levellers*, Cambridge, Mass., 1955.

Freshfield, Edwin, *Some Remarks upon the. . .History of the parish of St. Stephen, Coleman Street*, Westminster, 1887.

Gardiner, S. R., *History of England 1603–1642*, 10 vols., 1884.

History of the Great Civil War, 4 vols., 1901.

Gibb, M. A., *John Lilburne*, 1947.

Gregg, Pauline, *Free-born John: A Biography of John Lilburne*, 1961.

Grippen, T. G., 'Nicholas Lockyer: A Half-forgotten Champion of Independency,' *Transactions of the Congregational Historical Society*, IX (1924–6).

Haller, William, *Foxe's Book of Martyrs and the Elect Nation*, 1963.

Liberty and Reformation in the Puritan Revolution, New York, 1955.

The Rise of Puritanism, New York, 1957.

Hill, Christopher, *Antichrist in Seventeenth-Century England*, 1971.

Economic Problems of the Church, Oxford, 1963.

Puritanism and Revolution, 1958.

Society and Puritanism in Pre-Revolutionary England, 1964.

The World Turned Upside Down, 1972.

Hill, G. W. and W. H. Frere, eds., *Memorials of Stepney Parish*, Guildford, 1890–1.

Hine, Reginald L., *History of Hitchin*, 2 vols., 1927–9.

Howell, Roger, *Newcastle upon Tyne and the Puritan Revolution*, Oxford, 1967.

Ivimey, Joseph, *A History of the English Baptists*, 1811.

Jones, A. T., *Early Days of Stepney Meeting* [1887].

Klaiber, A. J., *Bewdley Baptists 1649–1949*, 1949.

Knox, S. J., *Walter Travers: Paragon of Elizabethan Puritanism*, 1962.

Lamont, William M., *Godly Rule, Politics and Religion 1603–60*, 1969.

Marginal Prynne 1600–1669, 1963.

'Richard Baxter, The Apocalypse and the Mad Major,' *Past and Present*, no. 55 (1972).

Liu, Tai, *Discord in Zion: The Puritan Divines and the Puritan Revolution 1640–1660*, The Hague, 1973.

MacCormack, John R., *Revolutionary Politics in the Long Parliament*, Cambridge, Mass., 1973.

Matthews, A. G., *Calamy Revised*, Oxford, 1934.

The Congregational Churches of Staffordshire [1924].

Maclear, James Fulton, 'The Making of the Lay Tradition,' *The Journal of Religion*, XXXIII (1953).

McLachlan, H. John, *Socinianism in Seventeenth-Century England*, Oxford, 1951.

Miller, Perry, *The New England Mind: The Seventeenth Century*, Cambridge, Mass., 1954.

The New England Mind: From Colony to Province, Cambridge, Mass., 1953.

Orthodoxy in Massachusetts 1630–1650, Boston, 1959.

Morgan, Edmund S., *Visible Saints: The History of a Puritan Idea*, New York, 1963.

Morison, Samuel E., *The Founding of Harvard College*, Cambridge, Mass., 1955.

Morton, A. L., *The World of the Ranters*, 1970.

Neal, Daniel, *The History of the Puritans*, ed. Dr Toulmin, 5 vols., 1882.

Newton, A. P., *The Colonizing Activities of the English Puritans*, New Haven, 1914.

Nobbs, D., 'Philip Nye on Church and State,' *Cambridge Historical Journal*, v (1935).

Nuttall, Geoffrey F., 'Some Bibliographical Notes and Identifications,' *Transactions of the Congregational Historical Society*, xvi (1949–51).

Visible Saints: The Congregational Way 1640–1660, Oxford, 1957.

The Welsh Saints, Cardiff, 1957.

Paul, Robert S., 'Henry Jacob and Seventeenth-Century Puritanism,' *The Hartford Quarterly*, vii (1967).

Pearl, Valerie, *London and the Outbreak of the Puritan Revolution*, 1961.

'London's Counter-Revolution,' in G. E. Aylmer, ed., *The Interregnum: The Quest for Settlement 1646–1660*, 1972.

'London Puritans and Scotch Fifth Columnists: A Mid-Seventeenth-Century Phenomenon,' in A. E. J. Hollander and William Kellaway, eds., *Studies in London History*, 1969.

Plomer, H. R., 'Secret Printing During the Civil War,' *The Library*, new series, v (1904).

Richards, Thomas, *A History of the Puritan Movement in Wales 1639 to 1653*, 1920.

Rogers, Edward, *The Life and Opinions of a Fifth-Monarchy-Man*, 1867.

Rowe, Violet A., *Sir Henry Vane the Younger*, 1970.

Schenk, W., *The Concern for Social Justice in the Puritan Revolution*, 1948.

Seaver, Paul S., *The Puritan Lectureships*, Stanford, 1970.

Thomas, Keith, 'Women and the Civil War Sects,' *Past and Present*, no. 13 (1958).

Tibbutt, H. G., *Colonel John Okey 1606–1662*, Publications of the Bedfordshire Historical Record Society, xxxv (1955).

Trevor-Roper, H. R., *Religion, the Reformation and Social Change*, 2nd edn, 1972.

Trout, A. E., 'Nonconformity in Hull,' *Transactions of the Congregational Historical Society*, ix (1924–6).

Underdown, David, *Pride's Purge*, Oxford, 1971.

Vann, Richard T., *The Social Development of English Quakerism*, Cambridge, Mass., 1969.

von Rohr, John, 'The Congregationalism of Henry Jacob,' *Transactions of the Congregational Historical Society*, xix (1962).

'*Extra Ecclesiam Nulla Salus*: An Early Congregational Version,' *Church History*, xxxvi (1967).

Wedgwood, C. V., *The Trial of Charles I*, Fontana edn, 1967.

White, B. R., *The English Separatist Tradition*, Oxford, 1971.

'How did Kiffin Join the Baptists?', *The Baptist Quarterly*, xxiii (1970).

'John Traske (1585–1636) and London Puritanism,' *Transactions of the Congregational Historical Society*, xx (1968).

'Samuel Eaton, Particular Baptist Pioneer,' *The Baptist Quarterly*, xxiv (1971).

Whitebrook, J. C., 'Sir Thomas Andrewes, Lord Mayor and Regicide, and his Relatives,' *Transactions of the Congregational Historical Society*, xiii (1937–9).

Whiting, C. E., *Studies in English Puritanism from the Restoration to the Revolution, 1660–1688*, 1931.

[Whitley, W. T.], 'Benjamin Stinton and his Baptist Friends,' *Transactions of the Baptist Historical Society*, i (1908–9).

'The Jacob-Jessey Church, 1616–1678,' *Transactions of the Baptist Historical Society*, i (1908–9).

Whitley, W. T., *A Baptist Bibliography*, vol. i, 1916.

Williams, Dorothy Ann, 'London Puritanism: The Parish of St. Stephen, Coleman Street,' *The Church Quarterly Review*, clx (1959).

Wilson, John F., 'Another Look at John Canne,' *Church History*, xxxiii (1964).

'A Glimpse of Syons Glory,' *Church History*, xxxi (1962).

Pulpit in Parliament, Princeton, 1969.

Wilson, Walter, *The History and Antiquities of Dissenting Churches...in London*, 4 vols., 1808–14.

Winslow, Ola E., *Master Roger Williams*, New York, 1957.

Wood, Anthony, *Athenae Oxoniensis*, ed. P. Bliss, 4 vols., 1815–20.

Woodhouse, A. S. P., *Puritanism and Liberty*, 1951.

Worden, Blair, *The Rump Parliament*, Cambridge, 1974.

Yule, George, *The Independents in the English Civil War*, Cambridge, 1958.

Zagorin, Perez, *The Court and the Country*, 1969.

'The Authorship of *Mans Mortallitie*,' *The Library*, 5th series, v (1950).

Ziff, Larzer, *The Career of John Cotton: Puritanism and the American Experience*, Princeton, 1962.

INDEX OF SEPARATE CHURCHES IN LONDON

Separate churches are listed by type, and, within each type, in order of formation, under the names of the successive pastors.

Independent gathered churches

Jacob-Lathrop-Jessey (1616), 3–4, chapters 1 and 2, 55–6, 58–60, 90–1, 99, 102, 108, 116, 121–2, 133, 154, 156, 171, 188, 192–5

Thomas Goodwin (1641), 92–3, 104–6, 120, 122, 141, 188, 196

Sidrach Simpson (1641), 93, 104–5, 141, 187–8

Cradock-Simpson (1643), 94, 109

Lockyer-Cokayn (1643), 94, 103–4, 154, 187, 189

Burton (1643), 66, 94, 109–11, 122–3

Homes (1643), 94, 109–11, 123

John Goodwin (1643), 66, 94, 111–16, 119, 139–40, 145–6, 149–50, 152, 171, 179, 184, 187

Carter (1644), 61, 95, 108

Greenhill (1644), 66, 95, 98, 107, 141, 171

Bartlet-Huntley (1645), 95, 108

Briscoe-Venning (1645), 95, 108–9

Nye-Loder (164?), 106–7

Brooks (1648), 118

Separate churches with lay pastors

Barrowist (1587?–1632), 3, 15, 35–6

Hubbard-Canne-How-More (1621), 17, 36, 46, 59, 66–7, 155

Duppa-Chidley (1630), 17, 21–2, 25–7, 36–7, 39, 46–7, 49, 65–7, 98, 122–4, 147, 156, 178, 188

Eaton (1633–9), 18–19, 22–7, 37, 43, 155–6, 161, 192–5

Green-Spencer (1639), 26–7, 59, 66–7, 156

Rogers (163?), 37, 47

Barbone (1640), 19, 26–7, 38, 65, 67, 147

Rosier (1641), 36–7, 66–7, 147

Banks-Bolton (1641?), 37, 67–8

Highland (164?), 67, 147

Fenton (164?), 67

Particular Baptist churches

Spilsbury-Richardson (163?), 24–7, 47, 58, 60, 192–4

Blunt-Shepard-Munden (1642), 26–7, 54, 58, 60, 156

Kilcop-Webb-Cox (1642), 26–7, 58–60, 155

Kiffin-Patience (1644), 55–8, 156, 165, 175, 182, 188, 194–5

Gunne-Mabbatt (1644), 59

Hobson-Goare (1644), 59, 133, 156

Phelpes-Heath (1644), 59–60

Knollys-Holms (1645), 59–60, 147, 150, 171

General Baptist churches

Helwys-Murton (1612), 70–1

Tookey-Garbrand-Clayton (1624), 71, 75, 80

Lambe (1640), 64, 72, 74–9, 81–2, 153, 170

Barber (1640), 75, 78–9, 134

Griffith (1646), 79

Loveday (164?), 80

GENERAL INDEX